Lost in New Orleans

ALSO BY LYNN KEAR

Laurette Taylor, American Stage Legend (2010)

BY LYNN KEAR AND JOHN ROSSMAN

The Complete Kay Francis Career Record: All Film, Stage, Radio and Television Appearances (2018 [2008])

Kay Francis: A Passionate Life and Career (2006)

BY LYNN KEAR WITH JAMES KING

Evelyn Brent: The Life and Films of Hollywood's Lady Crook (2009)

ALL FROM McFARLAND

Lost in New Orleans

*Friendship, Desire and Self-Destruction
in Four Jazz Age Lives*

LYNN KEAR

McFarland & Company, Inc., Publishers
Jefferson, North Carolina

ISBN (print) 978-1-4766-8985-2
ISBN (ebook) 978-1-4766-4752-4

LIBRARY OF CONGRESS AND BRITISH LIBRARY
CATALOGUING DATA ARE AVAILABLE

Library of Congress Control Number 2022057296

© 2023 Lynn Kear. All rights reserved

No part of this book may be reproduced or transmitted in any form or by any means, electronic or mechanical, including photocopying or recording, or by any information storage and retrieval system, without permission in writing from the publisher.

On the cover: *clockwise from left* Walker Ellis and Katty Stewart married in Paris in 1930; Walter Stauffer; Moosie White from the early 1920s (all photographs courtesy Maunsel White); *background* a recent photograph of the Buckner house shows little change since the 1920s (photograph by Camille Lilly)

Printed in the United States of America

*McFarland & Company, Inc., Publishers
Box 611, Jefferson, North Carolina 28640
www.mcfarlandpub.com*

In memory of Kimber Herndon (1965–2020)
and Mindy Hill (1954–2021)

Acknowledgments

This book would not have been possible without the help of many people. Special thanks go to John Rossman, my research partner on my books about Kay Francis, who was responsible for reading and recording her diary entries at the Wesleyan University archives.

Photographer Camille Lilly graciously traveled to New Orleans to take contemporary photos of the Buckner house. Special thanks to Jeannette McCurnin for helping with New Orleans probate and succession records. The Louisiana Secretary of State's office was wonderfully efficient when I requested marriage records, death certificates, etc.

Sylvia Hernandez, archivist, the Texas Collection, Baylor University, was friendly and helpful when I needed information about, and a photograph of, Pauline Breustedt. Like Sylvia, Heather Green at the Historic New Orleans Collection was a joy to work with. She was thorough and a lifesaver at a time when I worried I would never find any photographs of Walker Ellis. Thanks also go to Joan Miller at the Reid Cinema Archive at Wesleyan University who once again helped me with Kay Francis' diary.

Katrina Callahan, friend, artist and photo wrangler, helped prepare the images for the book, cheerfully taking on a job that my late wife once did. I am grateful for her advice and good humor. I'd still be working on the photos if it weren't for her.

I contacted Steven Eustis through Ancestry.com when I came across a photograph he had posted on one of his ancestor's pages. I had a feeling almost immediately that the little girl in the lower right-hand corner of the family portrait was Katty Stewart. I contacted Steven, and he confirmed it. He was enthusiastic about my project and generous with information, records, and photos.

Maunsel White was a tremendous help in piecing together the lives of Moosie and Walter. He patiently answered my questions and went above and beyond the call of duty in terms of time, resources and insights. I am enormously grateful. The book is better because he contributed so much.

Table of Contents

Acknowledgments — vi
Introduction — 1
Prologue: That Time a Movie Star Visited New Orleans to See Katty Stewart — 3

1. The Buckner House and the South — 11
2. Society Columns — 17
3. Katty and Moosie — 22
4. Baby Dances — 33
5. *Let's Not and Say We Did* — 36
6. Walker Mallam Ellis — 41
7. Walter Joseph Stauffer — 52
8. Walker and the French Quarter — 64
9. A Trip to Europe — 76
10. Debutantes — 87
11. 1924 — 102
12. A Surprise Marriage — 108
13. 1925 — 114
14. Oak Alley — 117
15. The Lost Generation — 124

16. 1927	130
17. Illusions	135
18. Kay and Katty in Hollywood	138
19. The Beginning of the End	146
20. The Wedding	150
21. The Marriage	156
22. The Houseboat	160
23. Restless	165
24. Walter Stauffer and New Orleans	175
25. 1940s	179
26. Everything Ends	185
27. The End	189
Epilogue	193
Chapter Notes	195
Bibliography	213
Index	217

Introduction

I first learned about Katty Stewart when her name appeared in Kay Francis' diaries. Katty intrigued me. In the 1920s, she was a relatively open American lesbian who enjoyed a wealthy lifestyle that included frequent travels to Europe and a love affair with a Hollywood film star.

Years passed, and I found myself thinking about Katty, hoping she had recovered from her doomed affair with Kay. I envisioned her moving to Los Angeles, New York, maybe Paris, hooking up with a woman, and living a long, happy life. Perhaps she had lived long enough to see the gay rights movement achieve some victories.

I researched her on Ancestry.com. It was slow at first, but the pieces started coming together. Unfortunately, it wasn't the story I wanted. It reminded me of when I first began researching Kay Francis. As with Katty, I wanted Kay's life to be happy, but Kay's story, like Katty's, turned out to be a sometimes sad, self-destructive one.

My plan for this project was to focus on Katty, but I quickly realized that Elizabeth (Moosie) White, Walker Ellis and Walter Stauffer's lives were enmeshed with Katty's. They grew up together, enjoying privileged childhoods in New Orleans. The four were also part of the restless lost generation of Americans in the 1920s, sharing a relentless path to self-destruction, some more so than others.

My goal was to discover what happened to Katty Stewart, and I did. I also found out about the lives of Moosie, Walker and Walter and learned a lot about New Orleans high society and its many eccentric characters. Their stories are compelling and human.

Katty Stewart and Walker Ellis apparently left behind no journals, diaries, letters, photographs, documents or other papers. Following their deaths, their personal effects were likely destroyed, perhaps to protect their family from scandal and embarrassment. Or maybe surviving family members just weren't interested.

Fortunately, Elizabeth (Moosie) White Stauffer left photographs, letters, newspaper clippings, etc., to her nephew, Maunsel White. These materials include photos of husband Walter Stauffer and Katty.

Walker Ellis, though largely unknown today, was enough of a public figure to be occasionally mentioned in books and magazine articles, especially in connection to his years at Princeton and his links to F. Scott Fitzgerald, Gerald Murphy and other Jazz Age figures.

New Orleans newspapers, especially society columns, documented the lives of all four for decades. I found thousands of mentions of Katty, Moosie, Walker and Walter. All were celebrities in their hometown, and their activities and accomplishments were regularly reported.

Between newspapers, Kay's diaries, books, magazine articles, interviews and public documents, I follow the lives of Katty, Moosie, Walker and Walter from birth to death. In addition, I paint a picture of the New Orleans upper class during their era.

For clarity and readability, I have corrected typos, misspellings, etc. I have tried to be as accurate as possible; I apologize for any errors.

Prologue: That Time a Movie Star Visited New Orleans to See Katty Stewart

It wasn't easy being in love with Kay Francis. Loaded with charisma, charm and jaw-dropping physical beauty, she broke many hearts in her 63 years. In the spring of 1930, she was on a train to New Orleans to dash the hopes of Katharine Stewart, better known as Katty to her friends and family.[1]

The movie star's arrival in Katty's hometown on March 22 was eagerly awaited by many New Orleanians. Perhaps no one was more anxious than Katty. They had last seen each other the previous year when Katty helped Kay settle in California after Paramount relocated their new star from New York. After Katty met Kay at the train station in Chicago, they had traveled together to Los Angeles where Kay reported to studio executive B.P. Schulberg.[2]

Before Kay's arrival in New Orleans, a local newspaper blandly recapped Katty's May–June stay with Kay in California. "Last summer Miss Stewart visited Miss Francis in Hollywood, taking a long automobile trip through Yellowstone Park."[3] A lot happened during that wild visit, perhaps least of all a visit to Yellowstone. Katty and Kay lived together as lovers for a couple months, attended parties with stars like Clara Bow and Walter Huston, hung out at the studio, adopted a dog, and discussed plans for their future.[4]

On her last night in Los Angeles, in June 1929, Katty worked up her nerve and poured her heart out, telling Kay she was madly in love with her and wanted to live with her. It was a long night, but the next morning when Katty departed, she was confident she had made headway with Kay. Katty fell in love with her years before, when they were goofy, awkward teenagers at an all-female Episcopal boarding school in New York.[5]

Still, Katty was likely nervous about Kay's New Orleans visit. Almost a year had passed. She worried that Kay had moved on. Though they'd kept in contact, Kay Francis' world had dramatically changed.

When Kay asked Katty to accompany her to Hollywood, Kay lacked confidence and was in awe of Katty. Sophisticated, possessing a strong, self-assured personality, Katty came from a wealthy, powerful Southern family. She had been written about often—and glowingly—in the society columns. She was a celebrity, at least in New Orleans.

On the other hand, Kay had been born poor. Her actress mother, Katherine Clinton, struggled to support herself and her daughter after husband Joe Gibbs abandoned them. Scrounging up the money to put Kay in a private girls' school was a strategy. Even if Kay had no money, she could hang around the rich and connected. Good things were bound to happen. One of the good things was meeting people like Katty Stewart, who taught Kay to navigate the society world.[6]

By March 1930, Kay Francis was no longer poor. She was wealthy, famous and a big movie star. She no longer needed Katty Stewart as a chaperone.

Kay and Katty's positions were, if not reversed, certainly askew. Katty was never as glamorous as Kay, but she'd been treated like a star due to her personality and her family's prominence. Now Kay was the star. It must have thrown Katty for a loop.

Still, Kay felt loyal to the woman who had been an on-and-off friend and lover for more than ten years. She'd promised Katty a visit to New Orleans, and she meant to fulfill that promise. Katty's birthday was March 3, so perhaps the visit was a belated birthday present. Letters between the two women no longer exist, but one can imagine a frantic exchange, along with extravagant, expensive phone calls that led up to Kay's arrival on March 22.

Kay's three-day trip started early on March 20. She left Los Angeles at ten a.m. She'd recently finished making *Raffles*, a movie with matinee idol Ronald Colman, and was looking forward to a break. She not only had a busy professional life, she also led a hectic personal and romantic life, juggling various flirtations and sexual relationships with actors Kay Johnson, Kenneth MacKenna, McKay Morris and others.[7]

In her diary, Kay described the long first day on the train as dull and confessed to getting drunk. Despite Prohibition, drinking to drunkenness was not unusual for Kay or Katty. Kay's diary entry for the next day, March 21, simply said: "Still on damn train."[8]

Saturday, March 22, began with thunderstorms rolling through New Orleans. Finally, at 7:35 p.m., Kay's Southern Pacific train rolled into the New Orleans Union Station. The press, alerted to the arrival of a movie star, awaited. Also hanging around were several giddy employees of Saenger Theaters who had been assigned to welcome Kay.[9]

Kay, smartly dressed, strolled off the train, and the looky loos checked her out. "Miss Francis who has the greyhound figure so much sought after by members of the New Orleans Junior League ... has grayish-green eyes, a straight nose, a slightly receding chin, and a laughing personality.... Dressed in a green coat suit with a black fox fur, a tan hat, tan shoes and stockings, the winsome Miss Francis was carrying a tennis racket when she made her personal debut to New Orleans."[10]

Katty, however. was late. Kay didn't mention it in her diary, so perhaps she expected it. While waiting for her friend, the star calmly chatted up members of the press. When someone from Saenger expressed concern for Katty, Kay laughed it off. "Katty will be here any minute now. I am sure she was delayed and I am in no hurry."[11]

Sure enough, Katty soon arrived, and it *was* an entrance. Perhaps Katty had coached herself to be cool, but the idea quickly went by the wayside when she spied her lover. "Katty dashed through the crowd and grabbed Miss Francis in her arms. The young women are close personal friends, having been classmates in St. Mary's College in Los Angeles."[12]

No, Kay and Katty did not attend college together in Los Angeles. However, both had attended Holy Cathedral School of St. Mary, an Episcopal private girls' school in Garden City, Long Island, New York.

Katty brought along several friends to meet Kay, including Elizabeth Werlein, one of the Saenger employees who worked as a censor. Known as Betty to her friends, she was the previous owner of 2228 St. Charles Avenue, which was now the Stewart family home.

Elizabeth's bio sounds like a character Kay might have played in one of her films. Born in Michigan in 1883, she studied opera in Europe; was briefly engaged to a Russian; became one of the few women to ride in a hot air balloon; and scandalized London when, as a young woman, she wore an outfit that showed her shoes. Elizabeth later became an activist who focused on New Orleans restoration and preservation, especially in the French Quarter.

Many people wanted their photograph taken with Kay. During the photography session, Kay was peppered with interview questions. The Hollywood publicity machine had trained her well. Regarding marriage, Kay said, "I think ... that marriage is the greatest single career in the world and that is the thing all girls should strive for. It is the alpha and omega of happiness unless a girl has a real profession in which to put her energies."[13]

Interesting advice, considering Kay's own marital history. She had already been married and divorced twice, both times to men from wealthy families. Fiercely independent, Kay refused alimony from both husbands.[14]

Several photographs of Kay's arrival in New Orleans exist. Perhaps the most intriguing is one of Kay and Katty.[15] Kay, beaming and beautiful, looks *exactly* like a glamorous Hollywood star: poised and posed, head tilted upward. Katty, in contrast, appears unsure. Her hands are clutched together. Her smile is forced and too large. Furthermore, the angle is unflattering, revealing a double chin and matronly pose. Even the buckle on her belted dress is slightly crooked. Katty had just turned 27, and Kay was 25. But Katty looked much older.

Katty likely had fantasized about their meeting. After the hubbub of Kay's arrival in New Orleans, she took Kay back to 2228 St. Charles Avenue, where they could finally be alone. Located in New Orleans' Garden District, it was, and still is, one of the finest homes on the block. Katty lived there with her divorced father Will, 53, a cotton broker, and brother Andrew, nicknamed Buddy, 25. Buddy, who had been deaf for much of his life, worked at his father's company.

According to Kay's diary, the two women got settled, and then got drunk and had sex. Kay, not for the first time, claimed it wasn't her idea: "Had to sleep with her because she wanted me."[16]

In her lifetime, Kay Francis had hundreds of sexual experiences with men and women. She was bisexual, but most of her bed partners were male. Her lovers included Maurice Chevalier, John Meehan, Kiki Preston, Kay Swann, Otto Preminger and many others. Her three marriages were brief and unhappy. She preferred a succession of dramatic, romantic flings that fizzled out quickly. She admitted she was "a lousy wife—happy lover."[17]

For the next few days, Katty took Kay to places she frequented, including the Country Club and the Patio Royal. Katty wanted to show off Kay—and also let Kay see how important she was in New Orleans society.

The Patio Royal was on Royal Street in the heart of the French Quarter. A favorite of the smart set, it was a hangout for Katty and her friends. It was crowded the night Katty brought Kay, with people craning their necks to get a look at her companion. A society columnist described how gaga the New Orleans crowd was over Kay:

> Katty Stewart entertained Kay Francis, the actress, this past week and hostess and guest alike were the center of gay, informal parties. Last Sunday night Miss Francis caused quite a stir at the patio, a lovely figure in a black lace dinner dress with long sleeves and the full flared skirt, and last Tuesday Katty had a number of people in for a late tea to meet her. The glamour of movie life makes such people interesting to begin with, but Miss Francis' glamour is individual, entirely due to her charming personality.[18]

Katty's best friend, Moosie White Stauffer, hosted a party at her parents' home on Second Street. She and her husband, Walter Stauffer, had lived in the house since their marriage the previous year. "Mrs. Walter Stauffer entertained informally for luncheon Friday afternoon at the family residence ... having a few friends to meet Miss Kay Francis, the guest of Miss Katherine Stewart."[19] Among the guests were Katty's mother Kittie Eustis, who lived in a French Quarter apartment; cousin Jo LeBlanc Gibert, and friend Burdette Waldo Huggins.

Katty also took Kay to Oak Alley, a former plantation that had been bought by her aunt and uncle, Andrew and Josephine Stewart. It had become a second home for Katty. In fact, she was such a frequent visitor that a cottage was named for her.

Kay and Katty attended movies and ate lunches and dinners at Arnaud's and Galatoire's. They drank coffee at the French market, attended a Junior League revue, and even went to an Italy-America Society meeting where the main event was the lecture "The Spirit of Florence and Sienna During the Thirteenth Century," given by Dr. Franco Bruno Averardi.[20]

Most of these events were attended by Katty's family members and friends, including Walker Ellis, Katty's future husband. He, like Katty, was gay; they had known each other for many years. Walker was an actor who had appeared on Broadway, so it's likely that he was interested in meeting Kay.

Kay, who had become obsessed with tennis, was disappointed when it was too windy one day to play at the country club. Instead, she and Katty retreated to the St. Charles Avenue house and drank. Kay admitted in her diary that she and Katty were "woosies after dinner."[21]

Prohibition started in 1920, "but New Orleans did not seem to have heard of it."[22] Katty's circle of friends drank oodles of bootleg liquor. Genevieve Pitot, who attended many of the same parties that Katty did, "remembered 'well-lubricated' parties.... Liquor was a social necessity.... 'We drank because they told us we couldn't.'" Elizabeth Anderson, Sherwood Anderson's third wife, said, "We all seemed to feel that Prohibition was a personal affront and that we had a moral duty to undermine it."[23]

That night, Kay and Katty stayed up until 3:30 a.m., drinking absinthe.[24] Banned in 1912, it was remarkably easy to procure. Nicknamed the Green Lady, it's a high-proof alcohol made with wormwood. A component of the wormwood is thujone, a hallucinogen that is toxic in high doses. Oscar Wilde, who knew from firsthand experience, described the drink's effects: "After the first glass of absinthe you see things as you wish they were. After the second you see them as they are not. Finally you see things as they really are, and that is the most horrible thing in the world."[25]

Kay and Katty liked absinthe. More importantly, Katty knew where to get it. She probably used the man that artist William Spratling and other gay French Quarter residents used. "A Swiss man living in the Quarter made it himself, and at six dollars a bottle [about $72 in today's money] it wasn't cheap."[26] Katty, who had a generous allowance, didn't care what it cost.

Katty probably served it the way Spratling did at his parties. "When it was poured over crushed ice with just a touch of water to make an 'absinthe frappe' ... it had very little taste of alcohol, so 'it was consumed in quantities.'"[27]

On March 27, Katty introduced Kay to Walker Ellis. In her diary, Kay noted that they went to Walker's sister's house.[28] This was likely Hazel Ellis Woodward, who lived with her dentist husband Joseph and their children on Audubon.

After a week or so in New Orleans, Kay was homesick, pining for boyfriend Kenneth MacKenna, and perhaps bored. Katty decided she needed to keep Kay interested, so they took a three-day boat trip into Bayou Teche country.[29] A newspaper blurb provided more details: "Katty Stewart and her celebrated guest Kay Francis of the movies, stole away to the land of Evangeline where they will be received by Weeks Hall, artist owner of a famous Colonial home. They will return to New Orleans via steamboat."[30]

Hall, described by John Shelton Reed as "master of and slave to Shadows-on-the-Teche plantation, painter, [and] deeply strange,"[31] was born in New Orleans and inherited Shadows-on-the-Teche. Architect Richard Koch modernized the structure, while Hall focused on the gardens. Many films were shot there, including D.W. Griffith's *The White Rose* in 1923.

Hall, who kept an apartment in the French Quarter in the 1920s, likely knew Katty from her gay circle of friends. Author Will Fellows met him when he photographed his estate. "Weeks Hall was rather notorious. My partner and I were over at Shadows-on-the-Teche in New Iberia photographing it one day.... One of the gardeners, a black man, was telling us about 'Mr. Weeks' boys'—all these good-looking, tall black men who had worked for him."[32]

Hall gave most people the creeps. "Novelist Henry Miller reported that some of Hall's 'imperative impulses' were so 'spectacular and weird' that even Miller found them 'impossible to describe in print'; an evening with him was 'like a private seance with Dr. Caligari.'"[33]

When Kay and Katty returned to New Orleans on April 5, it was almost time for Kay to leave. Kay originally thought she might stay for three weeks but decided she'd had enough fun and made plans to return to Los Angeles. Paramount also was eager for her to return to work.[34]

Kay's last night in New Orleans was April 6. She wrote in her diary that she had dinner with Walker Ellis and others and ended with: "God!"[35] Whatever that meant, it was not a good sign for Katty and the future of their relationship.

Also on April 6, society columnist William G. Wiegand proclaimed that New Orleans "has found a new darling and is doing its very best to see that she has a good time."[36] Wiegand, like many other Orleanians, expressed surprise that Kay wasn't like her film roles:

> This newest social lioness is a rather tall, slim, close-cropped brunette with greenish-gray eyes, a flare for wearing clothes, a natural quick wit and ability to step out of the original character in which the movies cast her.... If you saw her in a night club or near a tea table, you would not think her a vamp.... It is not often that a girl knows she has "it" and is good enough sport to keep her bulldog muzzled.... It is no wonder that New Orleans, in the full spotlight of her personality, should react favorably to this school chum of Miss Katharine Stewart, St. Charles Avenue society girl, whom she is visiting "between pictures."

Wiegand interviewed Kay in Katty's beautiful St. Charles Avenue home. "Beneath the ancestral portraits in the Stewart salon, Miss Francis, attired in a blue and white suit of lounging pajamas having a natty Navy anchor embroidered on the chest, answered questions." Wiegand was smitten. He described how she answered his questions in "the throaty voice that makes many movie fans 'feel that way.'"

Kay talked about how nice it was to have a break from work. "I finished *Raffles* just before coming to New Orleans. The studio will be calling me in a week or so and then I'll be working my head off again. The visit to New Orleans is really a Godsend because I am run down, because of long hours on the studio lots."

This was true. Kay regularly worked until midnight or later, and often didn't have weekends off. However, she was not entirely truthful in the interview: "People are all wet about the wildness of Hollywood.... The Hollywood folk are much too busy to throw wild parties."

Kay Francis, a former model, was one of Hollywood's most glamorous stars throughout the 1930s (author's collection).

Kay and her Hollywood friends partied hard, using drugs and alcohol with abandon.

At 11 a.m. on April 7, Kay said goodbye to Katty, got on her train and left New Orleans. In her diary, her final words about the trip were "Gee: Katty was terribly boring and unhappy."[37]

Kay may have told Katty they had no future. Even if she didn't say it in those words, Katty apparently got the message. Though the relationship ended, Katty and Kay had had an on-again, off-again affair for more than a decade, one that had a profound influence on both women's lives.[38]

Kay arrived in Los Angeles at 9:15 p.m. on April 10. Future husband Kenneth MacKenna met her. "God, I am glad to see Ken, missed him! Made me come on the road going 40 miles—rather like old times!"[39]

Kay never again mentioned Katty in her diary. While postcards and letters likely were sent and phone calls made, Kay's visit to New Orleans was the period at the end of the sentence.

Their lives went in different directions. Kay's movie career exploded in the 1930s, and when it ended in the 1940s, she went on to have a successful stage career. Meanwhile, Katty's relatively brief life in New Orleans ended in obscurity. There was not even an obituary when she died.

Surprisingly, though perhaps not coincidentally, both Kay and Katty married soon after their last meeting. Kay wed Kenneth MacKenna in January 1931. It was a brief marriage.

Katty married Walker Ellis in October 1930, a few months after Kay left New Orleans. Though the couple remained married until his death in 1948, it was not a happy marriage, and they were estranged for most of it. What at first seemed like the perfect solution to a problem she and Walker shared turned out be something that satisfied neither.

❮ 1 ❯

The Buckner House and the South

> All the dwellings are of wood ... and all have a comfortable look. Those in the wealthy quarter are spacious; painted snowy white, usually, and generally have wide verandas, or double-verandas, supported by ornamental columns. These mansions stand in the center of large grounds and rise, garlanded with roses, out of the midst of swelling masses of shining green foliage and many-colored blossoms. No houses could well be in better harmony with their surroundings, or more pleasing to the eye, or more home-like and comfortable-looking....[1]
> — Mark Twain on the Garden District in New Orleans

Houses are important in New Orleans. They are not only shelters but also symbols of a family's importance.

On March 3, 1903, Katharine Eustis Stewart was born in the Garden District of New Orleans to Katharine (Kittie) and William (Will) Stewart. She probably breathed her first breath in perhaps the largest and most magnificent mansion in New Orleans.

Unlike Kay Francis, who had a rough, disadvantaged childhood, Katty was born into New Orleans royalty and enjoyed all the trappings that came with it, including wealth, privilege and a grand house. Katty grew up in the Buckner Mansion. Its address is 1410 Jackson Avenue, and it is located at the corner of Jackson and Coliseum. The house gained recent fame when it was the setting for the third season of the American TV show *American Horror Story*. In the FX show, the house became Miss Robichaux's Academy for Exceptional Young Ladies, a fancy name for a coven of witches.

Katty would have been amused, but her grandmother, Laura Buckner Eustis, would have clutched her pearls, thinking it scandalous. Laura, known as Mumsie, was born in New Orleans in 1847. Her father, Henry Sullivan Buckner, born in Virginia in 1797, built the mansion in 1856.

Katty Stewart was born and raised in the Buckner house, built by her great-grandfather, Henry Buckner. The house has been used many times as a set for films and TV shows. This is a recent photograph (by Camille Lilly).

Buckner made his money from cotton, which meant the family wealth depended on slavery.

The mansion was a spite build. Buckner held a grudge against former business partner Frederick Stanton, who had built Stanton Hall in Natchez, Mississippi. Intended to replicate his ancestral home in Ireland, Stanton's house was large and showy. Buckner wanted a bigger, better home, thinking this would "stick it" to Stanton.

Architect Lewis E. Reynolds constructed a 20,000-plus-square foot antebellum mansion with lots of bling: dozens of columns, numerous verandas and large floor-to-ceiling windows. While it was larger and more opulent than Stanton Hall, Buckner only had a few short years to taunt his former colleague: Stanton died in January 1859.

Laurance Eustis, Katty's cousin, was the son of Kittie's brother, also named Laurance. The younger Laurance wrote about the Buckner mansion in his autobiography *One Lucky Fellow*, "It was perhaps the biggest house in the city at the time, on a lot that extended from Jackson Avenue through the block to Philip Street."[2]

The mansion had many rooms, and Laurence claimed his father literally could not remember all of them:

1. The Buckner House and the South

The 12-foot-wide hall ran down the middle of the house, and on one side were the parlor, library and a huge dining room with two chandeliers. The upstairs had the same hall and three bedrooms on each side. The nursery was the same size as the dining room below. The attic must have had ten rooms, and four of them were pitch-black with no windows in them. Above the attic was the cupola from which we always watched fires in the city.

It's likely that Katty slept in one of the six bedrooms on the second floor.

The house's furniture was imported and expensive:

The ballroom had four magnificent mirrors, one at each end and each side. You could look in one of the mirrors at the end of the room and see for hundreds of yards from the mirror at the other end of the room. These huge mirrors all came from France and cost, I believe, about $1000 each. It was a beautiful room, and two of my sisters [Maude and Kittie] were married in this room.[3]

Behind the house were slave quarters. It took many slaves and, later, servants, to maintain the property. Legend has it that a free black woman named Miss Josephine was in charge of the household. Other sources described her as a slave. Josephine had many responsibilities, including midwife, nurse and governess.

Of course, the house is haunted:

The broom of Ms. Josephine can still be heard in many of the rooms in the mansion. A lemon scent can also be smelt, a scent that was her favorite to smell as she worked in the house. Visitors to the mansion have reported seeing the chandelier shake, lights go on and off, and doors opening and closing.... Her apparition has been seen walking up the stairs and walking the galleries. Miss Josephine has also been seen staring out the window onto the street. Many psychics have come to visit Ms. Josephine's room and report overwhelming feelings of sadness, and the sound of a woman praying.[4]

The mansion was always a busy place with

interesting tradespeople ... constantly arriving at the gate at the rear of the property. One was the "Tin I Fix Man," who was called that because he hollered out, "Tin I fix!" Most of the cooking utensils and many other items were made of tin, and he repaired them. Then there was the "Ting-a-Ling Man," who rang a bell and sold ice cream. And the "shrimp man," who came by selling river shrimp. Another fellow selling junk came by yelling, "Any rags, any bones, any bottles today?" The "fig man" sold fresh figs and all kinds of other fruits and vegetables.[5]

Henry Buckner was not a cotton planter, but a factor, someone "who purchased from upriver planters and sold the crop to brokers for the best available price, usually for a 2.5 percent commission."[6] It was a lucrative business.

In 1835, Buckner married Catherine Allen, born in Kentucky in 1805. Mumsie, one of nine Buckner children, married Confederate veteran Cartwright Eustis, who was born in Natchez, Mississippi, in 1842. Their wedding was held in the Buckner mansion on May 3, 1870. Like her father, Mumsie and Cartwright also had nine children, including Katty's mother Katharine Eustis. Born on January 2, 1879, she is listed as Kate in the 1880 census; she later became known as Kittie.

Neither of Katty's grandfathers were living when she was born in 1903. Her mother's father, Cartwright Eustis, died in 1900. Her father's father, Irish immigrant Andrew Stewart, died on February 7, 1903, less than a month before Katty was born. Grieving turned to jubilation when Kittie and Will's first child was born.

For some reason, perhaps because Mumsie was widowed, Kittie and Will Stewart, from a wealthy family himself, moved into the Buckner Mansion after their marriage. Katty grew up in the house and didn't leave it until it was sold in 1923 when she was 20.

The first time Katty Stewart appears in the U.S. census is 1910. She, her parents and younger brother Andrew (nicknamed Buddy) lived with Mumsie Eustis. Katty was seven, Buddy five. Kittie was 31 and Will was 33.

Fortunately the house was huge because in 1910 Mumsie's sons Richard, 28, Laurance, 25, daughter Maude, 22, and Richard's wife Alice, 22, lived there. Another occupant was Betty Kingsley, a 40-year-old mulatto widow. She was unable to read or write; her occupation was listed as nurse. Since it was common for African American women to be employed as wet nurses for wealthy white Southern women, Betty might have nursed Katty and Buddy. Most certainly, she was responsible for caring for them. Considering the fact that she was born around 1870, it is likely that her parents were slaves for much of their lives.

Enslaved and emancipated blacks lived with white families and made their lives comfortable.

> How were the houses a part of the slave system? In every way. They would not stand were it not for the labor and lives of enslaved people. Enslaved people extracted lumber and clay from the land and converted them into building materials. Enslaved people helped import the materials that did not come from the land. Enslaved people cut, laid, erected and pieced the materials together. Enslaved people built the houses. Enslaved people made and brought in the items that furnished the houses once construction was done. Enslaved people cleaned and maintained the houses once they were furnished. Enslaved peopled helped expand and renovate the houses when their owners wanted more.[7]

After emancipation, enslaved people's descendants had many of the same duties: Discrimination and Jim Crow laws kept them under the control of white people.

Katty and her friends were born into a white supremacist, patriarchal society. White men held virtually all positions of power. However, one place where women wielded power was in the home. On the 1910 census, Mumsie, not Will Stewart, was listed as head of the household.

The Civil War had ended only 38 years before Katty's birth. Despite the end to slavery, African Americans continued to suffer under institutional racism in the South. In addition, the Confederacy and its "heroes" were still revered, and annual pageants and parades celebrated "The Lost Cause." Brought up to believe the South had been wronged, Katty and her friends participated in many of these activities.

Katty knew many people who vividly remembered the Civil War. Cartwright Eustis, her grandfather on her mother's side, fought for the Confederacy. "[Cartwright] and two of his brothers [Horatio and Richard] were at Harvard when the Civil War began, and the three of them left college to come home and fight for the South." According to Laurance Eustis, "My grandfather, a captain in the Confederate Army, was wounded twice, once in the leg at Shiloh and again at Murfreesboro, Tennessee. Each time he was injured, he came home to his father's cotton plantation in Issaquena County [Mississippi] to recover. When he was healed, he went back to fight. Both of his brothers were killed fighting the war, Horatio in 1861 and Richard in 1864."[8]

The plantation Eustis referred to was Eustacia Plantation. "Eustatia Plantation was located in the southwestern part of Issaquena County near the Mississippi River. Owned by Horatio Sprague Eustis (Katty's great-grandfather), the plantation was home to 101 slaves.... The plantation included 26 slave houses."[9] Prior to the Civil War, Issaquena County had the highest concentration of slaves in America. Almost 93 percent of the county's population were slaves, working on some of the country's largest cotton plantations.

In New Orleans newspapers of Katty's time, racism is pervasive. Racial epithets are casually used. An individual's race is mentioned only when they are African American, often in cases where that person is accused of criminal activity.

In a passage from a society column in 1925, white author Natalie Scott explains how nice it is to return to the South:

> You feel a touch of home, when a black-faced, white-coated negro porter gives three ceremonious flicks with a napkin at non-existent crumbs on your tablecloth, and asks your order, with an ecstatic chuckle over the joy of serving you. And you know you are there when two little shabby pickaninnies shoot coins against a wall. They pick them up at the end of the toss, calling it even. When

one adds, with belated inspiration, munificently with an added gesture of mammoth drooping coat sleeve, much frayed—"I had yeh by a little bit; but I leave it be."[10]

Scott, who later traveled to Europe with Katty, was an educated, well-traveled intellectual, active in artistic circles. However, she did not believe in equal rights for African Americans. When she was in Europe during World War I, she volunteered with the Red Cross. While working with a Frenchwoman at a small field hospital near the end of the war, she was upset to see the woman's

> coziness with an African-American lieutenant stationed with his all-black unit in the area. So emboldened, in Scott's view, the man "breezily" flirted with her as well. Here was precisely the racial apocalypse many Southerners in particular dreaded: give the black man authority and he will convert it to sexual license—or at least that's what many white supremacists claimed to anticipate when withholding political, social or economic equality. "Just imagine," Scott wrote to her mother, "the time we will have with these people after the war."[11]

While Anthony J. Huebner hastened to add that Scott's views on race "evolved," this shows how common racist views were in the South at the time.

2

Society Columns

> Palms and ferns and pink carnations decorated the rooms and in the dining room the table was embellished with pink carnations and pink-shaded lights in silver candelabra. The ices and confections were served in rose color and white.

Katty's mother, Kittie Eustis Stewart, was an important part of the New Orleans social scene, which, of course, was only for rich white citizens. From a young age, Kittie, considered one of the great beauties of New Orleans, was often mentioned in society columns. For example, in 1898, Kittie was chosen queen at the annual ball of the Knights of Momus,[1] an important Mardi Gras event held every year. "The King's float always stopped in front of her home and toasted her each year for decades."[2]

The rich liked to think of themselves as quasi-royalty, and social events, including Carnival balls, often included dressing up and engaging in a kind of cosplay where they pretended to be kings, queens, pages and squires. It was expected that Katty and her generation would also become involved in this family tradition.

Katty's father, William P. Stewart, was born in 1876 in New Orleans. Will's family also had tremendous wealth that depended on slavery. His father, Andrew Stewart, born September 26, 1827, in Stribane, Ireland, came to America at the age of 20 and made a fortune in the cotton industry. When he died at age 75 of heart failure in his Philip Street home, he was a "senior member of the cotton firm of Stewart Bros. and Co., of this city, and of Stewart, Gwynne & Co., of Memphis."[3] Another obituary described him as a "cotton man [who] did a big business in cotton and served as president of the Cotton Exchange."[4]

Almost a year before Andrew's death, Will and Kittie married on April 16, 1902, in an Episcopal service at the Buckner mansion. The wedding was a major event in New Orleans society:

> [It] was the nuptial event of the week marked in attendance by a large family connection and intimate friends. The ceremony took place at the residence

of the bride's mother ... at 8 o'clock in the evening. The spacious home, a typically Southern mansion, is remarkably well adapted for entertaining and especially so for the celebration of a wedding. The residence throughout was made beautiful with hundreds of white flowers including roses, lilies of the valley, syringa, carnations, jasmine and other snowy blooms. Arching the doorways and windows were tall tree palms, which flanked the entrance of each.[5]

The article mentioned that Kittie was still grieving her father, who had died in December 1900: "The bride, who is just laying aside her mourning for her father, the late, generally beloved Mr. Cartwright Eustis, was given into the keeping of the groom by her mother." As was common in society columns of the time, much was made about Kittie's beauty. "She made a most exquisite bride in her gown of white chiffon...." Mention was also made of the bride's taste and manners. "Though an unusually large number of costly and artistic gifts were received by Mr. and Mrs. Stewart, the bride adhered to the very good form of not displaying her collection of beautiful bridal souvenirs and remembrances."

Katty was born less than a year later. Since Katty was the only granddaughter living with Mumsie, it's likely she received much attention and affection. In fact, she was probably spoiled.

Laurance Eustis, one of 23 grandchildren, described his grandmother as generous and loving. "Every December she ... sent us a huge package of Christmas presents, and opening the box was the highlight of the holiday for our family of three in Memphis. Mumsie always sent me three or four presents."[6]

Katty was born into a world of rigid social mores and rules, including gender conformity, which she would have been taught by her mother and grandmother. There would have been enormous pressure on Katty to behave in a certain way. In addition, Katty also realized at a young age that her family was special, or, as Laurance Eustis described them, "prominent ... socially and financially."[7]

Katty Stewart was groomed to follow in the footsteps of her grandmother and mother. At a fairly young age, she was pushed into social activities with people who belonged to her social class.

Society columns in twentieth-century America newspapers were the Instagram, Twitter and Facebook of their time. They existed for wealthy white people of the city to inform others of their activities and events. As with social media of our time, they were often used to show off, to make one's life appear glamorous, important and successful. Society columns also could have been, and likely were, a place to lie, exaggerate and fabricate. They provided a do-it-yourself public relations campaign that women, and some men, participated in. Katty learned from her mother, who learned it from her mother. The Eustis women were masters. Kittie, a real pro, could have taught a Udemy course on it.

Society column editors relied on self-reporting. It's quaint to think that the editor relied on eager, enthusiastic reporters who fanned out over the city to discover interesting tidbits about the town's citizens. But no.

New Orleans enjoyed a number of different newspapers, and each had its own society column.

> There were three [newspapers] in the early 1920s, four after 1924, and no single paper was comfortably dominant. The morning *Times-Picayune* always led in sales, but the combined circulation of the afternoon papers, the *Item* and the *States*, was great, and when the *Item* brought out a morning edition called the *Morning Tribune* in 1924, soon *those* two papers together outsold the *Times-Picayune*. *Time* magazine described New Orleans as "one of the hottest competitive newspaper towns in the country." The resulting scramble for readers led to extensive coverage of local news … and created jobs for reporters to cover it.[8]

Writing a social column was one of the few jobs available to women, and it was given to those who were white, wealthy and socially connected. Society editors often employed staffs of women. Their job wasn't easy. For one thing, the columnists were required to be flattering to the point of sycophancy. In addition, columns covered many square inches, often spread out over two pages or more, and thick with names. The only way it was possible to fill the column was for the staff to receive phone calls or pieces of paper with the information written out. In some cases, the staff likely received a copy of guest lists or, like college students in assembly halls, the attendees were asked to write their names on a sign-in sheet.

It's important to remember that what appears in the society columns is information the subject wants readers to see. While it does provide a kind of record of a person's life, it's a carefully curated account.

It would be a while before Katty's name appeared in society columns. However, there is an interesting family photograph of the Eustis family which probably dates from around 1910. It includes Katty (approximately seven years old), Will, Kittie and Buddy, along with other relatives. Fortunately, someone took the trouble to write down the names. Before she was nicknamed Katty, Katharine Stewart was called Coddy.

Katty is confident, butchy and, frankly, looks like a handful. Considering her influences, she is surprisingly tomboyish and not particularly feminine.

One of the first mentions of Katty in a society column was December 17, 1911. Katty, eight, was referred to as Katharine. The event was a tea for Althea Winship, and Katty was one of several young women "presiding in the dining room."[9] The tea was sponsored by Althea's grandmother, Mrs.

Ernest Puoch, which was typical. Relatives, usually but not always women, hosted parties for family members. The Puoches were acquaintances of Katty's parents. Names of attendees at this event numbered into the dozens.

Several names stand out because they appear many times throughout the years alongside Katty's. Katty grew up with these children, and some friendships lasted for decades. First was Josephine LeBlanc, Katty's cousin. Her mother was Jane Stewart LeBlanc, who was Will Stewart's sister. Jo's father was local businessman Alfred LeBlanc, who married Jane in 1881. LeBlanc owned and managed a steamship company. Jane died in 1920, but Katty continued her warm friendship with Jo for the rest of her life.

The Eustis family portrait circa 1915 includes Katty and Buddy Stewart and their parents, Will and Kittie Eustis Stewart. First row, from left: Jimmy Eustis, Buddy Stewart, Binks Eustis, Coddy (Katty) Stewart; second row, from left: Kittie Eustis Stewart, Adele Britten Eustis, Nellie Eustis Dearborn, Herbert Eustis, Jr., Laura Buckner Eustis (Mumsie), Lollie Eustis Russell; third row, from left: George H. Russell, Dr. Allan Eustis, unknown, William Dearborn, Herbert L. Eustis, unknown, Richard Eustis, Will Stewart, Laura Russell Van Brunt, Alice Aldice Eustis (courtesy Steven Eustis).

Another name was Ellene White, daughter of Albert Sidney White and Ellen Tobin White. Ellene, nicknamed Tita, was the sister of Moosie White. Moosie was a year older than Katty and became a close friend and confidante. The New Orleans society world was a small community with lots of connections. For example, Moosie and Katty became relatives when Josephine LeBlanc married Leon Gibert, whose mother was Moosie's aunt. Yes, it's complicated.

There were no boys at the tea party. In fact, the only male name listed in the article was Mrs. *Ernest* Puoch. Like every woman of that time period, Marie Ernestine Baudoin lost her surname upon marriage. In most cases, adult women were only referred to by their husband's first and last name in newspapers. Whatever identity they had before marriage disappeared.

It's likely, of course, that there were young boys who would have loved to attend a tea party. It's also likely that some young girls, despite the event being described as a "delightful afternoon," reluctantly attended. Gender conformity, like white supremacy and the patriarchy, was the world that

Katty grew up in. It's likely Katty chafed against the ultra-femininity she was expected to display.

Most of the tea parties, even for children, included a detailed description of the setting and flora. All of this seemed important, perhaps because it suggested the wealth of the family. Plants and food were expensive. It also pointed to the important role of the woman of the house. Someone had to plan, set up and organize these parties, and in more cases than not it was the lady of the house. Of course, much of the actual work relied on poorly paid servants.

Another early mention of Katharine Stewart was in 1912 when she was a flower girl in the wedding of Maude Eustis (Kittie's sister and Katty's aunt) and Harold Seaman. Katharine was described as "the charming little daughter of Mr. and Mrs. William P. Stewart, who was the dainty flower girl."[10] "Charming" and "dainty" suggest prized female qualities. The *New Orleans Item* society editor also noted Katty's outfit: "The flower girl … wore an exquisite frock of blush pink hand embroidered mull trimmed with lace, and carried a French basket tied with fluffy bows of pale pink tulle."[11]

A frequent way to get mentioned in a society column was to announce travel plans. Later that year, around June, Katty and her brother Buddy traveled with their mother and Grandma Eustis to Milwaukee, Wisconsin, where they stayed with Maude and Harold Seaman. It was typical for the wealthy to leave hot, humid New Orleans in the summer and head for cooler temperatures. When Katty was older, she too, often accompanied by Moosie White, regularly left New Orleans in May or June and stayed away until fall.

Mumsie particularly enjoyed visiting Wisconsin. According to Katty's cousin Laurance, "They went up on the Illinois Central with servants. I'm certain that at that time, around the turn of the century, there were no dining cars, so my grandmother packed huge baskets of fried chicken to eat on the train."[12]

3

Katty and Moosie

> Women are like canaries, born and raised in a pleasant cage,
> After awhile, they forget that a sky is above them.
> When chance leaves the door open, they venture a little way out
> But are afraid to fly;
> They shrink from the strength of the wind in the coming storms,
> Nor do they trust their wings.
> What if the cage door shut![1]

Bell Lawrason was a poet, artist and architect born in New Orleans in 1889. Natalie Scott described her as "that courageous and hauntingly pretty architect."[2] She was friendly with Walker Ellis and other gay New Orleanians. She was ten years younger than Kittie Stewart and 14 years older than Katty. Her poem "Canaries!" illustrates the conflicting feelings many women felt about their role in society.

Young women featured in society columns likely found the attention flattering and welcome. However, after women married and took their husband's names, it must have been a shock when they became invisible and ignored. Some women tried to re-establish their identities and visibility. For example, in 1913 when Katty was ten, an odd profile on Kittie Stewart appeared in the *New Orleans Item*. Accompanied by a large photo, the text read:

> Mrs. William P. Stewart, before her marriage, was Miss Katharine Eustis, the daughter of Mrs. Cartwright Eustis. Golden-haired and blue-eyed, with the slender grace of a girl, Mrs. Stewart possesses to a marked degree the charm of manner that characterizes all the women of her family. Mrs. Stewart is considered by many people to be the loveliest exponent among New Orleans women of the new dances.[3]

Kittie herself was likely behind this newspaper article and may have written most of it. She missed the attention she had received before marriage and may have felt ignored by her husband. Whatever the reason, Kittie, now the mother of two young children, wanted New Orleans to know she existed and was still one of its "loveliest." This was out of character for most wealthy New Orleans society women and did not bode well for the Stewart marriage. Kittie's disappointment with life after marriage also created tension with her mother.

In that same year, 1913, Katty appeared in an article about a tea for a young girl named Marion Souchon. Organized by Marion's mother, the event took place on St. Charles Avenue in the Garden District. Elizabeth (Moosie) White's name was on the list of dozens of names of young girls who attended. Katty was ten, Moosie 11.

Nicknamed Moussie (it evolved into Moosie), Elizabeth grew up with Katty, and their names appeared hundreds of times together. In fact, columnists talked about the two as though it was common knowledge that they were a couple. Later, when Katty began to travel to Europe, New York and other places, Moosie often accompanied her. Their close friendship lasted years. It's unknown if their relationship was sexual, but there is no doubt that Katty and Moosie shared a long-term, intense connection, almost from the time they met.

Katty and Moosie's generation was different from their mothers.' For one thing, they were better educated. Most went to finishing schools, and some attended college. They also had more freedom in terms of who they would marry and when. This generation had fewer children, and some even chose not to have kids. None of the four subjects of this book—Katty, Moosie, Walker and Walter—had children. Furthermore, Katty and Moosie grew up during the suffrage era and were the first generation of women allowed to vote.

Elizabeth (Moosie) White was born Elizabeth Bradford White on July 26, 1902, in New Orleans. Her parents were Albert Sidney White and Ellen Virginia Tobin White. At the time, the White family lived at 1631 Esplanade Avenue in New Orleans' Garden District. The house was a beautiful white-frame mansion (it's now converted into condo apartments) with columns, a large front porch and a second floor balcony. Moosie was a sensitive girl who loved music and the arts.

Moosie's ancestors were wealthy and well-known. Her great-grandfather Maunsel White, born in Ireland in 1783, was a self-made businessman who owned several plantations and hundreds of slaves. He married a French Creole New Orleans woman named Celestine de la Ronde. White was friendly with Andrew Jackson and Walter Stauffer's grandfather, Zachary Taylor. He is also known for inventing two sauces: a hot pepper sauce and a wine sauce. A rumor suggests that the McIlhenny family stole the hot sauce recipe and used it for their Tabasco sauce. The McIlhenny Company strongly denies this.

The wine sauce, called Maunsel White's 1812 Sauce, commemorated

Elizabeth (Moosie) White was raised in this house on Esplanade in the Garden District of New Orleans (courtesy Maunsel White).

Andrew Jackson's victory at the Battle of New Orleans. The story goes that White served it in Jackson's honor for the first time at White's Deer Range Plantation. White's descendants still sell it in the New Orleans area. "The Colonel" (that was his honorary title) died in New Orleans in 1863.

The parents of Moosie's mother were John William Tobin (1827–1888) and Mary Frances Scott (1837–1915). Tobin owned a steamboat business and served with the Confederacy during the Civil War. He was proud of the fact that he turned down several hundred thousand dollars from the Union and instead ordered that his steamboat be burned. After the war, Tobin ran a cotton factory in New Orleans and helped found the Rex and Proteus carnival groups. Mary Frances Scott, Moosie's grandmother, was the daughter of Judge C.C. Scott, a member of the Arkansas Supreme Court.

Called Mummy by her children and others, Ellen White has been described by various relatives as "imperious" and a "stupendous snob."[4] Mummy had favorites among her children, and Moosie, her youngest daughter, was one of them. More conventionally attractive than the plainer Maudie, Mummy "cruelly taunted" Maudie. The favoritism led to "friction"[5] between Moosie and Maudie.

3. Katty and Moosie

Portrait of Ellen Tobin White with her five children. From left, Moosie, Maudie, John, Ellen, Sid, Ellene (courtesy Maunsel White).

There was other family drama. In 1912, Moosie's father Sid was named Comus in a Mardi Gras event, "which was about the pinnacle of New Orleans society at the time."[6] Maunsel White, son of John White, Moosie's nephew, explained,

Maudie was in line to become the Queen of Comus in 1917, but because of the war, Comus elected not to hold a ball that year. A subgroup [Krewe of Carnival Revelers] formed that was opposed to the hiatus, and they held a ball that had Maudie as queen. It resulted in a schism in the Comus organization, the net result of which was a big come-down for Maudie's and my grandparents' social aspirations.[7]

The money train derailed in 1912 [i.e., the family had a reversal of fortune] when my great uncle Maunsel White died. He was a famous metallurgist who co-invented high-speed steel which revolutionized the iron and steel industry. He co-signed the loans that underpinned my grandfather's sheet metal business. When "Uncle Man" died, all the loans were called, and my grandfather had to sell everything he had to satisfy the creditors. In those days, bankruptcy was *not* an option for any "respectable" person. He became a manufacturer's agent, basically a traveling salesman.[8]

Moosie's name began appearing in newspapers before she turned four. In April 1906, she attended an Easter egg hunt for Althea Winship. Moosie's sisters, Maude and Ellene, were also there.[9] Yes, this is the same Althea who Katty knew, and it illustrates what a small world New Orleans society was at this time.

In the 1910 census, nine people are listed as residents at the Esplanade address, including Moosie's parents Sidney and Ellen, oldest daughter Maude, 12; Ellene, 10; Elizabeth (Moosie), 7; oldest son Sidney, 5; and the youngest child and son John, 2. There are three servants listed. Octavia Andrey was a 45-year-old mulatto, Ada Hanson an 18-year-old of Norwegian descent, and Charles Ross, the coachman, a 42-year-old black man.

Like Katty, Moosie was socialized to understand a female's role in her culture. In 1913, she attended a children's birthday party for Eliska Tobin. "Seated at either end of the table were Miss Elizabeth White and Miss Marie Olive Carriere, two charming little misses who served the tea and chocolate, both of whom wore white lingerie dresses with sashes and hair ribbons of pink."[10]

* * *

On February 27, 1915, Katty's grandmother, Theresa Josephine Pharr Stewart, died at the age of 74, and Will Stewart and his siblings received a healthy inheritance. Will splurged on a yacht, *Sunshine*. This delighted Katty because she loved being around water, and in the coming years she and her family and friends spent much time on the yacht.

When Katty became a teenager, she was finally allowed to attend events that included boys. One such occasion was in May 1915. Her cousin Edwa Stewart, daughter of John and Edwa Stewart, hosted a party at her parents' Napoleon Avenue house. The *Picayune-Times* covered the event: "Though informal, it was a very beautiful party of the spring.... The porches were enclosed with canvas and the supper table was arranged on one, and lovely with flowers. An Aolian Vocalian [phonograph] furnished the music for the dancing."[11]

Katty's parents were among the chaperones, along with aunt and uncle Andrew and Josephine Stewart, the childless couple who would eventually purchase Oak Alley Plantation. Among the male attendees was Richard Orme, who continued to socialize with Katty and Moosie throughout their childhoods and into adulthood. Orme had a brief show business career and then became an antiques dealer. He had a long friendship with Tennessee Williams.

No matter the era, gay people will find other gay people. Orme was just one of many acquaintances who Katty met in social situations and realized they had something in common.

In the summer of 1916, the closeness between Katty and Moosie grew, and Katty spent part of her summer with the White family. "Mrs. A. Sidney White has been having a number of young girls as her guests for more or less short visits this season, at her cottage at Mandeville [located on the north shore of Lake Pontchartrain], where the family is spending the summer."[12] From this point on, Moosie and Katty usually spent their summers together.

Katty was now allowed to attend dances at the Country Club, where her parents were members. Over the coming years, Katty spent much time at the Club. A typical event was a 1916 Christmas party. Also attending were Moosie and Ellene White, Jo LeBlanc and Edwa Stewart. Katty would have been one of the youngest girls there. "Miss Ellen Henderson gave a beautiful Christmas party in the evening Thursday, at the Country Club, in honor of her young nephews, William and Sylvester Labrot. The club was reserved for the evening.... The dance was one of the largest and liveliest of the many private parties of the young set, planned in fashionable circles for Christmas week, and found many of the younger college and school sets attending."[13]

By 1917, Katty and Moosie were fully immersed in New Orleans social activities. One big event that year was a Red Cross benefit held at the French Opera House. A newspaper critic went above and beyond in his praise for the production:

> The French Opera House wore a festive aspect last night when the "Gambol of the Gods" was presented.... The audience was reminiscent of the gala opera nights of bygone years.... The entire entertainment moved in professional style and ended before 11 o'clock. It was elaborate and spoke eloquently of the time and energy expended on it.... The scenic effects were charming, the costumes very attractive and the stage pictures were, on several occasions, of a really striking beauty.[14]

The production featured a cast of hundreds of locals. Katty and Moosie were among the many young girls who portrayed snowflakes.

When Katty turned 14, she finally got an opportunity to host her own party—the first of many such events that she hosted in her life. It was held in the Buckner mansion, which had to be a special thrill. "Mr. and Mrs. William P. Stewart entertained Saturday evening a number of the college set at a farm dance at their home in Jackson Avenue, in honor of their daughter, Katharine Stewart. The guests wore farm costumes with sun bonnets, aprons and overalls. A large number of guests were present."[15]

In the late spring of 1917, Katty continued a long tradition of visiting her aunt Jane and cousin Jo LeBlanc at their Pass Christian, Mississippi, summer home. Many Orleanians had summer homes in the Mississippi Gulf area, according to Maunsel White: "The Mississippi Gulf Coast had been a watering place for New Orleanians for a very long time—since early in the 19th century. The same people who socialized at the clubs and balls in New Orleans also 'took the waters' together on 'the coast' together. In fact, there was a significant contingent of people who commuted to and from New Orleans and the coast on a daily basis via train."[16] That summer, Katty was accompanied by Anne Hardie, Burdette Waldo, Katherine Thomas, Edwa Stewart and Moosie White.

Later that month, Katty and Moosie attended a dance celebrating the commencement of Miss Miller's School, a New Jersey finishing school which many young, wealthy New Orleans girls attended. It was customary for the wealthy to send their children outside of New Orleans to attend boarding schools.

Before the summer ended, Katty, who loved to travel, went with a group of New Orleans girls to Camp Quinibeck in Vermont. It was a popular girls' camp, and Katty stayed through August. She loved the outdoors and especially enjoyed swimming, riding and hunting.

Beginning in 1918, Katty and Moosie were often seen together at the Southern Yacht Club dances. "The dance given Monday evening at the Southern Yacht Club by members of the Tau Sigma, a club composed of the school set of girls, was a particularly delightful event for very young members of society."[17]

Katty and Moosie also attended events related to engagements and weddings. For example, in April, Katty and Moosie were at a tea in honor of bride-to-be Helen Dufour. "Maude White was hostess very informally Tuesday afternoon, at tea…. Miss White entertained at the home of her parents, Mr. and Mrs. A. Sidney White, in Esplanade Avenue, and the tea table, lovely with sweet-pea blossoms, was presided over by Miss Heda Kock. The tea-girls were: Misses Elizabeth White, Maude Fox and

Katharine Stewart."[18] The term "very informally" was occasionally used and apparently an important distinction to make.

The *The New Orleans Item* society column was written anonymously by "Louisianne." When covering this particular tea, the writer got cutesy: "I want to tell you about the lovely tea Maudie White gave Tuesday for Helen Dufour. We had just lots of fun and Heda Kock poured tea at the loveliest flower-filled table, and there was Ruth Wood waving her hand gracefully ... as she took her cup from the tray of one of the cute little serving girls, Maude Fox, I think it was, or perhaps Katharine Stewart? ... I took a delicious cake from a plate Maude's dear little sister Elizabeth held up to me...."[19] It goes on and on, naming and commenting on as many young women as possible, showing the importance of getting one's name into a society column.

Katty enjoyed dances and soon graduated from simply attending them to planning them. For example, in 1918, she, Burdette Waldo and Anne Hardie were on a committee to host several junior dances at the Suffrage House. Located at 1109 St. Charles Avenue, the House's mission was to get women the right to vote.[20] Katty and Moosie were part of a generation of women who came of age with the Suffrage movement, and it influenced them. In 1922, Moosie and Katty's debutante year, Moosie was quoted as saying that she believed that it was "every woman's duty to vote as often as the law allows."[21]

In August 1918, it was announced that a boarding school had been chosen for Katty. "Mrs. Stewart and Miss Katharine Stewart will ... leave for New York, where the latter will enter Miss Masters' School at Dobbs Ferry, to be a student there this winter."[22]

Here's where it gets interesting. Katty, now 15, did not enroll at Miss Masters' School. There were several New Orleans girls who did, but for unknown reasons, Katty ended up at a different school. On Tuesday, September 17, Katty and her mother left New Orleans for the Hotel Biltmore, a New York luxury hotel. "Miss Stewart will remain North as a student at the Cathedral School at Garden City, Long Island."[23]

The decision to change schools was life-changing. It was at the Cathedral School of St. Mary where Katty met Katharine Gibbs, later known as Kay Francis.

Katharine Edwina Gibbs was born in Oklahoma City, Oklahoma, on January 13, 1905. Father Joseph Sprague Gibbs gave Kay her last name and towering height, but her mother made a terrible mistake when she married him. He came from a good family but was not a good man.

Twelve years older than Kay's mother, Joseph Gibbs had already been married and divorced more than once. He was a bad catch and eventually doomed Kay and her mother to years of poverty by abandoning them.

Although an accomplished, trained actor, Kay's mother struggled to make ends meet. Kay later intimated to friends that her mother resorted to prostitution to provide for her.

Kay's mother had many secrets. Her stage name was Katherine Clinton, but her real name was Katherine Clinton Franks. Her parents were Isabella Clinton and Edward Gay Franks. Born in Pennsylvania in 1832, Edward Franks moved to Chicago where he became a merchant. After his first wife Henrietta died in 1869, he married Isabella on January 20, 1875, eight months after Katherine's birth on May 17, 1874.

In 1883, when Katherine was nine, Isabella died. Three years later, in 1886, Edward died, making Katherine, not yet 12, an orphan. Fortunately for Katherine, her half-brother Edwin, a criminal lawyer in Colorado, stepped in and provided for her, including paying for her education. Edwin died unexpectedly in 1909 when Kay was four.

Many have speculated about Kay Francis' ancestry because of her dark, exotic looks. Some thought she might be part African American, Cuban, or Spanish. The truth, however, was a secret that Kay and her mother successfully kept hidden.

Kay Francis had deep Jewish roots on her mother's side. Kay's mother, fearing anti–Semitism, changed her last name from Franks to Clinton and never publicly discussed her Jewish background. She likely convinced Kay, too, to keep it secret.

This was at a time when most people were clueless about their genealogy. It's doubtful that Katherine Franks had any idea how far back the Franks line went—and that it leads to prominent American Jewish men and women, including Moses Benjamin Franks who helped build the first synagogue in New York. Other ancestors were persecuted for their religious beliefs.

Kay, for obvious reasons, didn't think much of her father. Despite being the son of a successful man, Joe never amounted to anything despite privilege and opportunity. Still, his family lineage, especially on the Sprague line, leads to American roots that may, in fact, lead to a man who came to America on the *Mayflower*.

No matter what Kay's ancestry might have been, the reality is that Kay's childhood was difficult, and her mother struggled. Katherine Franks got the idea, and it was a good one, that placing Kay in private schools where she could mingle with children of wealth might provide connections and lead to an easier life. It worked. Kay's private school education, combined with her charm and good looks, helped her gain entry into high society.

The Cathedral School was not Kay's first school. She admitted that her academic career was checkered. "St. Mary's school at Garden City, where I met Katty Stewart, was only one of about 15 schools I attended.'"[24]

3. Katty and Moosie

Kay's disadvantaged childhood ended up being an advantage in her career. Knowing real poverty and desperation, she was determined to make it. She had grit. Giving up was not an option. She famously said, "As long as they pay me my salary, I'll sweep the stages if they give me a broom."[25] Katty, and many of the privileged young women she grew up with, had a safety net and a surplus of options. They had a plan B, C and the whole alphabet.

Katty and Kay quickly became friends at the boarding school. Katty was 15, Kay 13. Kay looked up to Katty and was impressed with her wealth and position. She listened with rapt attention to Katty's stories about life in New Orleans among the elite.

* * *

Unlike Katty, Moosie stayed in New Orleans for her schooling. She admitted to a newspaper during her debutante year that her academic record was, well, not good. This was due, likely in no small part, to an eventual diagnosis of bipolar disorder. She finally ended up at Newcomb College which, in addition to its college for women, offered high school classes.

By 1917, Moosie was appearing at most of the same events—dances, wedding, parties—as Katty. They were children of wealthy, white New Orleans parents, and their friends had the same background. The same names appear over and over again: Claire Parkhurst, Kingsley Black (one of the coolest names in this social clique), Burdette Waldo, Amelie May, Emily Hayne, Genevive Pitot, Anne Hardie, Rebecca Perkins, Katharine Thomas, Dorothy Clay, Josephine LeBlanc *et al*. From that time on, Katty Stewart and Moosie White often had their names adjacent to each other in listings of attendees.

Katty usually came home to New Orleans for holidays and summer breaks. When Katty returned on December 17, 1918, a party was held to celebrate her arrival. "Mrs. Cartwright Eustis [Mumsie] will entertain members of the younger set at 'The Dansant,' the afternoon of Saturday, December 28, from 4 to 7 o'clock, complimentary to her young granddaughter, Miss Katharine Stewart, who will arrive from school on Long Island for the holidays."[26] A dansant was a French term that simply meant a small, informal dance.

The event was "one of the smartest events of Christmas week for very young members of society.... Mrs. Eustis entertained at her home in Jackson Avenue, which was additionally pretty with holly poinsettia and other Christmas decorations. In addition to Miss Stewart, the young guests present were the daughters of prominent members of New Orleans' fashionable world."[27] On that return trip home, Katty also had a separate party planned in her honor hosted by Moosie White and her parents.[28]

Katty returned to New Orleans in the summer. She spent much of her time at the Country Club and Southern Yacht Club and attended various teas and other social activities. Her near-constant companion was Moosie.

The following summer, Katty and her parents traveled again to Pass Christian where they stayed at the Miramar Hotel, a resort hotel that catered to the wealthy[29]:

> The Gulf Coast resorts nearby are not wanting for gaiety, in either younger or married circles, and much of the entertaining done is very elaborate, with the many beautiful homes of the villa community proving attractive settings. One of the very picturesque parties at Pass Christian last week was given by Mrs. John G. O'Kelly, who entertained for her niece, Lucille O'Kelly.... It was an al fresco tea, with the tea table set under the vines of the pergola on the lawn of the home."[30]

Among the guests were Katty, Moosie and Moosie's sisters Maude and Ellene. According to the society column, "There is no more attractive coterie of young women than these three charming young sisters. The youngest, Elizabeth White, is still a member of the college set, however, and is one of the very handsome and attractive of the younger girls in the society circles here."

4

Baby Dances

"Mr. Eustis is no more."

Behind wealth and privilege, there are dark family secrets. While Katty was at school, a family tragedy struck. Her uncle, Richard Eustis, Kittie's brother, a man with whom Katty had once shared the Jackson Avenue home, died on October 27, 1919. The first newspaper article, on the front page of the *New Orleans Item,* incorrectly reported, "Richard Eustis Murdered at Harvey Mill." Rumors circulated that a former worker who had been involved in a recent strike was the murderer. It wasn't true. Another rumor was that Eustis had died in an accident. This also wasn't true.

The family remained tight-lipped for several days. "A brother [likely Dr. Allan Eustis, who appeared to be the family spokesperson] of the mill manager refused to give the details of Mr. Eustis' death. He would say no more than that 'Mr. Eustis is no more.'"

In reality, Eustis shot himself in the head at his workplace, the Louisiana Cypress Lumber Company. He was 37. "Eustis was found dead when employees went to investigate the cause of a shot they had heard. A few minutes previously he had been joking with members of the office force." The newspaper pointed out that Eustis was wealthy, suggesting that money woes were not the cause of his suicide. "His salary was a large one and he had ample means aside from it." Allan, a medical doctor, blamed the flu. "Since he suffered an attack of influenza a year ago he had been subject to mental lapses. At intervals he was extremely melancholy."[1] The previous year, 1918, had seen the start of a flu pandemic, and its effects had stretched into 1919.

Services were held for Richard, and his remains were placed in the family tomb. "Only relatives and close friends of the family attended the ceremony."[2] It's not known if Katty came home for the funeral, but it's doubtful. Still, it had to be deeply upsetting for the 16-year-old. It was probably the first suicide that touched her. It wouldn't be the last.

At the end of the school year when Katty returned to New Orleans, she was on a committee, with Jo LeBlanc and Marion Souchon, for Tau Sigma, the social club for school girls. It held its annual dance at the Grunewald Hotel on Saturday, December 20. These types of dances were often referred to as "baby" dances to distinguish them from adult dances. According to the newspaper, "This is always an important event for young folks."[3]

The Whites were now living at 1530 First Street, a beautiful home in the Garden District with lots of wrought iron and many gorgeous rooms.

From a young age, Moosie was interested in art, music and drama. She also had a strong interest in France and all things French, largely because of her ancestry. Her parents enrolled her in the Classe de Conservation, and she regularly participated in recitals and performances. In March 1918, she performed in a skit at the home of Mrs. Miriam Crusel and later served refreshments.[4]

At the end of 1918, Moosie participated in a small performance at Jo LeBlanc's house. "Oh, what a delightful time we had last week at the meeting of the Causerie du Lundi at the pretty and artistic home of Mrs. Alfred LeBlanc.... The little tea girls came dancing in upon us—Josephine LeBlanc, Elizabeth White and Burdette Waldo."[5] The translation of Causerie du Lundi is Monday Chatterings and was taken from a weekly literary column written by Charles Augustin Sainte-Beuve. The name was used for salons, hosted in private homes, that featured music, lectures, readings and other highbrow entertainment. Katty's aunt, Jane Stewart LeBlanc, was president of the club, which was a branch of L'Alliance Française. Meetings were held in her home at 1296 First Street until her death on March 15, 1920, of pneumonia at the age of 60.

In January 1920, Moosie, who loved performing, had a small role in a Le Petit Théâtre du Vieux Carré production of *Big Kate*. She appeared with several others as one of the ladies of the court.[6]

The Le Petit Théâtre sprung from "a group of friends who called themselves the Drawing Room Players [who] had begun performing for their own amusement in the Garden District house of Rhea Loeb Goldberg."[7] That was in 1916. Within a few years, they rented a small second floor on St. Ann Street for $17.50 a month. They also changed the name to Le Petit Théâtre du Vieux Carré. Natalie Scott, who had recently returned to New Orleans after serving with the Red Cross in Europe, was a member of the group, which was a good thing because her public support was amplified through her work as a journalist.

In December, Moosie gave another performance at a dinner held at the Quartier Club. "Little Elizabeth White, known by the unique nickname of Moosie, recited a Creole monologue that Mrs. Christian Schertz had written."[8]

4. Baby Dances

Helen Pitkin Schertz, called "The Lady Helen," "was almost a caricature of the benevolent clubwoman, active in a score of social, cultural, civic, charitable and ancestry-based organizations, ranging from the DAR to the ASPCA, often as a founder or officer."[9] She was one of the founders of Le Petit Théâtre and a close friend of journalist Dorothy Dix.

Katty returned to New Orleans for the holiday break at the end of 1920, arriving in time for a December 21 debutante party for Dorothy Clay. She and Moosie attended the dance at the Country Club with hundreds of others. Of course, the newspaper proclaimed the event "one of the most handsome and elaborate private parties ever given in New Orleans society." (They always were.)

> The Country Club was beautifully and artistically decorated for the occasion. The Lounge, which was cleared for the dancing, was brilliantly lighted and decorated with a profusion of roses and palms…. There were two orchestras for the dancing and later a set supper was served. All of the tables in the dining room were laden with gifts, favors and trinkets…. After supper the guests all participated in a cotillion figure, the boys all receiving walking sticks and the girls fancy paper parasols.[10]

The expense had to be exorbitant, but the debutante circuit was an important part of New Orleans society. It was expected that wealthy parents would spend beaucoup bucks for their daughters to be introduced to society.

{ 5 }

Let's Not and Say We Did

Elizabeth White's nickname, like Katty's, was often mangled by New Orleans newspapers. Newspapers sometimes called her "Mousie." This one seemed to make sense, especially since Katharine Stewart's nickname was Katty. Her actual nickname was Moussie.

In 1932, a society columnist claimed to know where the nickname came from, though in typical fashion, she misspelled it. "Once upon a time her hair resembled the foamy white mousse on champagne, so Mrs. Walter Stauffer went through her maidenhood as Miss Moussey White. (What was her name? We can't even remember it ourselves.)"[1]

One of the first times Elizabeth was referred to as Moussie was in December 1920. Natalie Scott had recently begun writing a society column called "Peggy Passe Partout's ['Peggy Who Goes Everywhere'] Letter." In the column, she pretended to be writing to her dear friend Cynthia, wittily briefing her on New Orleans news and gossip. "Engaging anecdotes about local people and events, inside news about visitors to the city, details on cultural events, plays, operas, debutante parties, weddings and Mardi Gras balls were her staple subjects."[2]

In December, Scott promoted a one-act play in her column that featured all female roles. "It's called *A Game of Hearts*.... Mrs. Schertz, Moussie White, Jessie Tharp and Natalie Scott are in the cast, and Mr. Flood ... is doing the coaching."[3] Yes, Scott herself was in the cast. Scott often pretended that she and Peggy were two different people. They weren't. It also should be pointed out that Scott often reported on events, publications and businesses with which she had a financial or personal interest without revealing it. "'Full disclosure' was not yet the norm for journalists,"[4] and Scott took full advantage.

Elizabeth immediately objected to the nickname, probably at her mother's urging. In a different column, Scott first commented on Elizabeth's performance. "It was delightful to see Elizabeth White's voice and personality twisted so cleverly to interpret her part." But then Scott announced that Elizabeth did not like the nickname. "Please notice the

'Elizabeth': she's announcing to the world in general these days, in a most aggrieved style, that her name is *not* Moussie—remind your memory!"[5] Needless to say, Natalie ignored her own advice, and Elizabeth was referred to as Moussie hundreds of times. For example, in April 1921, Elizabeth appeared in a second play at the Little Theater. Natalie Scott grudgingly referred to her as Elizabeth but also used the nickname. "Elizabeth (alias Moussie) White had only to be herself to be the perfect ingenue heroine 'so cool and white.'"[6]

The nickname stuck, though the spelling changed to "Moosie." Even Elizabeth often signed her name "Moosie" in letters to family and friends in the early 1920s.

By the way, *Game of Hearts* was performed "before a large dinner dance audience at the New Orleans Country Club.... The play kicked off a series of parties that began at the country club, moved to two downtown restaurants (with drinks she [Natalie Scott] called New Years Volsteads), and ended at a place called Child's followed by daybreak French Market pastry and coffee as a postscript."[7]

In 1921, Moosie turned 18, and in February she was one of the performers at the Quartier Club. "There was singing and 'stunts' and clever Elizabeth White gives a 'mimic' talk and others equally clever amuse in different ways and it is all very jolly and 'sans facon.'"[8]

During the time that Katty and Moosie came of age in New Orleans, a literary-social renaissance took place in what came to be known as the French Quarter. Elizabeth Werlein, one of the cultural leaders, helped found the Quartier Club:

> The Quartier Club, which soon found a site in the lower Pontalba building, enrolled a group of society women who were already meeting and socializing in other settings. It was primarily a ladies' luncheon and supper club (albeit New Orleans–style—the twice weekly supper dances began at 11:00 p.m.).... The club had a Committee on Literature, and Arts and Distinguished Guest Committee, and a Lyceum series.... Its founders' unstated goal may have been to bring uptown society women to Jackson Square, to introduce them to the charms of the Quarter, and to build an influential constituency for preservation.[9]

Lunches and dinners were catered by renowned chef Arnaud. Alcohol was discreetly served. When the Club was raided in 1924, "President Werlein fooled no one when she claimed the discovery was a 'revelation' to her."

* * *

Before Katty graduated from the Cathedral School of St. Mary, she and Kay collaborated on a play. Kay was 16, Katty 18. The play was presented on June 14, 1921. In a 1936 interview, Kay admitted,

I guess I always had it in my mind to be an actress..., and with Katty Stewart wrote a play for our class. It was called *Let's Not and Say We Did*, and there were songs in it. Katty had the feminine lead and I had the masculine lead. It must have been a success because after we gave it the first time, they made us stay over another day and give it for the alumni. Each one of us had the right to bring two guests and I remember that we invited the boys from St. Paul's school and there was a lot of talk about it.[10]

By 1921, Katty and Moosie were inseparable—and adorable together. They were a comical team, and some of their antics were described in the social columns. During construction of the Quartier Club, "Moussie White and Katty Stewart joined the interested group who were observing and supervising the painting the other day, and a few minutes later they had corralled an organ grinder from somewhere and the painters and watchers were serenaded insistently."[11]

Another example of the many reports of Katty and Moosie cavorting in public: "Helene Israel and Mrs. Maurice Goldstein were having tea together—Katty Stewart and Moosie White were laughing deliciously when I looked their way—with Victor da Cuhnua [sic]. Mrs. Stewart chaperoned them from a distance."[12] By the way, the correct spelling of Victor's name is da Cunha. Stick a pin in that name because da Cunha will eventually play a major role in Katty's life and, more specifically, her mother's.

Natalie Scott often wrote about Katty and Moosie, separately and together:

> Katty Stewart, of college age but not collegiate inclinations, lends a decorative effect wherever she happens to be, with that shock of irrepressible curls that lends a piquant touch to any hat she happens to wear. She is quite a help in the Paul Morphy Book Shop, which is one of her favorite haunts. Very often with her is Elizabeth White (one must call her that sometimes not to forget that it really is her name, but Moussie is delightfully appropriate for that effervescently young person). Her debut seems inevitable, but it must await Ellene's.[13]

In the same column that referred to da Cunha, the columnist described 18-year-old Katty:

> Really there's a great deal of enjoyment to be gotten from the mere sight of a girl like Katty. The tallest girl in New Orleans, she calls herself. She isn't that—quite. But she is such a joyous person—from the tip of her little tilted nose to the slippers that are scarcely ever still. A lovable person. Quick on the up-take, as the boys say. Her goldy brown hair bobs out delightfully from under the close-fitting hats she affects, her mouth is so poutingly pretty as a child's—her teeth as even and white—her eyes are blue—dark with mischief though.[14]

One of the oddest references to Katty and Moosie was in a July 31, 1921, *New Orleans Item* column titled "The Diary of Diana." It was a breezy narrative that named names:

Someone told me Ellene White [Moosie's sister] was coming home from Europe—very reluctantly—in September. She's been over there for ages with the Leon Giberts [Maude Gibert, Leon's wife, was Ellene and Moosie's aunt on their mother's side], who've just lately bought a chateau in southern France. And Ellene adores southern France. But—this being the true inwardness of the debut— Moosie refuses to be held back any longer. She and Katty Stewart are as impatient as two little ponies for the blare of social trumpets and the anticipated triumphs and conquests. These complications will arise when there are several roses on one stem as one delightfully sentimental old lady expresses it.[15]

This photograph of a confident young Katty was found in Moosie's collection (courtesy Maunsel White).

Meanwhile, a new gathering place had opened in New Orleans. The Patio Royal, located in what had once been the Paul Morphy home, served tea and lunch. It quickly became the most popular place for debutante parties.[16]

In what was soon to become a regular activity for Katty and Moosie, Katty was in a wedding party for a friend. Walter Pierre Stouse married Margaret Ferrier in November.[17] Katty knew Margaret through the Bridle Club, whose headquarters were at the Fair Grounds.

Katty was an avid horsewoman. She and Peggy (Marguerite) Mason Smith once arrived at a wedding reception in their riding clothes. Mildred and John Baldwin had a

> quiet and unexpected wedding, [and] no one was willing to miss the reception in their honor, which was really equivalent to a belated wedding reception, and certainly quite as elaborate. Katty Stewart and Peggy Mason Smith found themselves still in their riding clothes with the hour perilously late, so they rushed on, even as they were, for fear of missing it. The handsome Prytania street-home was crowded to the full of its stately rooms, spacious even as they are with the generous proportions of the days before the servant problem.[18]

Meanwhile, Katty and Moosie made it clear that they wanted careers. Ideally, together. A society column mentioned that the girls dreamed about opening a fashion shop. "Katty Stewart and Moussie White … play with the idea of starting some sort of shop or other.... I am sure they would have record sales!"[19]

On Christmas Eve 1921, Katty attended a debutante party at the Louisiane in honor of Marion Souchon. Marion was described as "chic, exceptionally pretty and attractive." No expense was spared. "The decorations throughout the room was Christmas in every detail and to one end was a large brilliantly illuminated Christmas tree from which a Santa Claus distributed attractive favors during the evening."[20]

Events like this provided Katty and Moosie a hint of 1922. Both probably had mixed emotions about their debutante year. It would turn out to be a madcap, wild, mostly fun jumble.

6

Walker Mallam Ellis

Walker Ellis is Fi-Fi.

Walker Mallam Ellis, born in New Orleans on April 29, 1893, was the youngest child of a prominent couple, Caswell and Nellie Ellis. Nellie was born on June 1, 1864, in Vicksburg, Mississippi. She came into the world almost exactly a year after Vicksburg fell to Union troops.

Caswell, born March 13, 1858, at Oak Hill plantation in Louisiana, was the son of cotton planter and slave owner Richard Ellis. According to Caswell's obituary in 1924, he was "descended from an old English family coming to the South in the early days.... Receiving his education under private tutors in New Orleans after the manner of sons of rich and prominent families of that day, Mr. Ellis entered business life in 1876, with a wholesale grocery firm." Caswell ended up in the cotton industry and started the C.P. Ellis and Company firm. "His firm was widely known throughout the cotton world. He was a member of the Boston, Pickwick and County Clubs, several Carnival organizations, and practically all civic bodies aiming at the advancement of New Orleans."[1]

On paper, young Walker sounds almost perfect. For example, when he was not yet a teenager, he attended Dixon Academy in Louisiana and won awards. Then the over-achiever was valedictorian of his prep school, Hill School in Pottstown, Pennsylvania, where he also participated in the drama and gym club and edited the school newspaper. When he attended Princeton, he was treated like a rock star by no less than F. Scott Fitzgerald. After graduating from Princeton, he was a war hero. Then he attended Harvard Law School. Still, despite being handsome and winning awards and accolades, he was gay. Though he enjoyed a close, loving relationship with his mother, Walker struggled with approval from his father.

From a young age, Walker's name frequently appeared in the newspaper. His proud mother, who enthusiastically served as his press agent, like Kittie did for Katty, and Ellen for Moosie, submitted frequent reports.

Nellie, who delighted in her last-born child, wanted people to know that Walker had an acrostic published in *St. Nicholas*,[2] a popular children's magazine published from 1873 to 1940. In a December 17, 1897, article, Walker and his brother Richard each contributed $2.50 "for dolls, toys, books and money for a Christmas for the children of the poor."[3]

Tragedy struck the Ellis family when Walker's older brother, Erl Mallam, died on October 7, 1901:

> Tulane University, New Orleans and a loving family, consisting of father, mother and five brothers and sisters, lost a star when young Erl Mallam Ellis died.... He was 18 years and eight months old.... Young Ellis ... went to Milwaukee to attend the convention of one of the college fraternities, and on his way home stopped at the home of his grandmother in Birmingham, where his sisters [Nellie and Hazel] were, intending to visit there and come home with the other members of the family. While there he was attacked with typhoid fever and brought home quite ill, with the hope that good care would restore him. All the efforts of doctors and nurses, failed to save him, however.[4]

Another newspaper described him as "bright, popular and [as] promising a young man as could be found in New Orleans.... The young man had completed his studies in the Boys' High School ... and by the excellence of his marks earned a scholarship in Tulane University."[5] Erl was "studying engineering and on Tulane's football team." Walker was eight when Erl died. The loss to the family was profound.

In 1907, Walker's parents enrolled him in Dixon Academy in Covington, Louisiana. "A medal for being the best drilled cadet was awarded to Walker Ellis.... This is quite an honor when it is considered that the company to which the young man belongs is one of the best drilled in the State and that several of its members hold medals for proficiency in this art."[6] The school, founded in 1899, closed in 1909 due to a lack of students. It was sold to a nearby abbey in 1911 and reopened as St. Paul's.

The first time Walker shows up in the census is 1910 when he was 17. His name was mistakenly recorded as "William M." Also residing in the house were his cotton merchant father, Caswell, 52; mother Nellie, 45; sisters Hazel, 25, and Nellie, 23; and brother Richard, 19, a clerk in a cotton office. His older brother Caswell, Jr., born in 1889, moved out of the house and married the previous year. There were no servants residing in the home. The address was 8 Audubon Place. The neighborhood, located near Tulane University, is still one of the most exclusive in New Orleans.

In 1911, Walker attended Hill School in Pottstown, Pennsylvania. Nicknamed "Cupid," Walker was president of his class, active in Glee Club, Choir, Drama and Debate and won awards for elocution, "Best Speaker" and "Song Leader." In the yearbook, his saying was a slightly altered quote from Oliver Goldsmith: "And still they wondered and still their wonder grew, That one small head could carry all he knew." The private boys' boarding school, first opened in 1851, was known as a feeder school for Princeton, and sure enough, after graduating as valedictorian from Hill, Walker was accepted at Princeton in 1911 when he was 18.

From a young age, Walker toyed with the idea of becoming a stage actor. While a freshman at Princeton, he appeared in the Triangle Club's 1911–1912 show *Main Street*. Of course, Princeton, like other Ivy League schools of the time, accepted only men. That did not change until 1969. So all the roles, including feminine ones, were played by male students. In *Main Street*, Walker played wealthy widow Mrs. Philander Pringle, president of a small midwestern town's Woman's Club. Donald Marsden, who wrote a history of the Triangle Club, described the play as "tightly

Walker Ellis was around 18 when he was photographed for the 1911 yearbook *Hill School Dial*.

constructed and sensitively written."[7] Donald Clive Stuart, who taught at Princeton and directed many of the Triangle Club productions, noted that "the standard of production…[was] so high that one does not hesitate to criticize it from a purely professional viewpoint."[8] Stuart did complain that the clever lines were not always heard because of the "wretched accoustics of the garage known as the Casino."[9] This was a common complaint during the time Walker attended Princeton. The Casino was torn down in 1924.

In 1913, when Walker was 20, he came home from Princeton for summer break and brought a friend. "Mrs. Thomas Pearson, of Asheville, N.C., who accompanied Mr. Walker Ellis on his return from Princeton College, where they were both students, will be the guest here of Mr. Ellis for two weeks."[10] Such an odd blurb. Thomas Pearson was no Mrs. The Mrs. was changed to Mr. when the *Times-Picayune* reprinted the blurb the following day. Pearson indeed attended Princeton and graduated with Walker in 1915. He visited Walker and his family often, traveled with them to Pass Christian, and attended Country Club events with Walker.[11]

He was born James Thomas Pearson in 1893 at Richmond Hill in Asheville. His parents were Richmond Pearson, a Congressman and ambassador, and Gabrielle Thomas Pearson. After graduation, Pearson served in World War I and then became an economic consultant to Persia, Haiti and the Dominican Republic. He never married, retired in 1951, and died in 1963.

Also in 1913, a newspaper reported on a party for Bayne Denegre, a Yale student home for the summer, hosted by his parents at their Biloxi summer home.[12] Walker and Yale student Walter Stauffer, who would later marry Moosie White, attended the party together.

Stauffer, born June 3, 1893, in New Orleans, had a lot in common with Walker. They were the same age, born within a few weeks of each other, and came from prominent, wealthy families. The two men also served in World War I. This event in 1913 was not the first or last time that they were seen together.

Back at Princeton, Walker appeared in *The Pursuit of Priscilla*, the Triangle Club's main play in the 1913–1914 season. Walker co-wrote a smaller piece with James H. Legendre, *The Scar*, which was performed at the end of *Priscilla*.[13] According to Triangle Club historian Donald Marsden, "*The Scar* was the forerunner of the story-line ballet ... which became a regular part of shows under Dr. Stuart after World War I and which still continue as one of the more consistently good features of the shows of recent years."[14] The play's program describes part of the plot:

> She sits at the fountain—a woman grown old in youth—dreaming of the days when all the demi-monde of Paris lay under the strange spell of her beauty; dreaming of him whose heart she caught and crushed, with whom she lived and played for five short months before she tired; dreaming with brooding hate of the night he proved her false, struck her unmercifully across the face and left her bleeding on the floor. And as she dreams, her eyes grow steely with the hardness of revenge—for o'er her face she wears a black lace scarf, beneath which hides a long and jagged scar, the living mark of his brutality and the lifelong ruin of her beauty.[15]

The soapy plot climaxes when she and the man she hates—and who hates her—meet. Donald Marsden points out that "it is rumored that from this plot several long-running radio soap operas were built."[16] After the first performance, Walker, Legendre and composer James M. Beck were summoned to President John Hibben's office. Hibben and other faculty members objected to a dance. According to Beck, "In the dance ... she is supposed to stab him to get revenge, but unfortunately the knife could not be found at the last moment, and she simply glared at him and he falls dead." The faculty interpreted his demise to "an excess of sexual passion," and "when the curtain fell there was dead silence." Beck remembered that Hibben "praised my music ... [but] heartily condemned the story. He then sent us to see Henry Van Dyke, who lectured us for about an hour on the evil philosophy of Oscar Wilde and others of the ilk. However, the dance was permitted to continue under the title of 'A Mexican Dance' although I never discovered what Mexico had to do with it."[17]

The play had enough good press that President Woodrow Wilson, who had many ties to Princeton, attended the Triangle Club performance in Washington, D.C., and invited the players to the White House. The play also traveled to Chicago, New York, Philadelphia, Newark and Pittsburgh. "The complete transportation bill—for touring the 70-plus–man troupe on a special train with a dining car, baggage car, and two Pullman sleepers, and including meals on the dining car—came to $4800. Apparently all of *Priscilla*'s running around stimulated hearty appetites, for the dining car bill consistently lists more meals served than there were members of the troupe."[18]

In the summer of 1914, Walker traveled to Asheville to visit close friend Thomas Pearson, who lived in the Richmond Hill House.[19] The Queen Anne mansion, built in 1889 by Thomas' father Richmond Pearson, sat on a bluff overlooking the French Broad River. Years later, after the deaths of their parents, Thomas and his sister Marjorie inherited the house and turned it into a museum. After Thomas and Marjorie died, the property eventually became an inn. The house was destroyed in a fire, believed to be arson, in 2009.

A popular and influential student at Princeton, Walker Ellis enjoyed "a brilliant undergraduate career."[20] While there, he was a member of Phi Beta Kappa, the Glee Club, the University Cottage Club and the Senior Council. In addition, he was president of the Triangle Club, contributed to the *Nassau Literary Magazine*, was awarded the R. Percy Alden Memorial Prize in French, and won the Baird Prize. Walker, who roomed in 8 National Bank Building, was valedictorian of his 1915 class, a self-declared Democrat, and "has always lived in New Orleans."[21]

Walker's work with the Triangle Club earned praise from fellow student and future Jazz Age novelist F. Scott Fitzgerald. "The Triangle Club (acting, singing and dancing) is Princeton's most characteristic organization. Founded by Booth Tarkington with the production of his libretto, 'The Honorable Julius Caesar,' it blooms in a dozen cities Christmastide…. Its best years have been due to the residence of such talented improvisers as Tarkington, Roy Durstine, Walker Ellis, Ken Clark or Erdman Harris."[22]

In fact, the Triangle Club was one of the reasons Fitzgerald attended Princeton:

> He was drawn to the university by its air of aristocratic ease and privilege, by its handsome Collegiate Gothic buildings, by its prestigious eating clubs (which he'd seen pictures of in *Collier's* magazine), and by the Triangle Club, an undergraduate theatrical group that produced an original musical comedy each fall and sent it on tour over the Christmas holidays.[23]

There was a strict hierarchy at Princeton in terms of extracurricular clubs. "After football, which stood at the top of the list, the most sought-after campus organization was the Triangle Club."[24] In his novel *This Side of Paradise,* Fitzgerald explained the main character's thought process about which club to join: "Amory found that writing for the *Nassau Literary Magazine* would get him nothing, but that being on the board of the *Daily Princetonian* would get any one a good deal. His vague desire to do immortal acting with the English Dramatic Association faded out when he found that the most ingenious brains and talents were concentrated upon the Triangle Club."[25]

Fitzgerald was desperate to get into the best clubs and realized it was important to learn the game and play it well. "Failure to make a club or making a weak club meant that a sophomore had failed at Princeton and that his life would be clouded by this rejection—or so it seemed.... He had decided that he wanted the University Cottage Club, which he regarded as the most powerful as well as the most socially prominent. Walker Ellis ... was president of Cottage."[26] Fitzgerald decided that Ellis would make a good friend. "He met and befriended the suave Walker Ellis '15, who served as president of both Triangle and Cottage."[27]

Fitzgerald's strategy worked:

> His book and lyrics for *Fie! Fie! Fi-Fi!* won the competition over the submission of Lawton Campbell '18 from Montgomery, Alabama. The selection of the script was up to Walker Ellis '15, the Triangle Club president, who may—as Campbell believed—have picked *Fie! Fie! Fi-Fi!* because it had a good part for him. Ellis, whom Edmund Wilson charged with "brazen duplicities," revised it with the author until he decided to award himself credit for the dialogue and characters. The published libretto credits Fitzgerald with only the plot and lyrics. It is impossible to determine from the acting script how much of the produced play Ellis changed.... Ellis cast himself in the female lead as the manicurist, and the role of the dancer Celeste was reserved for Fitzgerald.[28]

There is disagreement about who wrote what. The play "was written in collaboration with Ellis, although Fitzgerald actually did most of the work."[29] According to Donald Marsden, "Lyrics of the show were written entirely by Fitzgerald. In the program, the book was attributed to President Walker M. Ellis '15, though Fitzgerald complained ruefully for the rest of his life that the idea for the book—if not the book itself—had been his. In his own copy of the program, Fitzgerald revised the credits for the show to read: 'Book and lyrics by F. Scott Fitzgerald, 1917. Revision by Walker M. Ellis, 1915.'"[30]

> "If Fitzgerald did, in fact, write the book for *Fi-Fi*, his reluctance to protest aloud at the time may be explained by his status as a lowly freshman—as a socially conscious freshman who had already anticipated Ellis' election to the

presidency of the Cottage Club, the socially desirable eating club which Fitzgerald wanted to, and eventually did, join.[31]

Like Fitzgerald, Walker also knew how to play the game. He has been described as "a brilliant young man and a clever politician."[32] The reality is that he used Fitzgerald and his work to promote himself.

While there may be controversy about authorship of the work, most critics agreed that Walker was the star of the show. *The Princetonian* singled out his performance, declaring it "undoubtedly the best piece of 'tough girl' acting ever seen in Princeton."[33] On December 19, 1914, the play opened at Princeton and subsequently went on a 3500-mile tour. The *Baltimore Sun* wrote, "The lyrics of the songs were written by F.S. Fitzgerald, who could take his place right now with the brightest writers of witty lyrics in America."[34]

Joshua B. Everett, who traveled with *Fie! Fie! Fi-Fi!*, described a tour that may have had more drama than the play:

> Many were the smitten Princetonians that were wrenched away, and many were the enamoured young beauties left behind…. We also survived many side trips of considerable interest such as a large brewery tour in St. Louis, a view of a new thing called an assembly line in Detroit…. Sleeping was a misnomer, for Pullmans in 1914 merely had uppers and lowers and curtains were never hung to protect one from traffic…. The Freshmen and some Sophomores were assigned the uppers but at least they had a berth alone. The more elegant upperclassmen drew the lowers but in most cases had to share that narrow berth with another and struggle for room. Local movements in the cities were by streetcar, and often by foot as autos were few and far between.[35]

Not surprisingly, and not for the first or last time, there were problems involving alcohol and obnoxious behavior among the Princetonians. Complaints were common and in some cases so egregious that some Princeton faculty members wondered whether the Triangle Club should be allowed to tour in the future.[36]

The *New York Daily Tribune* provided details that give the flavor of the production:

> The plot, as much as such things as Princeton playwrights care to bother with in a production that is built mainly on fun, tuneful music, clever dancing and amusing dialogue, centers around the designs of Fi-Fi—a manicure girl—of course of alluring beauty to get even with her adventurer husband, Bill Tracy, gambler, who has deserted her to palm himself off in the usurped job of Prime Minister of Monaco. She uncovers him, and while doing it has a good deal of sport with the audience, telling the confessions of a manicure girl in the vernacular.[37]

Walker, of course, played the manicurist role in drag. It's doubtful his father was thrilled. Still, Walker threw himself into it and did a great deal of research:

> Walker Ellis is Fi-Fi. Campus gossip has it that he is going to get his Ph.D. for the original work he did in collecting local color for the part.... Long absences from Princeton were explained by the discovery of Ellis in a grand tour of New York's best manicure parlors, from Wall St. to 42nd St., and as Ellis is as good-looking and entertaining off stage as on, New York's most gorgeous wielders of the nail-polisher have been unstinted in their confessions of experiences.[38]

On April 27, 1915, the *Times-Picayune* reported that Walker's parents were traveling to New York to see him perform. Nellie, who probably prepared the press release, gave Walker full writing credit: "[They will] attend the performance of a clever play written by ... Mr. Walker Ellis of Princeton college, which is to be presented at the Astor House in New York City. The party will remain North for the graduation of Mr. Ellis, June 18, from Princeton. Next year the latter will enter the law department of Harvard University."[39]

By 1916, local newspapers were raving about their hometown boy, his accomplishments and bright future:

> In a class of '15, Walker Ellis is among the very leading leaders. His scholarship record won for him the always coveted Phi Beta Kappa. He has written and also played leading parts in several clever, well-done Dramatic Club plays. He was Master of Ceremonies at the Class Day exercises last Monday. Of course, everybody's awfully proud of him. And, my word ... he's good-looking! I believe that next year he plans to enter one of the great law schools in the East. And after that is over, let us hope that New Orleans will once more be something more to him than a place to come at Christmas time![40]

Walker's world and fortunes changed, however, on April 6, 1917, when the United States joined Britain, France and Russia to fight in World War I. Like many young American men who held a romanticized idea of war, perhaps due to Civil War stories told by old soldiers, Walker quickly enlisted. "Mrs. Caswell P. Ellis will leave Wednesday for Boston where she will join her son, Mr. Walker Ellis, who is at Boston Tech studying with the aviation corps, having joined the first squadron taken from Harvard, where he has been a student in the law department since graduating from Princeton."[41]

It was a brave and patriotic decision, but World War I changed Walker Ellis. He saw too much death, chaos and madness. After aviation school, he was appointed Officer in Charge of Training at Clermont-Ferrand. Many of the young men he trained were killed. For example, on May 25, 1918, William Stearns and George M. Martin died in a training accident. Stearns, who graduated from Harvard in 1917, was trained by Walker, who thought so much of him that he had made him an instructor.

> Though [Stearns] didn't like it, he accepted his assignment cheerfully and did splendidly as an instructor.... We soon grew to have absolute confidence in

him. He was above all things reliable. He never did any spectacular flying, but every movement in the air was perfect, and he knew what he was doing every instant of the time.... There were two or three Fiats, which were ready for testing.... It seems he had taken up one.... The immediate cause of the trouble was a vertical bank at about 2000 feet, during which the nose of the machine fell, which resulted in a tail-spin.... He was instantly killed.... No other accident ever did, or will, affect me as that one did. He was such a dear boy; and he represented the very best in young American manhood.[42]

It's difficult to grasp the amount of loss Walker experienced in his wartime service. It led to a death wish. "As survivors attempted to make sense of lives lost and spared, many expressed admiration for the Christ-like dead and despair over a missed opportunity to be counted among them."[43] Walker wrote a particularly poignant letter to the father of a friend who died in combat. The dead soldier, Hamilton Coolidge, 25, was killed in action on October 27, 1918, in France. In a letter, Walker wrote, "The incalculably dear deaths which have come to some of them were the destiny of all of us ... those of us who remain have missed our calling." Jonathan H. Ebel wrote:

> His destiny, his calling, as Ellis understood it was not merely to face death for the cause, but to be "merged in the greatest tradition the world has known since Christ." By surviving, he had irreversibly failed his Seegerian "rendezvous" and missed forever the chance to consummate fully his imitation of Christ.

Perhaps. However, there's no doubt that his wartime experiences added to Walker's depression and increased thoughts of suicide.

The 2015 novel *Villa America* by Liza Klaussmann[44] is a fictionalized account of Gerald and Sara Murphy and their life in Antibes in the 1920s. One of the main characters is World War I pilot Owen Chambers. Although he is from New England and grew up on a farm, he appears to be at least partially based on Walker. The character, a handsome gay American, ends up in the Murphy world after a harrowing wartime experience. He eventually becomes Gerald's lover. In the novel, the character struggles with feelings that he'll never reach his potential, and that the world would have been better off had he died during the war. "Sometimes, lately, he wondered about that boy he'd killed in the tunnel. What if it had been the other way around; what if he had died and the boy had lived? Would the boy have gone on to do better than him? Be a better person than he was? But Owen hadn't died. He'd lived."[45]

In August 1918, the *New Orleans Item* reported that Walker was returning to the States. Later that month, one of the local columnists provided a flattering report on Walker:

> Hoping that he will never know I said it, I must tell you ... that the most perfectly wonderful and beautiful person I have seen for a long time is Walker

Ellis.... [He] has always been handsome. Add to this the wonder of his uniform with the aviator's cap, a physique in the most perfect condition, tanned skin and the splendid color in his cheeks that comes from being much in the very high altitudes. Then add to this splendid physical fitness the certain spiritual something that puts the shine in his eyes and the strength in his whole bearing, the something that tells its own story of all that this beautiful youngster has seen and done and felt; take all this together and perhaps you will have some idea of Walker Ellis, first New Orleans aviator to come back and tell us about it, and otherwise a very perfect model of that most splendid soldier, the American fighting man of today.[46]

In addition to being a competent actor, Walker was also an excellent public speaker. After returning to New Orleans, he was asked to speak at a luncheon at the Boston Club. A columnist reported that he hit it out of the park: "[Ellis] made his audience laugh and cry almost at the same moment.... New Orleans is very proud of her young flyer and I say to you again that it is from such as these that the Hun had best be wise enough to run away."[47]

Walker was soon back at Harvard to study law.[48] In December, he returned home for the holidays. Now 25, he and 15-year-old Katty Stewart attended a party for their mutual friend Virginia Downman.[49] Katty would have been aware of Walker much earlier, of course, since both their fathers were in the cotton industry, and Walker was already a notable local figure.

When Walker returned to New Orleans, he moved back into his parents' mansion. A 1919 article, printed below a blurb mentioning a giggly 16-year-old Katty hanging out at the Country Club, reported that he had graduated with a law degree from Harvard on June 9.[50]

Walker never had a burning desire to practice law. It was his father's dream, not his. He did, however, reluctantly join a local law firm. "'Home is the best place after all,' so the old song goes, and it looks, after 12 years absence, as if Walker Ellis thought so, too.... In June he completed his interrupted course, and came home ... and his many friends are wishing him the success that is due him."[51]

Walker joined a law firm that included Edgar Farrar, Abraham Goldberg and H. Generes Dufour. The office was located on the 18th floor of the Hibernia Bank Building. It was a top Louisiana law firm and showed Walker's connections, or at least the powerful influence his father had in the city.

By the fall of 1919, Walker, perhaps missing the theater, became involved with Le Petit Théâtre du Vieux Carré. At this time, its members included Florence Pugh, Olga Kaufman, Rhea Goldberg, Natalie Scott and Virginia Parker.[52] The theater would become important in Walker's future.

6. Walker Mallam Ellis

Like Katty and Moosie, Walker enjoyed concerts and other live performances. In November 1919, he attended an Isadora Duncan dance performance, which was accompanied by pianist George Copeland.[53] Copeland, born in 1882, lived openly as a gay man most of his life. A few years earlier, in 1913, he told a newspaper reporter, "I don't care what people think of my morals. I never think anything about other people's morals."[54] Although Copeland was ostensibly talking about drinking alcohol, the entire article made it clear what he was about with lines like this: "Carefully he smoothed out the wrinkles in his lavender silk pajamas and straightened the silver and lavender stone ring on the baby finger of his left hand."

Near the end of 1919 and into 1920, Walker was often in the company of Tommy Farrar, Edgar Farrar's son (and Maude White's future brother-in-law when she married Stamps Farrar, Edgar's other son). For example, they attended a Mary Garden concert and several other events.[55] They were both young gay men who were interested in art and culture. Tommy had attended Tulane and studied architecture before turning his attention to stage design.

Near the end of 1920, Walker appeared to be in a good place. A columnist reported seeing him out and about. "I shall follow Walker Ellis' very good example … and take to walking to clear my head of the fumes of jazz and rose color…. He was seen this morning hiking along the road to the Country Club, an apparently utterly happy individual in knickers, bound for a game of golf."[56]

In the 1920 census, the family was still at 8 Audubon Place. Walker's father, now 61, was retired. Also residing in the home were Walker's mother Nellie, 54; cotton broker brother Richard, 29; nephew Richard, five, and niece Helen, two. (Richard's first wife Helen had died in 1919.) Walker's occupation was described as lawyer, which seems wishful thinking on his parents' part. One servant, Victoria, a 56-year-old black widow, lived in the home. She could neither read nor write.

7

Walter Joseph Stauffer

> These books are the result of an intelligent accumulation of years, a cultivated and watchful taste for Mr. Stauffer and the members of his family are lovers of literature.

Walter Joseph Stauffer, Jr., the son of wealthy, influential Walter Robinson Stauffer, was born on June 3, 1893, in New Orleans. Although referred to as Walter Jr., he and his father had different middle names.

The family home, located at 1506 Jackson Avenue, on the corner of Jackson and Prytania, was one of the Garden District's largest mansions, once described as "an old mansion that is greatly admired and about which frequent inquiries are made."[1] It was a wedding gift to Walter's father, Walter Robinson Stauffer, and mother, Elizabeth (Betty) Myrthe Taylor, from *his* father, Isaac Hull Stauffer.

Betty, born July 8, 1854, on the Hermitage Plantation in New Orleans, was the daughter of General Richard (Dick) Taylor, a Confederate "hero," and Louise Marie Bringier. The Hermitage Plantation was named after Andrew Jackson's Tennessee plantation by Louise's father Michel Bringier, one of Jackson's war buddies.

The Stauffer mansion, built before the Civil War, is "a three-story brick building, painted a gray color. It is enclosed on two sides by a handsome iron fence, eight feet high.... The property has a measurement of 128 feet on Jackson Avenue and 120 feet on Prytania Street."[2] The Stauffers were particularly proud of their furnishings and interior decoration. "Rare china, plaques, plates, tapestries, rich rugs, etchings, paintings, vases and sculpture abound. In the library the bookcases are filled with the choicest literature, handsomely bound and in perfect keeping with their surroundings."

Young Walter would have felt watched by his famous ancestors. "In the beautiful double parlor are the portraits of General Zachary Taylor, the hero of the Mexican war, and subsequently president of the United States; a large photo-engraving of General Dick Taylor, son of President Taylor; a large picture of Mr. I.H. Stauffer, the father of Mr. Stauffer."[3] It was a lot to

Walter Joseph Stauffer, born in 1893, was the great-grandson of former U.S. president Zachary Taylor and grandson of Confederate general Dick Taylor (courtesy Maunsel White).

live up to. While it's likely Katty, Moosie and Walker also gazed at images of their ancestors, the ancestor worship was extreme in the Stauffer home.

Walter's father, Walter Robinson Stauffer, was born in New Orleans on March 26, 1854. He attended Jesuit High School, Mount St. Mary's

College in Maryland, and Fordham University in New York. He also studied for a year at Oratory College in Reading, England. He began working at a hardware importing company when he was 19. Eventually the company took on his name, becoming Stauffer, Eshelman and Company.[4]

Walter R. and Betty Stauffer were socially prominent. When the Country Club was organized in 1903, Walter's father was its first president. In the 1900 census, there were 16 people residing in the home. The head of the household was Walter R. Stauffer. He was 46, as was his wife Betty. The oldest child, Myrthe, was 17, and then came Alice, 15, Anita, 14, Dick, 12, Celeste, eight, Walter Joseph, six, and Willie, three. Then there was a sister-in-law, also named Myrthe, 33; Ike, a 14-year-old nephew, and Louise, a 13-year-old niece. The servants included Sarah Thornton, a 20-year-old single black woman; Julia Egues, a 28-year-old single black woman, and Elizabeth Burns, an 82-year-old widowed black woman. Based on her age, it is assumed she was a former slave. She was the only one of the servants who could neither read nor write.

At the time Walter was growing up, there was still a reverence for the Confederacy, but even more so in the Stauffer family. General Taylor was described as one "of those who, believing the cause of the Confederacy a righteous cause ... took up arms against fearful odds, and persevering under untold difficulties, was distinguished for his undaunted gallantry and achievements in battle and for his unforsaken fortitude in defeat."[5]

Walter was the grandson of President Zachary Taylor, Richard's father. Countless newspaper articles mentioned this relationship through the years, and it was a source of pride within the family. Taylor grew up on a plantation and became a war hero. Nicknamed "Old Rough and Ready," he served in the War of 1812, the Black Hawk War, the Second Seminole War and the Mexican-American War. Although he had no political experience, he was enlisted to run for president by the Whig party and won. He died a little more than a year after his election.

Walter Stauffer's upbringing was different from his contemporaries because he was raised Catholic. It wasn't unusual for the Stauffer family to entertain cardinals, bishops, priests, etc., in their lavish home.

Like many of his male contemporaries, Walter was sent away to school. He attended the Lawrenceville School in New Jersey, beginning in 1907 when he was a teenager. The school was one of America's first prep schools and is one of the most expensive. Alumni include Lowell P. Weicker, Jr., Huey Lewis, Malcolm Forbes and Michael Eisner.

Walter's name was often included in the society columns, but there was not a constant barrage of news about him, as there had been with Walker, Katty and Moosie. The 1912 Lawrenceville School yearbook did provide some information about him. His nickname was "Stauff." A quote from Shakespeare's *As You Like It* appeared below his rather stern-looking photo: "You have a nimble wit; I think it was made of Atlanta's heels." According to the yearbook entry, he was studying science and intended to go to Yale.

Walter was the class' historian, on the Prom Committee and baseball team, in Mandolin Club, and a member of the Calliopean Society. The Calliopean membership is an intriguing one. It was a kind of literary and debating club, originally founded at Yale in 1819, and a secret club with limited membership, rituals and initiations.

Walter returned home from school for the holidays as well as the summers. His family, like other wealthy New Orleans residents, frequently traveled to Pass Christian, Mississippi.

Walter Stauffer, nicknamed Stauff, attended Lawrenceville School in New Jersey. From there, he moved on to Yale University (courtesy Maunsel White).

By 1912, Walker Ellis and Walter Stauffer were often seen at the same social events during their prep and college years. Walter eventually attended Yale and was on the rowing team. He did not have the kind of celebrated academic career that Walker had at Princeton. He graduated from Yale and later became involved in a New Orleans Yale alumni group.

Like Walker, Walter also brought male friends home with him from college. For example, in 1912 it was reported that he had returned to spend the Christmas holidays with his parents, "accompanied by Mr. Rumlin, who will be his guest during his stay in New Orleans."[6]

At some point, Walter began working at his father's hardware company. Unlike Walker, who wanted nothing to do with the business world, Walter realized the opportunity was a good one. He apparently did not have any desire for a creative career and chose to follow in Dad's footsteps. It worked out for him, and he stayed in the business world for decades.

In 1915, when Walter was 22, he was appointed to the National Security League by New Orleans Mayor Martin Behrman. "Propaganda urging the nation to strengthen its land and naval forces is to be carried on by the committee. Speakers nationally prominent will be brought to New Orleans to speak on preparedness under the auspices of this organization."[7] This would eventually lead to a future interest and involvement in the military.

By 1916, Walter's name was often included in the long lists of attendees at social functions. In January, he was one of the "dukes" at a Carnival ball. "The ball of the Mittens held Friday evening was the center of attention for apparently all of the smart world…. The ball, always a notable event among the fashionable here, was strikingly beautiful this season."[8]

A more serious side of Walter appeared in March 1916 when he joined the Washington Artillery. He was not quite 23 but obviously felt a need to do something other than attend social functions. He may also have felt family pressure because his grandfather Zachary Taylor once led the Artillery during the Mexican-American War. Formed in 1838, the organization had a long history, including being on the wrong side during the Civil War.

Walter was made a lieutenant in Battery C and went through a 90-day training period. In 1916, the Artillery was recruited to protect the Mexican border after Pancho Villa and his militia attacked a New Mexico town. The conflict, known as the Mexican Expedition, officially began on March 14, 1916, and ended on February 7, 1917.

Battery C was led by Captain Bryan Black (father of Kingsley) and, along with Batteries A and B, were mustered in late June. A local newspaper explained that many of the volunteers were giving up quite a lot to defend the border:

> Some of those going to the front as targets for prospective Mexican bullets are giving up salaries by the side of which solders' pay amounts to no more than cigarette money…. Battery C, of Washington Artillery, probably is paying heaviest, or sacrificing most, for its patriotism. Its departure for the Rio Grande will reduce salary rolls in New Orleans several hundred thousand dollars. But the battery boasts that not a man hesitated in answering his country's call, even when that response meant the surrender, temporarily, of big-paying positions, or profitable professional practice, or big business opportunities just budding.[9]

Walter was specifically mentioned as being the son of a prosperous merchant.

On July 2, a photo of the commissioned officers included Walter, who now sported a mustache and a new toughness. The caption read: "Battery C is the so-called 'society battery,' of whom their acting captain, Lieutenant (Guy) Moloney, says, 'If those are the 'silk stockings,' God save me from the 'roughnecks'!"[10] It's likely that Walter may have started growing his moustache around the time he signed up for the Washington Artillery—and kept it for much of his life. Perhaps it made him feel—and look—more grown-up.

Within a couple weeks, the well-trained, fit Artillery arrived in Texas. "From battery commanders to 'high buck privates,' the belts have tightened up not one notch—but in some instances three or four."[11]

Journalists surrounded them in the Houston train station. "The 'millionaire battery,' Battery C, seemed to interest them most, and the New Orleans silk-stocking contingent were given the lion's share of attention. 'Not a man in the battery that isn't worth at least $100,000,' Lieut. Goldstein told one journalist. 'Quite so, we're all in it, because it's such ripping sport,' assured Lieutenants Walter Stauffer and George Clarke, Yale members of the battery."

Although they saw little action in Texas, the Artillery was prepared. "Armed with 12 three-inch field pieces, the battalion became part of the 13th Provisional Division, and was camped at Donna, Hidalgo county, Texas, nine miles from the Rio Grande, and 50 miles up the Rio Grande, from Brownsville, Texas.... During this period of eight months and 12 days of Mexican border service they had marched 385.4 miles and sustained no casualties whatever."[12]

In February 1917, the Washington Artillery returned to New Orleans where they received a warm welcome and were treated as heroes. Walter's mother was a member of a committee "of prominent New Orleans women ... to assist development of the plans for the gala welcome ... upon their arrival here from the Texas border."[13]

It was a big deal. "A dispatch was received Tuesday afternoon from General Frederick Funston's headquarters that the battalion of Washington's Artillery would be mustered out of active service Feb. 20. The men will come direct to New Orleans instead of proceeding to Camp Stafford, and it is desired that their movement will be so arranged that they may reach home during daylight so a suitable reception may be given them."[14]

State and local dignitaries were invited along with family members of the men. "Every mother who had a son in the service and each sister or wife or other kinswoman will be neatly decorated with an emblem, which will not only distinctively designate them, but which may be kept as souvenirs of the occasion." Years later, however, Walter "described his war experience as little more than 'taking care of a bunch of mules.'"[15]

A society columnist suggested that Walter had become a bit of a heartthrob to the young ladies of New Orleans. "Don't you think it would be a sensible idea for Uncle Sam ... to send squads of girls up to the camps? I would go to Nicholls, for it is there our Battery C is and Peter O'Donnell and Walter Stauffer are (oh sit still my heart!)...."[16]

Before Walter returned to New Orleans, an engagement to a Chicago heiress named Dorothy (her name is sometimes spelled Dorothie and Dorothey) Russell Dickason went sideways. The engagement was announced while Walter was involved with the Washington Artillery and then broken before Walter was due to return home. All of this was public and eagerly reported by newspapers across the country. Both Walter and Dorothy were from prominent, wealthy families. Dorothy was born in Chicago on August 14, 1894, and lived on the city's exclusive Gold Coast.

Interestingly, the families were on opposite sides of the Civil War. Considering the war was only a generation away, it's surprising this wasn't a deal-breaker. Dorothy's father was Livingston Dickason, who had enlisting at age 19 and fought with the 64th Ohio at Shiloh and other battles. He was discharged in June 1864 because of injuries.

He married his second wife Elizabeth Gilbert Barber on September 14, 1892. Their age difference was almost 24 years. They had two children, Dorothy and Livingston. He'd already had a daughter, Ada, with first wife Sybil Tinkham.

Dorothy's father, who had made a fortune in grain, mining and timber, was on a family trip when he fell ill and died on March 22, 1913, in Naples, Italy, at the age of 69. Dorothy, 19, became a wealthy heiress and a desirable marriage partner.

A frequent traveler, Dorothy was in New Orleans in 1916 when she met Walter. In November, about a week after Walter's sister Celeste married Harry Burnett, it was announced that Dorothy and Walter would also wed.

> Walter J. Stauffer, son of Mr. and Mrs. Walter R. Stauffer, prominent in society and presiding at Prytania Street and Jackson Avenue, is to marry Miss Dorothy Dickason of Chicago. Announcement of the engagement is made there Tuesday by ... the mother of the girl. Miss Dickason already is known to New Orleans society, having visited here. No date as yet has been set for the wedding, though it probably will take place this winter.[17]

The announcement was front-page news.

More details followed, describing it as "an engagement of prominence recently announced in Chicago and of unusual interest in smartest circles."[18] According to the article, "Miss Dickason will be remembered as the charming guest for a few weeks last winter ... when she was greatly admired and entertained during her stay in New Orleans.... Miss Dickason is a particularly beautiful young woman and is prominent in younger circles in Chicago's exclusive social world."

The couple did not marry that winter. In fact, much drama followed before the marriage finally took place.

Some time in February 1917, a few months after the engagement's announcement, Dorothy changed her mind and decided that, no, she didn't want to marry Walter. The story took on the feel of a Hollywood screwball film, perhaps starring Jean Arthur or Carole Lombard, and featuring an attractive American heiress who does something so zany and madcap that it makes news.

Here's a headline from February 8, 1917: "Stauffer's Fiancée Will Remain in the U.S.: Chaperon Refuses Trip and France Loses One Nurse." In the article, Dorothy is described as a "prominent Chicago society bud," and Walter as "scion of a wealthy old New Orleans family."[19]

The writer explained what Dorothy did—and didn't—do:

> Dorothy Dickason won't become a trained nurse in France. It wasn't the submarines that deterred her. When she slipped away from her home ... and left for New York, she had made all her plans for sailing for Europe. And then, a few hours before the boat sailed yesterday, Dorothy's chaperon decided to stay in the United States. Today Dorothy's mother, Mrs. Livingston Dickason, boarded a train for New York to bring her daughter back. She had just learned of her whereabouts.

The writer reminded readers that Dorothy was recently engaged to Walter, who was in Texas protecting the border. Here's what Dorothy had to say for herself: "I had made all arrangements ... to become an auxiliary nurse in the American ambulance corps. I arrived here [New York] from Chicago Monday with a chum, Miss Catherine Steele, but she did not intend to sail with me. I changed my plans because the woman under whose chaperonage I was to sail decided not to go." She left a lot out of her explanation, including why she wanted to escape in the first place. Was it marriage in general? Was it Walter specifically?

The drama was publicly humiliating for Walter. One has to assume that his family, especially his parents and siblings, were enraged at Dorothy.

On June 9, 1917, a New Orleans newspaper reported that Walter, accompanied by his father, traveled to Chicago to finally marry Dorothy.[20] And indeed the wedding finally took place.

However, the scandal had become national news, and the two became figures of ridicule. An Indiana newspaper included a photo of Dorothy with the headline: "Venus Bests Mars." The caption read: "Miss Dorothy Dickson, of Lake Shore Drive, Chicago, will wed Walter Joseph Stauffer, New York [sic], lieutenant in the Coast artillery, instead of becoming army aviatrix or going to France as a Red Cross nurse."[21]

A New Orleans newspaper also got in on the fun at the couple's expense:

> Miss Dorothy Dickason, of Chicago, who tried to go to Europe as a war nurse and failed, will become a matron of New Orleans.... The then Miss Dickason started for France as a war nurse and got as far as the Ritz-Carlton in New York. She decided that was far enough and returned to Chicago, announcing her intention of joining the aviation corps. About this time, however, her

fiance, who is an officer, obtained a leave of absence and hurried to Chicago, and Miss Dickason's plans changed again. The bride is wealthy in her own right through an inheritance left by her father.[22]

This was again front-page news.

The *Times-Picayune* took a shot at the hapless couple:

> Young Mr. Cupid today won a victory over ferocious Mr. Mars and in the victory transformed Dorothy Dickason, a budding war nurse, into Mrs. Walter J. Stauffer, a soldier's bride.... Since her debut two years ago, Miss Dickason has kept all her friends interested in her current activities and guessing as to her next move. Early in March she announced her intention of going abroad as a war nurse. While her friends were trying to dissuade her from attempting the voyage, she went to New York. Her arrival at the Ritz-Carlton was the first intimation they had of her departure. Finding it impossible to sail for France, she returned to Chicago and immediately announced her intention of joining the aviation corps. Just about this time her soldier-fiancé in New Orleans obtained a leave of absence and came swiftly to Chicago. He succeeded in persuading Miss Dickason to name the day.[23]

Another New Orleans newspaper wondered if Dorothy might change her mind again:

> Until recently Miss Dickason was disposed to go to France as a war nurse, and when she found sailing at that time impractical she decided to enter the aviation corps. About this time, Mr. Stauffer, who is a soldier, gained a leave and went to Chicago. He persuaded Miss Dickason to name the day. Whether she has changed her mind or will make further effort to go as a Red Cross nurse, according to Chicago dispatches, is a question.[24]

Walter and Dorothy married on June 14 in Chicago. Walter had just turned 24. Dorothy was not yet 22. The headline in a New Orleans paper read: "Chicago Society Girl Weds Mr. W. Stauffer."[25] According to the article, the marriage was

> *quietly* [emphasis added] celebrated Thursday morning at 11 o'clock in the presence of immediate relatives at the home of the bride's mother, Mrs. Livingston Dickason ... which was decorated with palms, ferns and flowers. The bride who is one of the most popular and attractive members of the younger set of Chicago wore a chic traveling suit of dark blue silk embroidered in cut steel, with hat and gloves to match.

Wedding announcements for the wealthy sought to stress how important and popular these people were. "Miss Dickason is a young woman of unusual beauty and charm. She has numerous friends in the smart world here.... She is also popular in the smart world of Chicago. Mr. Stauffer is a member of one of New Orleans' most prominent families and is himself popular in the social and business world.... He is now on a few weeks' leave furlough."

7. Walter Joseph Stauffer

The now-married Walter and his regiment returned to New Orleans, and he decided to remain with the Washington Artillery. Joining the Washington Artillery had been a good experience. He was a leader, and his parents and family were proud of him, especially when he was promoted to captain of Battery C.

In August, a society columnist reported that Walter and Dorothy were temporarily living at Tennyson Place and that Dorothy had become quite adept at the life of a housewife. "How very versatile is Madame to so completely transplant herself and plunge at once into housekeeping with methods so entirely different from those of St. Louis [she was actually from Chicago], her former home.'" The columnist depicted the couple as happy: "'No trouble at all,' replies our cheerful young hostess, serenely and with a shrug so calm as to slide off the slightest burden and why not? Such shoulders surely are made for other things. 'Walter is never very far off and messengers always available. The least problem brings him here,' with the most charming nonchalance."[26]

In September, Dorothy was reported to be an expert horsewoman. "Quite the most stunning thing seen recently is Mrs. Walter Stauffer as she sat on her handsome mount out at the camp the other afternoon. And, hurdles, my dear, she took seven without so much as winking her eye. She's wonderful, and between us, they say she leaps all obstacles as well as hurdles."[27]

The "happy family" talk was short-lived. Within a few months, Dorothy would be dead.

The last part of 1917 and the beginning of 1918 was a tragic time for Walter and the Stauffer family. The tragedies started on December 15, 1917, when Walter's brother-in-law, 47-year-old Albert Schwartz, husband of Walter's sister Myrthe, died of pneumonia in New Orleans. Then Walter's sister Celeste died of pneumonia on January 11 in Massachusetts. She left behind her husband, Harry Burnett, whom she'd married on November 18, 1916, and an infant, Peter, who was less than a month old. Celeste was only 26.

Then, less than two weeks later, on January 23, Dorothy died suddenly, only seven months after marrying Walter.

> The third death in the Stauffer family in the past month occurred Wednesday evening when Mrs. Walter J. Stauffer, formerly Miss Dorothy Dickason of Chicago, died in Lawton, Okla., where her husband Captain Stauffer, of the 141st Field Artillery (formerly Washington Artillery), is attending the Firing School at Fort Sill. News of Mrs. Stauffer's death was received Wednesday night by Captain Stauffer's family of 1506 Jackson Avenue. No details of the cause of her death were given. The body will be taken to Chicago for interment.... Mrs. Stauffer was a member of one of the wealthiest families in Chicago.[28]

A Rockford, Illinois, newspaper provided a few more details: "[Dorothy] died suddenly at Fort Sill, Okla., where her husband was stationed. She had been active in welfare work among the national army men. Before her marriage, Mrs. Stauffer was a popular Chicago society girl."[29]

According to the *Times-Picayune*:

> Advices [sic] telling of the death of Mrs. Walter J. Stauffer ... in Lawton, Okla., at 6 o'clock Wednesday evening, were received by members of the Stauffer family in New Orleans Wednesday night. Mrs. Stauffer left New Orleans just a week ago with her husband ... where he was attending the firing school. No details of the cause of her death were given in the dispatches. It was a decided shock to relatives here, as she was apparently in the best of health when she left New Orleans last week.[30]

Although the Stauffer family had several plots in New Orleans' Metairie Cemetery, Dorothy was interred in the Livingston mausoleum with her father in Chicago's Graceland Cemetery. Her burial record is under the name Dorothey D. Stauffer. Not one newspaper reported a cause of death. Oddly, there were two death certificates. One was included with Dorothy's probate papers. The other was apparently filled out later, and there are differences.

They both list the same cause of death—purpura hemorrhigica fulminans. This is a rare condition that usually affects newborns and children, not adult women in their twenties. Both death certificates misspell female as "femail." The probate certificate includes an incorrect birth year (1895 instead of 1894). This was corrected on the second certificate. The probate certificate puts the time of death as 5:30 p.m., and the other one says it was 6 p.m. Also, the second death certificate misspells Dorothy's last name "Staffer."

Dorothy's will was executed in Illinois on February 1, 1918, and probated in June. The cause of the delay, according to one newspaper article: "[A]dditional proof was required under the Louisiana law, and the document was returned to Chicago, with certain interrogatories to be answered."[31]

Dorothy's mother and Walter were executors. Her official name in the probate records was Dorothie D. Stauffer. Walter ended up with the bulk of the estate. Her mother would have received $50,000. However, she had remarried, which excluded her from getting anything. Dorothy's brother Livingston received $25,000. Jewelry and $10,000 went to friend Eleanore Chapman, and $5000 went to another friend, Nan C. Sutter of Pass Christian, Mississippi. Walter received "all of the balance of her estate, including animals, wherever situation, and of whatever character."[32] Walter ended up with around $150,000, which was a chunker. In today's money, it would be around $2.6 million.

7. Walter Joseph Stauffer

It does not appear that Walter had a warm relationship with Dorothy's mother, who was now married to Dr. Frank Walls. Interestingly, Katty and Moosie do appear to have been friendly with the Wallses and occasionally visited them at their Saratoga home. Walter did maintain a long friendship with Dorothy's brother Livingston, as did Katty and Moosie.

Regardless of how Dorothy died, the engagement, marriage and death were difficult, traumatic and tragic for Walter. Not only that, but these events occurred during a world war—and on the precipice of one of the worst flu pandemics in history. In early 1925, a columnist

Walter Stauffer served in the Washington Artillery and later in World War I (courtesy Maunsel White).

ascribed a saying to Walter that explained a lot about his philosophy of life, probably formed—and forged—during this difficult period. "Walter Stauffer remarked brilliantly with a flare of that inimitable Stauffer wit, that most of them had been through the war ... and of course nothing could seem very bad after that."[33]

By late June, Walter went to Europe to fight in World War I. That November, he was reported to be in Bannes, France, with several other young men from New Orleans. And then on November 17, it was announced that he and several others would soon return home.

Walter, restless and unhappy in New Orleans, promptly returned to Europe. "Captain Walter Stauffer, of New Orleans, commander of Battery C, seeking more action, was permitted to accept service in the Polish army."[34]

Walter had been through hell. Various friends later reported seeing him in France and England. In August 1919, he was at the Liverpool coastal home of John and Stella Little, among other travelers from New Orleans. No doubt he was carefully considering his options and what he would do with the rest of his shattered life.

8

Walker and the French Quarter

> I tell you that this town is aswarm and alive and
> criss-crossed with perverts.—Huey Long[1]

In the 1920 census, Walter was listed as a resident of the 1506 Jackson Avenue house. Also listed: Walter Robinson Stauffer, 65, head of the house; his wife Betty, also 65; their daughter Alice Hardie, 35; her husband Lewis Hardie, 46, and their son Walter and daughter, Betty, 11. Also living with the Stauffers was grandson Peter, now two. The son of Celeste and Peter Burnett, he was living with his father and new wife by the time of the 1930 census.

Walter Joseph is described as a 27-year-old widowed clerk working in a hardware company. There were no servants residing at the house. Also living at the home were Walter's two unmarried brothers, Richard, 32, and William, 23. Both would remain single until their deaths.

Meanwhile, Walker, who had been living with his parents on Audubon, decided he wanted his own place and was looking at a neighborhood called Vieux Carré, which came to be known as the French Quarter. According to Natalie Scott, "The Petit Theatre and the Architects' Club have ensconced themselves in the glamor of the Pontalba buildings.... I hear Walker Ellis is showing deep interest in 'For Rents' and 'For Sales' nearby. It seems that our Quartier Francais will soon be as artistically characteristic of us as the Quartier Latin is of Paris."[2] Walker bought a property at 723 Toulouse Street on April 28, 1920, for $2700.[3]

The building is variously referred to as the Valery Nichols house and Casa Flinard. Walker was not the only one who thought the neighborhood was perfect. Lyle Saxon, another gay man with a keen interest in architecture, wrote,

> The interest seems to be on Royal Street and in the cross streets between Conti and St. Ann Street. St. Peter is a popular street for artists, and Toulouse Street a close second. Interest at present centers in the charming old home recently purchased by Walker Ellis in Toulouse, near Royal, which he is repairing and

8. Walker and the French Quarter

This is a drawing of Walker Ellis' home in the French Quarter. It's still located at 723 Toulouse Street (Historic American Buildings Survey, Creator, and Hilaire Boutet. Valery Nicholas House, 723 Toulouse Street, New Orleans, Orleans Parish, LA. New Orleans Louisiana Orleans Parish, 1933. Documentation Compiled After. Photograph. https://www.loc.gov/item/la0021/).

> making into a bachelor quarters. This house is one of particularly beautiful design, embodying all the most desired features, wrought iron balconies, old arches and passages, a courtyard and fan-light windows.[4]

Saxon, who was also a friend of Katty's, was a writer for the *Times-Picayune*, a historian and a novelist. He also bought property in the French Quarter.

While the neighborhood quickly became trendy, it was sketchy when Walker bought the property.

> Almost all the elite Creole families had long ago abandoned the Vieux Carre for more favored uptown neighborhoods. The deteriorating Quarter was a downtrodden mixture of immigrants, tramps, prostitutes, peddlers pulling their wagons, and itinerants seeking a cheap place to lay their heads.... Streets and sidewalks lay broken and unimproved; stagnant water stood in drainage ditches. Delicate wrought-iron balconies served as improvised clotheslines;

Walker Ellis purchased 723 Toulouse Street in 1920 (Historic American Buildings Survey, Creator, and Hilaire Boutet. Valery Nicholas House, 723 Toulouse Street, New Orleans, Orleans Parish, LA. New Orleans Louisiana Orleans Parish, 1933. Documentation Compiled After. Photograph. https://www.loc.gov/item/la0021/).

and chickens, pigs, scrawny cows and old horses were stalled within ruins of once-elegant courtyards, even in broken-down sections of the old Pontalba buildings. Abandoned mansions, barely recognizable, housed cheap dives, flophouses and tenements.[5]

Around the time Walker was settling into his new home in June 1920, he and Walter became close friends again. This friendship led to the two co-founding the ill-fated Leon Soniat Post of the American Legion. Soniat, a member of the Washington Artillery, died in France of spinal meningitis. Most of the members, including Edgar Bright, William J. Gibbons, Jr., Shermon (Shine) Pardue and John M. Parker, Jr., the son of Louisiana's governor, were friends of Soniat.

Walker was elected commander and Walter was chaplain. The post became a new toy for Walker and Walter. They had lots of ideas about what they wanted to accomplish. "The post will hold meetings in the Association of Commerce building and proposed to take an active part in all questions that interest ex-service men."[6]

But the post immediately picked a fight with the American Legion—yes, *the* American Legion—which led to its charter being revoked in August. To say this was a rare event is an understatement. "This revocation of a Legion's post is the first in the United States—the first, in fact, in the history of the American Legion."[7]

The drastic action was due to a resolution the post passed in late June, within a week of founding the group. Proud of its resolution, the post telegraphed copies of it to the "platform committee of the Democratic National Convention and to the Louisiana Delegation in the United States Senate."[8]

Walker, Walter, and the post's other members wanted to stir things up, and they did. A headline referred to the post members as "Society Favorites."[9] Entitled, privileged Southern white men, they did not back down when called out.

The revocation was announced by State Commander T. Semmes Walmsley, who later became mayor of New Orleans. "The Louisiana Committee contends that the resolution tended to criticize and defame the House of Representatives of the Congress of the United States as well as to disrupt our organization."

Another representative, Michel Provosty, made it clear that the post's expulsion was not due to its opinion on the issue but "words and phrases that cannot be tolerated and the gross misstatement of facts."[10] Provosty pointed out that another post had also disagreed with the plan but its charter had not been revoked.

When asked for a reaction, Walker replied, "There is no statement to make…. I would only ask in fairness that the full resolution which has brought about this action by the Louisiana committee be printed in *The Item*."

Here are the good parts:

This post is opposed to the legislation recently passed by the Federal House of Representatives providing for a blanket cash bonus to all ex-servicemen, or to any legislation which contemplates the payment of any bonus to those ex-servicemen who returned to civilian life unscathed, and sound in mind and body. That war service is not and should not be undertaken with a view to pecuniary reward, and that no such reward could be commensurate to the service rendered.... The movement for a blanket cash bonus to ex-servicemen is sprung from unworthy motives and finds its chief support in the pandering of politicians to a supposed soldier vote.... The honor of our country demands that those wounded or otherwise in the late war and the dependents of the dead be given immediate and generous treatment, and that all bonus legislation should look to their welfare—not in a spirit of donation but as endowing the country with the privilege of caring for them.

The next part is probably what got them in hot water:

The easy and unscrupulous use of the name of the American Legion, by certain of its leaders, to foster such legislation in Congress without a referendum thereon to the full membership of the organization has, by creating a false impression of the unanimous approval in its ranks, operated to the injury of the Legion's interests, and is inconsistent with the high principles set forth in the preamble of its constitution.[11]

Even though Walker said he had no statement, he said more the following day. "We are content to have uttered our protest and to have published the fact that we are not in accord with the proposal.... Our experience as a post of the American Legion is ended but we intend to keep up our organization, probably as a private club."[12] That was probably for the best. That same week, a different post, the Allen Thomas Post No. 66, was formed. "One of the first official acts was to vote their support to the bonus plan."

It wasn't over. On August 11, an announcement was placed in the *Times-Picayune* by "Friends of the former Leon Soniat Post" that reproduced the resolution.[13] After saying that they were not interested in appealing the decision, they changed their mind. "It has developed that the Soniat Post has made an aggressive fight to prevent this action on the part of the national executive committee."[14] It didn't work. Finally, on September 27, at the national American Legion convention, the expulsion was upheld, and the charter was officially revoked.[15]

At the time of this drama, Walker and Walter were both 27 and war veterans. Yet they come across as smug, arrogant and immature. They had no inkling how inappropriate their actions were. Then they doubled down and suggested that they would just have their own private club. Sheesh.

Still, their scandalous behavior did not prevent them from continuing to dine, dance and luncheon in social circles. Both kept a busy social schedule in the early 1920s, and nobody seemed to hold it against them.

8. Walker and the French Quarter

However, while Walker stayed away from politics and civic activities, Walter learned the important lesson to keep his political activities mainstream and uncontroversial.

Walker poured his youthful energy into renovating his new house. Perhaps not surprisingly, his parents weren't pleased, though one suspects that some of the tension was due to Walker's behavior during the American Legion incident. According to Natalie Scott, "I hear interesting things about that charming old house of which the Ellises, Senior, are wont to speak with only scanty respect."[16] However, Scott, who also dabbled in real estate in the French Quarter and was at one time William Spratling's landlord (and rumored lover), was impressed, knowing that the

> clever and versatile Walker is going ... to make "a habitation and a home" after his own artistic promptings. They say the class of labor that is now engaged in painting the walls and performing various other difficult tasks under his scrupulous direction is of the very rarest.... I hear that the dainty feet which mount the rickety ladder there have moved rhythmically over the floors and the most brilliant balls in town: that the hands which wield so effectively the paintbrushes are slim, and shapely soft and well manicured. And they do say that Walker's trousers and a paint-bespattered shirt of Tommy Farrar's, open at the throat, sat with extreme becomingness on the graceful figure of a certain delightful young woman, who is usually marked by the elegance of her costumes and her distinguished air of quiet repose!

The young woman is not identified but might have been Elizabeth Wilkinson or Bell Lawrason. Still, Scott was perhaps providing cover because she had to be aware that Walker, Tommy—and Elizabeth Wilkinson—were homosexual.

In fact, many of the people moving into the French Quarter in the 1920s were gay. Others were artists and writers. Some were all of the above.

> New arrivals were attracted not only by architectural aesthetics and cheap rents but also, oddly enough, by the Quarter's offbeat inhabitants and the sense of escape to a quiet refuge. These ingredients produced a bohemian flavor that was creatively stimulating. A sense of liberation from society's rules resulted in a colony of kindred spirits passionately pursuing their artistic work.[17]

Walker's house became a hangout. Born in 1891, Charles Bein, nicknamed Uncle Charlie, graduated from Tulane in 1912. He was a teacher, painter, architect and a gay friend of Walker's.

> He is one of that little coterie who find the Vieux Carre the most attractive part of the city and you may find him on Sunday mornings busily lending his advice on color and decorative scheme to Walker Ellis in the interest of preserving the charm and atmosphere of the house that Walker Ellis has taken for his sanctum sanctorum. There is always an enthusiastic little group in the rooms of this new-old treasure and Walker's quaint house bids fair to rival the

coffee houses of olden days for gathering unto itself the men and women who look for the delights of pleasant conversation and artistic encouragement.[18]

According to John Shelton Reed, gay men were largely responsible for protecting and restoring the French Quarter. Specifically, he named artist William Spratling, writer Lyle Saxon, philanthropist William Ratcliffe Irby and architect Richard Koch as leaders who, "in alliance with elite women ... were a vital part of the movement that transformed the French Quarter from a slum to an artists' colony to whatever it is today."

Still, at the time Walker was living there, the Vieux Carré had "an underworld of opiates and prostitution.... Members of the circle patronized Celeste's, which Carl Carmer described as 'the lowest joint in New Orleans—filled with lesbians, homosexuals, and the rest of us.' It was across from the police station."[19]

By the fall of 1920, Walker was restless and traveled frequently. He and Charles Kock sometimes traveled together. "Mr. Walker Ellis returned recently from a three weeks' vacation trip, spent visiting Mrs. Theodore Pratt, at Glen Cove, L.I., in New York, attending the races at Saratoga, and in Greenwich, Conn. He stopped for a few days at White Sulphur Springs, Va., en route here."[20]

Even when Walker was out of town, his Toulouse Street residence continued to get attention and accolades.

> If you stroll down in the Vieux Carre, your eye will note Mr. Ellis' bachelor residence, which is quite the envy of every antique romancer. There is, apparently, both fascination and excitement in owning a home with modern comforts in this section of the city, particularly when the mosquito season is over. This part of our quaint old village is far more interesting in traditions than Greenwich Village in New York, and if the housing question continues to be as serious in the future as in the past, there is no doubt it'll become famous.

These were prophetic words. Vieux Carré, better known as New Orleans' French Quarter, is still one of the city's most popular places.

Considering his frequent trips out of the city, it is clear that Walker's job at the law firm did not work out. He quit or was asked to leave after just a few months. Apparently unconcerned, Walker continued to focus on decorating his home. "Walker Ellis is ... an aesthete. Who but an aesthete could have seen through the cobweb and dirt and grime of the old house in Toulouse St., its intrinsic beauty?"

Walker's house, a hangout and a place to party, was conveniently located near the Quartier Club and other sites where one could indulge in alcohol and other vices. A columnist described a typical weekend scene:

> We ... were much enlightened and encouraged last Sunday evening when chance led us through Toulouse St. and we saw a double-line for blocks of

smart touring cars and fashionable limousines.... A supper at the Quartier Club was a glorious beginning.... The big room of the Quartier Club was filled to capacity with the guests who were gathered about the handsome table, in the cozy candlelight.... And when the resources of the Quartier Club had been exhausted, the company, still at the zenith of enjoyment, gathered up the

A wrought iron gate leads to the garden at 723 Toulouse Street (Historic American Buildings Survey, C. & Boutet, H. *Valery Nicholas House, 723 Toulouse Street, New Orleans, Orleans Parish, LA*. New Orleans Louisiana Orleans Parish, 1933. Documentation Compiled After [Library of Congress]).

phonograph bodily, and marched in triumph to Toulouse St., to the house of Walker Ellis. And the second installment of the party was as wildly merry as the first. Certainly, the new setting was quite as entrancing.[21]

Walker's house was indeed special, and it's no wonder it became a favorite place of many.

> The old house came into existence under the dominion of the Spanish, in 1784,[22] and since that time its dignified construction and its aristocratic lines have known no change. The entrance is through what was once the covered carriageway, leading past the keepers' rooms which occupy the ground floor. Candles in brackets on the wall throw a flickering light that weaves odd patterns of shadow on the cold gray stone. The old rounded stone archway at the end of the passage gives out onto the courtyard, flooded Sunday night with transcendent and most opportune moonlight. Looking over the court at one side is a balcony with wrought-iron railings, and, if you mount to it by the old steps, you have the most delightful view of rounded stone archways, fan transoms, big heavy doorways, which reveal the massive 15-inch thickness of the walls, and all the charms that the old French quarter is heir to. A living-room stretches across the entire front of the house. At each end is a large fireplace, with handsome, old-fashioned mantels. It is illuminated only by the soft light of candles and lamps. Four tall, dignified French windows with heavy black velvet curtains that trail on the floor for two feet or so. It is a room with personality.[23]

At the end of 1920, Walker, still interested in theater and film, hosted a party for movie star Florence Fair, whose silent film *Clarence* was playing at the Tulane movie theater. "Miss Elizabeth Wilkinson entertained Sunday evening at a supper at the Quartier club followed by a dance in the studio of Mr. Walker Ellis in honor of Miss Florence Fair and other members of the cast of *Clarence*."[24]

By the way, party hostess Elizabeth Wilkinson is an interesting character in her own right. Born in 1877, she owned an interior design shop in the French Quarter. Wilkinson, who never married, traveled throughout Europe and at one point worked in New York with legendary interior designer Elsie de Wolfe, who lived with her partner Elizabeth Marbury.

By the end of 1920, Katty was 17 and Walker was 27. It was not unusual for the two to be at many of the same social functions. It's unlikely they had much contact. She was too young to attend his house parties, and he was too old to have much in common with her.

Katty would not have been invited to a New Year's Eve party hosted by Walker. Natalie Scott wrote about it in her persona of Diana:

> We are among those invited. Queer where the people come from. All of the hotels and restaurants are crowded days ahead—that is their reservations are all taken for New Year's Eve, dozens of people are going to the affair at the Country Club, and yet on every hand you hear them talking about

8. Walker and the French Quarter

This interior shot of 723 Toulouse Street shows one of many fireplaces (Historic American Buildings Survey, C. & Boutet, H. *Valery Nicholas House, 723 Toulouse Street, New Orleans, Orleans Parish, LA*. New Orleans Louisiana Orleans Parish, 1933. Documentation Compiled After [Library of Congress]).

week-ending across the lake.... I have heard tales that I might tell ... however, I won't. Everyone probably knows them already anyhow, and there's no sense in putting them on record.[25]

Scott suggests that Walker had a kind of notoriety. It appears that his queer life was an open secret, and most people did not care. "University of

New Orleans professor Kenneth Holditch reports 'an old saying' that his fellow New Orleanians 'don't care what you do. They want to know about it, but they don't care.'"[26] According to Maunsel White, "There was a 'don't ask, don't tell' kind of treatment in play. Social position contributed a lot toward acceptance or tolerance toward homosexuals in New Orleans."[27]

By 1921, Walker's house, or studio, as it was now called, had also become popular with wealthy tourists. "The DuPonts—the powder people … came over from Palm Beach in their private car and have absorbed French town as though it were an oyster *à la* Rockefeller, green sauce and all. They had been told en route not to miss the Walker Ellis studio. They didn't. They went there for tea this afternoon … sat on the gallery and watched the courtyard—found it delightfully artistic."[28]

Walker also often hosted parties for his siblings at his house, including one for his sister Hazel Woodward.

> Walker Ellis' house is one of the oldest in French town, sits right on the street, shops on either side of it, but the walls are so high you'd never know they were there after you get inside that large entrance and get a view of the beautiful courtyard through the curved arch at the end of the alley way. That courtyard reminds you of a moving picture of some place in southern France: perhaps, too, it is one of the largest in the city…. Walker has perfect taste and he rummaged for and selected every piece of furniture and decoration in that house, from the old grand piano that he had made into a desk to the fascinating lamps and candelabras that he has throughout the place.[29]

In another article, Walker was accused of buying up all the cool lamps in New Orleans. "I have followed duly in the wake lately of several friends bent on the quest of the kerosene lamp, and we have ransacked antique stores from one end to another…. Constantly we meet with this reply…. 'I had just what you would like, Madame. The very thing. But Mr. Walker Ellis bought it.' Truly, he is to be suspected to have a hoard of lamps stowed away, in a mysterious room of that fascinating Toulouse Street house of his."[30]

In the spring of 1921, Walker announced plans to return to Europe for the first time since the war. The rumor was that Walter would travel with him.[31] Later, a society columnist reported that Walker was headed to Paris "and expects to wear a pathway smooth between the Montmartre and the Latin Quarter, choosing those two extremes as his favorite Parisian haunts. He has designs on Spain for later on."[32]

Finally on July 29, Walker left for Europe, but apparently without Walter. Also, the local newspaper again referred to him as Mrs.: "Mrs. Walker Ellis will leave Friday, via Chicago, for New York, from which port he will sail to Europe early in August. He will make an extensive trip through Spain and will also visit several other countries before returning in the late fall."[33] The "typo" was corrected in the next edition of the newspaper.

8. Walker and the French Quarter

More details about Walker's trip came out in a different society column. "From Paris he takes a flying trip—to London to complete his wardrobe (Vanitus, vanitus, once again, my friend!) then on to Spain—or where the spirit moves him. A two-months trip.... I passed Elizabeth Wilkerson's windows this afternoon ... and looking through into the shop, saw him, apparently telling her something of all this. I wanted to hear it in his enthusiastic telling but someone came by to enter the shop and I hadn't the nerve to even linger longer at the glass."[34]

All things must end, and in the fall of 1921, Walker's beloved French Quarter house was for sale.

> The rumor still persists that the Walker Ellis house is still on the market. There have been various would-be buyers.... One in particular, poured into my ear a perfect Odyssey of wanderings, when he wanted to go through the house as a prospective buyer and went in search of the key. He was referred to the Farrars, to Miss Elizabeth Wilkinson, to Bell Lawrason, to Charlie Bein and various others ... and finally around the circle again, till he gave up in despair. Evidently Walker is not keenly enthusiastic about selling and he will find his big toy waiting for him when he returns from the devious ways of his European trip.[35]

When Walker returned to New Orleans in October 1921, one society columnist noted that he'd gained weight and wasn't in the mood to talk. "Met Walker Ellis on Royal Street today. The months have wrought their changes there. Fourteen pounds added to his manly weight. I wanted dreadfully to hear about his motor trip through Spain.... I wanted to ask him whether he hadn't changed his mind about selling his house now that French town was booming. But he rushed past me."[36]

9

A Trip to Europe

> A group of ... younger ... girls in fashionable circles in New Orleans, and not yet "out," ... left in a party last week for New York whence they will sail Wednesday for Cherbourg on a three months' tour in Europe.[1]

Katty and Moosie's debutante year was 1922. That year their names were mentioned in the newspapers hundreds of times. Not only were they feted, but in a cultural quid pro quo, they were encouraged to fete and attend other deb parties. It was an exhausting year.

The first major event in January was a themed event at the Quartier Club for Moosie White's sister, Ellene, who was also a deb. The Club "was decorated with a variety of posters. All the guests wore costumes representing some advertisement."[2] Katty's costume was the *Daily States* newspaper, which was bound to get her mentioned in at least one newspaper.[3] Moosie won a prize for "Saturday Night," another newspaper-themed costume[4]:

> [She] had the most fetching creation—I fall in with the judgment of the judges, who gave her costume first prize. She deserved it ... for it is surely a prize-winning feat to take two bath towels, hold them together with blue ribbons, tie washcloths and sponges about at random, and have a bewitching toilette. Katty Stewart was quite bewitching, too, and her costume was clever as could be made, if you please, of the Sunday States, and as saucily attractive a thing as you could imagine, pleated, with plaited standing jauntily up on the shoulder, a full-plaited skirt, and a piquantly pointed hat.[5]

Also in January, there was a black-and-white party held at the Quartier Club.

> An airy effect of a snow-bird was what Katty Stewart suggested, in a costume that was very full and feathery and dainty.[6]

> [Moosie White and her sisters] are wonders: it seems a triumph to achieve one costume in a family, but three, all very different is to marvel! Ellene was a picture; Maudie's was the dashing one, with black silk short "trou," a black bolero jacket and a fluffy white shirt, while Moussie's twinkling eyes sparkled

in their most mischievous, wise, probably because she suspected that her all-black with soft pompons of white fur at her throat, at her sleeves, dangling from black ribbons, was especially becoming.

During this time, Katty (as well as Walter Stauffer and Walker Ellis) was becoming more involved with the revitalized Bridle Club, a riding club for the wealthy. A photo appeared in the February 1, 1922, edition of the *New Orleans States* newspaper. showing seven members of the Bridle Club: Walter Stauffer, Will J. Gibbons, Katharine Stewart, Natalie Scott, Walker Ellis, Pierre Villare and Peggy Mason Smith.[7] "Among the valuable additions to outdoor life in the city during the past year, the New Orleans Bridle Club is perhaps the most cherished. The small group, numbering many people prominent in the social and business life of our city, banded together and have made horseback riding one of the permanent sports available to Orleanians. Every day, groups may be seen along the many attractive bridle paths contiguous to City Park and Metaire Ridge." Members hoped to add polo matches, horse shows and steeplechases with the goal "to make the New Orleans horse shows equal in fame to those of Virginia and Kentucky."

In New Orleans, the debutante season was closely tied to Carnival events. In February, Walker was chosen as king at the annual "Follies" ball, "a very important feature among the social activities of each season.... After the rise of the curtain, several members of the organization, which-by-the-way is composed of girls of the unmarried and younger married sets, gave a cymbal dance which was followed by a grand march and the choice of the king and dukes from the 'call out' seats."[8]

A popular annual event, the French Opera Society Trade Ball was held in February. In 1922, James Ewing was crowned king and Ellene White was queen. Katty, wearing a salmon-colored velvet gown, was a member of the court.[9] "The Ball of the Atlanteans, as usual, brought out an array of beautiful gowns on the floor for the maskers' dances. The gowns worn by the queen and other members of the court were glittering and gorgeous in the extreme."[10]

Walter and Walker were featured in a strange February column titled "The Marriage Market," which listed names of eligible bachelors and a brief description. The comment for Walker was: "Brilliant mind, wrapped in cotton wool." For Walter, it was: "Creole charm, but equal indifference."[11]

Walter also became involved in a dog giveaway that was offered through the S.P.C.A., an animal welfare organization. The dog's name was Brownie, and he was offered to a boy. A woman wrote in and asked why Brownie couldn't go to a girl or woman. In the same cutesy, conversational style, Brownie wrote, "I don't know exactly how to answer her letter. I'd like her all right and all that. I know, but—aw well, I'm just a boy's dog, that's all!"[12] Before he was finally given away (it was quite a saga), Brownie once again, and this time tersely, addressed why it could only be a boy after a couple of girls also wrote asking if they could be considered. "As I said before, I was just cut out to be some boy's pal."[13] New Orleans in the 1920s was a sexist society with lines clearly drawn.

The death of Juliette Hunter on February 16, 1922, signaled the end of an era. The 92-year-old, once a slave, was a longtime servant of many of the city's wealthiest families, including the Stauffers. "The death … marked the passing of New Orleans' oldest servant. Her service as a maid and cook for prominent New Orleans families dates back to antebellum days. She served as a slave in the Burbank family and worked later for Mrs. John W. Stone. For more than 40 years she was employed in the homes of T.D. Miller and Walter Stauffer."[14]

At this time, it was not unusual to have Walter, Walker, Katty and Moosie at the same events, often sitting at the same table. All were socially active in the same circles, and they often attended several events in a week. Walter also frequently socialized with Richard Orme. Often in lists of attendees, their names were next to each other, which usually indicated that they had come together.

Meanwhile, New Orleans had not forgotten that its very own Walker Ellis had once been a war hero. In March it was announced that he would be part of "the greatest aviation exhibit ever held in the South."[15] It was scheduled for October and "[t]here will be one race in which the entries are limited to New Orleans ex-aviators. Among the entrants will be Captain Walker Ellis, whose army record shows nine German planes brought down." This is surely an exaggeration. While Walker served honorably, his name does not appear on any list of World War I flying aces from the United States.

Also in March, Walker, Walter and several others went fox hunting in Mandeville, Louisiana.[16] The group was part of the Bridle Club and included Peggy Mason Smith and her sister Elise. "What loads of fun—and aside from the hunt, the thought of moonlight at Mandeville just now is wonderful. The moon—and the pines—and the water."[17]

Walker had a sense of humor and was likely aware, from a young age, that some questioned his masculinity. Like Katty, he was expected to follow gender conformity, but struggled with it.

> Walker Ellis tells this one on himself. Once upon a time he went turkey shooting on a plantation near New Orleans. There was much talk of the hunt and when he entered the blind with a wishbone blowing guide before dawn, he was in a state of nerves. Buckfever. When the first streaks of pink showed in the sky, the guide grabbed his arm and pointed. "There!" the guide whispered. "A

turkey!" Walker fired both barrels. When the smoke cleared he was delighted to see the bird prone, and, dropping his gun in his excitement, ran forward. When he stood over the turkey he noticed something white on its neck. Looking more closely he found the white to be paper tied to the turkey. He unfolded the paper and read, "Why did you shoot me, Walker? I was tame."[18]

In the spring of 1922, Walker's French Quarter home was finally sold. His parents likely pressured him to sell the money pit. "Father Hume bought the charming little house in Toulouse Street that Walker Ellis restored two years ago, and further repairs are in progress."[19] Father Hume was Monsignor W.W. Hume, who paid $4000 for the property on May 22, 1922.[20] Walker owned it for a little over two years and made a tidy profit on it, though, of course, he put a lot of money into it for repairs and furnishings.

In 1922, Katty and Moosie were inseparable. In April, the *New Orleans Item* described "a perfect riot of a party" at the Patio, "with everybody staying after the band had disbanded and obliging with vaudeville stunts of their own invention. Amazingly clever ones, too.... Parham Werlein

Katty and Moosie with unidentified men and women at a party, probably in the early 1920s. Katty is wearing the "Snappy" headband and Moosie is the blonde beside her (courtesy Maunsel White).

doing all sorts of clever card tricks—and Moosie White and Katty Stewart singing bowery songs in their own quaint idea of appropriate costumes."[21]

Katty was often on, in or around water, and newspapers took notice. She frequently used her father's yacht during the spring and summer of 1922. "Parties on Lake Pontchartrain and yachting generally is the usual favorite pastime for this season of the year. Mr. William P. Stewart is frequently out on his yacht the *Sunshine* with more or less small parties of friends. His daughter, Miss Katharine Stewart, who is a lover of out-of-door sports generally, is usually with him."[22]

In the spring of 1922, the *Times-Picayune* featured a photo of Katty by noted society photographer Anthony H. Hitchler. A flattering profile, it was used many times in the coming years. Hitchler, a favorite of the wealthy class, was born in Germany in 1835 and died in 1936 at the age of 81.

Alongside the Hitchler photo was a caption that again pointed out Katty's attractiveness and made an important announcement about her upcoming plans. "Miss Katharine Stewart, one of the most attractive members of a charming coterie in younger circles ... will spend the summer in travel abroad."[23] You really can't blame Katty for wanting to get away, and this trip would prove to be one of the most interesting experiences of her life.

The summer trip to Europe was chaperoned by Natalie Scott. "Naming the group 'Natalie Scott and Her Nine Muses,' the New Orleans press followed the trip. Scott's reports of their exploits regularly appeared in her 'Peggy Passe Partout' column, along with occasional feature articles."[24]

The group included Katty and other wealthy young Southern women. Surprisingly, Moosie White was not one of them:

> Miss Natalie Scott, having with her Edwa Stewart, Charlotte Reilly, Amelie May, Bessie Johnson and Elise Roussel, of New Orleans. Mary Janet Smith, daughter of Mr. Gordon Smith of Mobile, and Blanche Broussard ... will leave Saturday evening for New York. The party will be joined in New York by Miss Katharine Stewart, who will leave for New York this evening, and by Miss Josephine LeBlanc, who is at school in the East. They will all sail from New York June 7 on the steamer *St. Paul* of the American line for Cherbourg and will visit first in Tours, Blols and elsewhere in France, including a ten-day stay in Paris. They will visit in Italy, spending five days in Rome, a few days in Florence, and shorter stays in other places and will travel through parts of Switzerland, Belgium, Holland and England, and also will go to Oberamergau [sic] for the Passion Play. Miss Scott will conduct the tour and the party will be absent in Europe three months.[25]

Natalie Scott is an intriguing woman. Friendly with Katty, Moosie, Walker and Walter, she was born in 1890 in Bristol, Virginia. Scott was the *New Orleans States* newspaper's society columnist, using the *nom de plume* Peggy Passe Partout. John Shelton Reed described her as a "journalist, equestrian, real-estate investor, Junior Leaguer, social organizer."[26] She was a Newcomb graduate and part of the New Orleans literary circle.

Scott earned a master's from Tulane and "seemed to be headed for a quiet academic career. But when the United States entered the First World War, she went to France as a Red Cross worker, and she came back as a heroine," one of the few American women "to receive the Croix de Guerre (for rescuing wounded soldiers from the rubble of her hospital during a bombing raid)."[27] She never married, but was rumored to have been one of William Spratling's female lovers. She eventually moved to Mexico where she led an active life.

In many ways, Scott was the ideal guide. She was intelligent, educated, good-humored, patient, and had a good head on her shoulders. "Fancy imbibing Europe with such a wonderful person as Natalie. Among her numerous accomplishments, she possesses the gift of Cicerone, well informed in art treasures, operas, theaters, etc., that make up European culture. And then they will have her delightful sense of humor to carry them through any little hardships that might arise."[28]

Scott and her charges left for New York in June and stayed at the Wolcott in New York before sailing. One of the first things they did when they reached Europe was attend the Grand Prix. "The 'Grand Prix,' which means a very brilliant gathering of the ultra-fashionable world in Paris, France, besides its importance as a sporting feature of the season there, was attended this year by a large number of Orleanians."[29]

Later that month, newspapers received letters from the travelers. Letter-writing was one way the elite kept their names in society columns, even when they were away from home. "Interesting letters from our European travelers are pouring in and contain news of all sorts of wonderful adventures and excursions.... And they are continually seeing interesting and beautiful things, art galleries, theaters and operas, and we here at home can only use Christian Science and try to make believe we are experiencing the same sensations—and are enjoying the cool climate and snows of Switzerland or the Italian Alps!"[30]

On July 9, 1922, the Sunday *New Orleans States* newspaper included snippets of a Scott letter which described the activities of her companions: "[T]he New Orleans young women 'start things' wherever they may be found. This time they started a Carnival on a steam ship, with Rex and his Queen and all, and they made of the affair a marked event in the annals of a famous old ship."[31]

Scott, who had been in Europe during the chaos of World War I, revisited familiar places on this trip. The changes in just a few short years surprised her. "You would never know that this land had been fought over and looked like one of the principalities of Hades just a couple of years ago. It is perfectly marvelous.... In the little villages the people are working away tirelessly, patching up the houses, filling up the holes and getting things in order again."[32] Despite the renewal, there were still sobering vestiges of war:

> We did the usual thing of going to the fortress of Pompelle. The fort itself has been left very much as it was and of course it is interesting to the girls to see the dugouts, the line of communicating trenches, the two German tanks that are left there stuck in the mud and all the rest of it. There are still, even after all the combing of the place that tourists have done, pieces of shrapnel and other souvenirs. We slid down a dugout, went through a short one underground which was another thriller and then we climbed about the poor dilapidated place from one end to the other.

The New Orleans women included several who were first-time visitors to Europe. "The girls were so delighted with the strangeness and foreignness of everything when they landed at Cherbourg that they would simply stand still and stare whenever any man, woman, went by in everyday clothes—which of course are not American by any means."

Many Americans were touring Europe that summer, so it's not surprising that the group ran into people they knew. In Deauville, they came upon one of Katty's relatives: "As cold as it could be when we landed.... Did I tell you that Henry LeBlanc [Jo's brother] was standing on the pier at Plymouth when we put in there? Katty Stewart saw him and said, 'There is a man that looks just like Henry LeBlanc.' Then to be factious [sic], she made a little mock bow and said, under her breath, 'Hello Henry.' You should have seen her expression when she discovered it really was Henry!"[33]

They also ran into New Orleans artists: "Fanny Craig, the artist from New Orleans who was ... traveling in Europe that summer, tracked Natalie down in Paris and went with the group to Rheims and other excursions from Paris. Two other young New Orleans artists, Charlie Bein and Tommy Farrar, were also exploring Europe and they too spent much time with Natalie and her companions."[34]

Although the tour was in the summer, it was often unusually chilly. Despite the cold, Katty desperately wanted to swim. Scott apparently could not say no to her.

> We rented a little bath cabin, towels and the rest of the necessary paraphernalia and dressed for the bath. Katty went into shrieks of laughter over the bathrobe which is made of toweling and simply fastens around your neck by pulling a string. I have never in the world been so cold as when we started off down that hard beach! The wind was simply cutting through us and I thought I would never in the world have the courage to plunge in but finally made the break, and it was glorious!

The same letter mentioned the group's attendance at a Mass in a Rouen cathedral. "We went early in the morning and the girls had the perspective of the altar with the priest and the little choir boys and wonderful music, as soft as a breeze it seemed, stealing through all the service the dim light and all that could inspire and impress one. We all sat quiet as mice—the greatest tribute of awe that we could offer."[35]

Scott and her companions continued their tour. "Katty Stewart and I have been standing in the corridor watching the sun set over the flat even stretch of the campagna, the Mediterranean in the distance. We had a wonderful time in Nice."[36]

Scott also took the young women to Monte Carlo. "We went gaily into Monte Carlo, all the girls quite excited over the idea of seeing the games." Although several were underage, they finagled their way inside. "The rooms are enormous, tremendous halls all ornamented and gilded very elaborately." Albert I, prince of Monaco, had recently died unexpectedly, and the mood was subdued. Scott played roulette.

They ate dinner in Rome "at the Castello di Cesare, perched up on top of the Palatine hill where was formerly the palace of the Roman emperors—all ruins now.... We ate everything we could think of and then found our bill just about a dollar and a half. We had cabs that we kept all evening and then made them take us to the Coliseum and wait for us while we wandered around in there.... And our bill was just a little over a dollar. Hurray for the rate of exchange!"

An eerie Coliseum experience took place in darkness. "We were speaking in whispers and beginning to believe in ghosts. Then from somewhere in the shadows an Italian boy began to sing.... When he finished there was a perfect storm of hand-clapping and then we knew for the first time how many people were in the place!"

In late August, the *New Orleans States* received another newsy letter from Scott. "Today we change from train to steamer again and go across to Lindau, which is in Germany. More passports, customs officers and language-hash—or Hungarian goulash.... We finally arrive (if we do) at Kaufberen, where we spend the night. On to Fussen the next morning, where a motor will meet us and motor us all about. We are going to see the Bavarian hills with their crop of castles.... And then we end up again in Oberammergau."

In Kursall, they went to a vaudeville performance. They also visited the Pharos tables. Again Katty and other women ran into old schoolmates and other friends. "The Hangars of New York are friends of Kattie that we have met several times. We feel quite sociable in Europe!'" Katty may also have crossed paths with the future Kay Francis. Seventeen-year-old Katharine Gibbs was also in Europe at the time.

Natalie's letter included glimpses into the personalities of her fellow tourists:

> And now a hurried picture of our party for you—Jo is absorbed in Baedcker at present. A hot bridge game is going on in one corner. Charlotte is gazing out of the window and exclaiming over apple orchards and unexpected glimpses of lake…, Phro [Blanche Broussard] is poring over a map of Switzerland and Katty is looking out of the window and announcing Zurich every few minutes for the fun of seeing us jump.

Meanwhile, life was continuing in New Orleans. While Katty was out of town, the *Times-Picayune* stirred the pot with a bitchy blurb:

> One had so pictured Miss Katharine Stewart making her bow to society in the spacious drawing room of the old family home in Jackson Avenue, in which her mother, as Kittie Eustis, and her grandmother, as Laura Buckner, made their bows. But it is not to be, for the beautiful old home, one of the residence landmarks in the fashionate "garden" district, has been sold by Mrs. Cartwright Eustis, who was Laura Buckner. Keeping up such residences in these days is such a tax after all, and Mrs. Eustis, its chatelaine, is so much away from New Orleans visiting married daughters and sons. And pretty Katharine Stewart has sailed for Europe with a jolly party of young people, all duly chaperoned, to spend a few months in travel."[37]

Yes, in 1922, Katty's debutante year, Katty's grandmother, Laura Eustis, made the decision to sell the Buckner mansion to the Soulle Business School, which began teaching accounting, management, secretarial and other business-oriented classes in 1923. Perhaps Katty did not care one way or the other, but it was odd timing. Mumsie, who grew up in the house, explained that she wanted to visit her children and grandchildren. In fact, Mumsie and Kittie were feuding for reasons that will become clear later.

Laurance Eustis, whose father grew up in the house, was nine when the house was sold. He described how the furniture, dishes, pots and pans, clothing, etc., were disposed of. "When Mumsie sold the old home, she gave her children all they might want, then held an auction and sold the rest of the possessions. The auction was started with a drummer beating a drum in front of the house, supposedly to attract a crowd."[38]

Meanwhile, a different property, 2228 St. Charles Avenue, located between Philip and Jackson Avenue near the Buckner mansion, was listed for sale in the spring of 1922. It was described as a "Raised Cottage with a Finished Basement."[39] Features included a

> spacious front porch, reception hall, library, long stylish living room, dining room, butlery with built-in features, kitchen, large screened living porch

9. A Trip to Europe

The Buckner house as photographed by Arnold Genthe in the 1920s (Genthe, A., photographer. *Henry Sullivan Buckner House, Jackson Avenue, New Orleans*, between 1920 and 1926 [Library of Congress]).

overlooking the rear lawn, three bedrooms, two tiled baths, clothes closets. Upstairs: Hall, two bedrooms, bath. Hot water heat, hot and cold water, gas, electricity, hardwood floors in living rooms, etc. Handsome mantels and chandeliers. Basement: servants' rooms, servants' bath, laundry with stationary tubs, large lawn, flower garden, trees and shrubbery. Double garage on Philip Street.

The house was listed at $20,000.

Mumsie soon purchased the St. Charles Avenue home from Elizabeth Werlein for $19,270, and Katty, Buddy and Will Stewart moved in. By this time, Kittie and Will had separated, and Kittie was living alone in an apartment. Family members moved in and out of the home over the years, and this address remained Katty's official residence until her death.

It must have been a real treat for anyone, but especially society columnists, to receive a letter from Natalie Scott. She was an intimate, clever writer and often included photographs. A *New Orleans States* columnist described two Kodak pictures

> that I was lucky enough to receive from Natalie, one taken at Zermatt, just below the Matterhorn.... Katty Stewart is especially good in the photograph, an attractive scarf thrown carelessly across the shoulders of her coat suit.... And the other picture! Shades of censors are not needed for these bathing suits of Genoa—long loose hanging affairs, that envelope the wearers.... A trio of bathers—Katty Stewart, Natalie and Bessie Johnson—Katty's costume is particularly remarkable being a loose garment that hangs from the shoulder and seems to be made for any size wearer.[40]

When the European trip ended, Scott returned to New Orleans. "'Oh, it was a lovely summer,' said Miss Scott when she stepped from the train and greeted the group of friends who had been waiting to meet her. 'We had a splendid time. Adventures? Scores of them.... We never had a single unpleasant or annoying experience.... It was a splendid summer. I wouldn't take a million dollars for it. But I'm glad to get back.'"[41]

10

Debutantes

A debutante or deb (from French: *debutante*, "female beginner") is a young woman of aristocratic or upper-class family background who has reached maturity and, as a new adult, comes out into society at a formal "debut" or possibly debutante ball. Originally, the term meant that the woman was old enough to be married, and part of the purpose of her coming out was to display her to eligible bachelors and their families, with a view to marriage within a social circle.[1]

On September 24, 1922, Natalie Scott wrote about the upcoming reunion of Katty and Moosie:

All the curious passengers of the Philadelphia train last Wednesday were looking everywhere for a groom to go with the "bride." That is the way they diagnosed "Moussie" White—Moussie, by the way, blossoming with determination into the debutante "Elizabeth" (can we ever be quite sure of her by any other name than Moussie?). She was on her way to Philadelphia to visit the Gazzams and expects to meet Katty Stewart there. The reunion of that buoyant-spirited pair of friends would be worth witnessing. Anyway, Moussie (the name persists, for the season hasn't begun yet, anyway) ... was quite submerged in masses of flowers, hands spilling over with magazines, books, candies, laughing, chattering ... [a] very pretty island in a laughing, chattering sea of friends who had gone down to see her off.... The Giberts [Moosie's aunt and uncle] ... plan to spend the winters over here and the summers in France.... They will arrive in New York in early November, and Moussie will join them for a brilliant whirl in New York's gayest moment,—opera's first nights for theaters, all in the bright opening time of New York's winter. She makes no promise here before the first of December.[2]

Katty finally met up with Moosie. "Elizabeth White, still another prospective debutante and one of the very attractive members of the coterie, joined Mrs. Stewart and her daughter at the Schuyler for a few days."

While Katty was in Europe, Moosie had developed a friendship with Pauline Breustedt. "Elizabeth White ... is now back in New York, visiting

Miss Pauline Breustedt, who will be remembered as her guest here last winter."[3] Pauline, born in Waco, Texas, in 1898, would become the Queen of the Texas Cotton Palace in 1923. She attended Bryn Mawr and Smith College and developed a love of acting. She appeared on Broadway in September 1922 in *Wild Oats Lane*. It received poor reviews and closed that same month. In 1926, she was a member of the Stuart Walker acting company along with Kay Francis. Pauline never married and spent much of her life traveling the world. She died in Waco in 1978. In an oral history interview done for Baylor University in the 1970s, she referred to a six-week stay in New Orleans where she spent part of the time with her mother's cousins and the other part with "an intimate friend."[4]

After leaving New York, Katty and Moosie traveled together to Annapolis, Maryland. "Many and glowing are the accounts of that hospitable Labrot home. Tales of a yacht at the very door, almost, of swimming, of sailing, motoring along marvelous roads, and dancing—and a countless succession of guests."[5]

> New Orleans newspapers could not get enough of Moosie and Katty in the fall of 1922: Mrs. Gazzam writes from Philadelphia of a twin sparkle that is dazzling the eyes of that distinguished city: Katty Stewart and Moussie White, naturally. "One continuous triumph." "Taking the city by storm," and all that sort of thing.... There were a number of parties planned for them before they arrived and now that [they] are actually here, the number has increased till the days are fairly spilling over with parties. And the general sentiment of the Philadelphia swains seems to coincide with that of the particular one of them who took his hostess aside after a certain dinner-party to say, earnestly: "See here: I didn't know there was a girl in the world like that. Where did you get two of them? They have me all bowled over." A sensation, in regard to that pair, that is not wholly unknown in New Orleans![6]

Nellie Gazzam grew up in New Orleans and moved to Philadelphia with her attorney husband Joseph. A fierce advocate for Prohibition, she was particularly concerned about "the alarming increase in the use of liquors and cigarettes by so-called fashionable young women."[7] One has to wonder whether Katty and Moosie successfully hid their cigarette and alcohol use from her.

Katty and Moosie continued to have so much fun in the East that society columnist Alice Dameron wondered if the young ladies would ever return home. "Orleanians are fairly falling over each other in New York these days.... Ethel and Maude Fox, Stephanie Levert, Katharine Stewart, Emily Hayne and Elizabeth White are having no end of a good time going to luncheon and dinner parties, and also attending the numerous theater parties. One wonders how they will ever be able to leave such a thrilling and entertaining spot, except that they have the brilliant social season promised for New Orleans this winter to look forward to."⁸

Another newspaper echoed that sentiment:

> Moussie White ... and Katty Stewart are playing havoc with hearts in the Eastern Universities, and have notebooks full of dates for proms and football games, and fraternity teas and house parties. They go up soon to the Harvard-Princeton football game ... and they are pledged to a succession of college parties as sequel to the game. They have promised likewise to dance the Princeton Prom on November 18. Will we ever get them home to their debutante duties?⁹

While Katty was in New York, Kay Francis noted in an October 2, 1922, diary entry that she needed to call—or had called—Katty. She had lunch with Katty on October 18. There were no further entries in Kay's diary mentioning Katty in 1922.

Moosie's friend Pauline Breustedt was an actress who toured with Kay Francis when both were in Stuart Walker's repertory company. This photograph was used as Pauline's headshot for appearances and reviews (Pauline Breustedt collection, Accession #1832, Box 1, Folder 11, The Texas Collection, Baylor University, Waco, Texas).

Katty's return to New Orleans in October signaled that it was time for her debut. According to the *Times-Picayune*, the debutante list, "though not as large as at first predicted, is one of the most interesting in several years. It includes a lovely group of young women, members of especially prominent families in the social world of New Orleans, and several of whom will doubtless be belles at all of the gayeties of the coming season."¹⁰

In mid–October, Moosie's parents announced that she would make her debut on Saturday, December 23.¹¹ On October 22, they put out that Moosie's sister Maude Tobin White was engaged to Stamps Farrar, the son of the late lawyer Edgar Farrar and Lucinda Stamps Farrar. The newspaper felt it important to note, "The marriage will unite two of New Orleans' very prominent and well-known families."¹² By the way, Lucinda Farrar was the great-niece of Confederate Jefferson Davis (her grandmother was Lucinda Farrar Davis, Jefferson's sister) and was reportedly at his bedside when he died.

It's unknown how Katty and Moosie felt about their debut. They may have been looking forward to it or perhaps dreaded it, but the experience definitely provided stressful moments for them and their mothers.

The article mentioned that Kittie was still in New York and

> indulging in a series of despairs at each of Katty's whirlwind returns. Each time, she has hopes of holding Katty down to serious shopping, and each time Katty arrives so enmeshed and entangled and ensnared in wholly unbreakable engagements, that shopping is a thing of scattered, frantic moments, or is not possible at all. That, with a debutante trousseau involved, is a thing of importance; but the trousseau grows, somehow, and beautifully, in spite of Kittie's despairs—and probably because of her monumental efforts.

In October, the *New Orleans Item* reported that Katty "will be formally introduced this winter and will be one of the loveliest and most attractive of the buds."[13] The term "buds" was frequently used to refer to the debs. The implication was that they had not yet flowered—but would soon.

Throughout the rest of the year, the importance of this "coming out" event was reflected in hundreds of newspaper articles. Almost every week of 1922, Katty and Moosie had several social obligations. Even the most enthusiastic partygoer would have reached a point of exhaustion.

Kittie had lots of plans for her only daughter's debut and likely had been thinking about it for years. She announced that there would a dance in honor of Katty on Thanksgiving, November 30, and a Sunday, December 24 (Christmas Eve) reception, at the Patio Royal. In addition, Katty would host her own dance on January 6. "It will be an 'Oriental' dance and one of the delightful features of the winter in debutante circles."[14]

Katty returned to New Orleans on November 21, traveling with Ethel Fox, another debutante.[15] Almost immediately, Katty and Kittie had a blowup. The day after Katty's arrival, the Thanksgiving Eve party was canceled. "Mrs. Katherine Eustis Stewart has recalled the invitations for the dance at which she was to have entertained … in honor of her young daughter. The date for the dance was afterwards announced as changed to November 28, but Mrs. Stewart has now postponed the dance indefinitely."[16] No reason was given for the cancellation. This had to raise eyebrows in their small circle. It was one of those things that "simply wasn't done."

The first of the deb celebrations started on Thursday, November 23. It was for Virginia Downman, who, according to the newspaper, was "much feted and attractive."[17] The article went on: "There will be many receptions at which the attractive young members of this season's coterie will be formally introduced by relatives and friends. Receptions have come into their own again and are decidedly popular forms of entertainment … for the day, and dances for the evenings."

10. Debutantes

Once the deb season started, Katty attended so many events that it probably felt like a full-time job. She not only attended and hosted parties but also shopped, had fittings, and so on. One columnist suggested that the deb culture could be competitive. "There is no doubt about the elaborateness that is characterizing all receptions this season—with veritable flower gardens in full bloom transported into drawing rooms and reception rooms generally."

Finally, it was Katty's turn to be feted on Wednesday, December 5. Her uncle and aunt, Andrew and Jo Stewart, hosted a celebration for her and cousin Josephine LeBlanc, "two of the very much feted and charming debutantes of the season. The dinner-dance was one of the handsomest of the winter parties given in fashionable circles here and the Patio, with its attractive courtyard was lovely with special decorations for the evening. There was a profusion of yellow and blue flowers and of autumn leaves and ferns."[18]

Katty's father was in attendance, as were other debs, but Kittie did not attend. Another interesting guest at this event was Katty's future husband Walker Ellis.[19]

On December 6, Moosie's parents, Mr. and Mrs. Albert Sidney White, hosted "one of the smartest dinner parties of the season ... in honor of Miss Katharine Stewart. The table was exquisite with orchids and lilies of the valley, and with tall crystal candelabra holding fancy lighted tapers."[20]

Katty managed to squeeze in a swim during her deb months. A columnist for the *New Orleans Item* described a party on

> the inviting waters of Lake Pontchartrain. Such an absolutely balmy day—positively warm in the summeriest of sports clothes. But the water was icy! After the first wild shriek from the first two who went overboard we were simply driven to it…. The moon was rising—absolutely crimson seen through the mists and the bare willow switches of the swamp that edges the lake shore—as we came in. And the clubhouse was a scene of revelry undreamed of. I can't think when I've seen it so crowded. Certainly not in many months. Tables almost in the middle of the dance floor. Someone was giving a party for the debutantes and they were out in dozens, of course, in the blue room."[21]

Katty again shared a celebration on Sunday, December 10. It was a supper-dance at the Patio Royal: She and Burdette Waldo were hosted by the Maurice Goldsteins. "The table was particularly attractive with quantities of roses…. The place cards were chic little paper dolls in the latest styles."[22] The *Times-Picayune*'s description of the event added more details: "Miss Waldo wore a girlish frock with garlands of pink that was extremely pretty and Miss Stewart was in black, with steel beads as trimming."[23]

The *New Orleans States* also noticed Katty's outfit. "There was a momentary revelation of Katty Stewart in a delightful toilette. Clever girl, who knows how to be quaint and modish! This was black velvet, with a round neck very simple, a piece of real lace accentuating the becoming roundness of the line, and the demure sobriety of it gaily contradicted by the flash of a smart hat of geranium red."[24] Another society columnist added, "Katty Stewart in a black creation beaded magically in steel so that when Jimmy (I think the man of the moment was Jimmy Kock) whirled her on the floor she shimmered in a wonderful way. Not shimmied."[25]

Moosie, who had returned to New Orleans only that day, was there as well. "Miss Elizabeth White, also a member of the debutante set and a guest at the party, was being made much of at her first appearance at any event this season.... She was very stunning in a gown of coral-covered chiffon very much beaded and very Frenchy."

It all got to be a bit much, even for the columnists. "Parties and parties. And charming debs who were repeaters over and over. Josephine LeBlanc, Katty Stewart, Minnie Barclay, Amelie May, Nell Kearney, all duplicated, triplicated, quadruplicated, multiplicated the number of times when they were guests of honor."[26]

On December 17, the *New Orleans Item* published a large profile photo of Moosie, along with flattering words, which makes it apparent that columnists occasionally ran out of synonyms. "This exquisite profile belongs to Miss Elizabeth White, who is one of the season's most charming debutantes. In addition to an undeniable loveliness of features and coloring, Miss White is gifted with a clever wit and with a sparkling animation which are part of an unusually delightful personality. Miss White has been visiting in the North and East for the past few months, and returned only the past week, with her aunt and uncle, Mr. and Mrs. Gus Gibert, who have come back from abroad to make their home here."[27] By the way, the Giberts also came back with their son Gussie, who would eventually marry Katty's cousin Josephine LeBlanc, which made her a relation of Moosie's because Maude Gibert was Moosie's aunt on her mother's side. Got that?

Overwhelmed, Katty went out of town for a few days and traveled with cousin Jo to the LeBlancs' Pass Christian summer home. Fellow debs Emily Hayne and Ethel Fox accompanied them.[28] According to the *New Orleans Item*, the young women were "four of the very popular and much feted 'buds' this winter."[29] And they were also sick to death of it.

Another columnist commented on the departure to Pass Christian,

> Quelle Vie! Quelle Vie! No wonder four of the P—'n—P's (that, I am told is the latest abbreviation in debutantedom, meaning 'pretty and popular') went over to the Pass for a rest…. "A good night's sleep is essential!" was their terse explanation. So they made it two for good measure, leaving on Monday morning and returning only on Wednesday. Incidentally, they talked till two in

10. Debutantes

the morning.... The Debutante parties, meanwhile, were the poorer for their absence. They need a rest. We all do. Such a week as in store for us, my dear—such a storm, such a whirlwind ... go to the calendar ... it is crammed to bursting."[30]

Another society columnist wrote about Katty and her friends, "Someone said they were off for a rest cure at the Pass. Making haste slowly through the season and drawing a deep breath before diving late into the maelstrom of next week's festivities."[31]

Moosie probably would have gone too, but she was being feted at the Quartier Club. "Mrs. Joseph B. Simmons entertained Monday ... complimentary to Miss Elizabeth White, one of the most attractive of the winter's debutantes."[32]

A highlight of the following week was a ball at the Athenaeum:

"Les Pierrettes" entertained Thursday evening.... The event claimed the college sets' interest and was one of the loveliest balls ever given by younger organizations. The subject was "Paint," cleverly carried out by the cast wearing futuristic costumes in red, green, orange, blue and purple, and carrying palettes. The ceiling and columns of the ballroom were draped with streamers in the different shades and between the columns were small palettes. The stage represented an artist's studio. The cast represented the paint, and "two spirits of paint" danced in and out of large paint bottles, finally upsetting them. As the paint poured out the members marched, forming letters spelling "'Les Pierrettes' Greet You." A "Snake" dance was given by the cast, after which the maskers' dance started.[33]

Katty was on the dance committee, along with Edwa Stewart and a few others.

Finally, the day arrived for Moosie's debut. "A brilliant and notable event of the season ... was the debut-dance at which Mr. and Mrs. Albert Sidney White were hosts to formally introduce their youngest daughter, Miss Elizabeth White.... Receiving with her mother last evening, she was strikingly lovely in a French gown of orchid chiffon velvet trimmed in ropes of pearls. She carried orchids and lilies of the valley."[34]

Katty and her mother finally mended their rift when Kittie held a tea for Katty around Christmas. "Mrs. Katherine Eustis Stewart will be hostess at an afternoon reception to formally introduce her young daughter, Miss Katharine Stewart, a beauty of the debutante set and a decided belle. The affair will mean a large gathering of fashionables in most exclusive circles."[35]

On the same day, the *New Orleans States* newspaper featured a large, flattering photo of Katty, along with a short, effusive blurb. "Miss Katharine Stewart is an exceptionally lovely debutante of the season who has been singled out for many social honors and attentions. Miss Stewart is a member of an old New Orleans family, widely connected here, and is personally much admired for her piquant beauty and for her ready wit. She will be formally introduced this afternoon by her mother ... at one of the handsomest receptions of the season."[36]

On the last day of the year, the *New Orleans Item* provided profiles of the debutantes including Katty. In an article titled "Who's Who Among the Debutantes," the newspaper quoted Edna St. Vincent Millay: "My candle burns at both ends; It will not last the night; But, ah, my friends, and, oh, my foes—It gives a lovely light." The columnist solemnly concluded: "That might be the Class Song of the New Orleans debutantes of 1922."[37] Indeed, this appears to be a haunting prophesy about Katty Stewart and Moosie White.

The article singled out several women as being, well, more beautiful than the others. "Of course, each one of these debutantes has various degrees of personal beauty and individual charm. And while 'naming names' is invidious, and sometimes downright dangerous, the other debutantes are unanimous in voting the palm of beauty to Emily Hayne, Virginia Downman, Amelie May, Katherine Stewart, Eileen Slidell, Elise Camors, Elizabeth White, Burdette Waldo, and Maude Fox."

The anonymous columnist also opined about the experience of being a deb in New Orleans in 1922:

> They are ... naturally and frankly thrilled at being feted and featured and flourished in the friendly face of a gay world.... However modest and demure, however girlishly gay and unaffected they may seem on the outside, inwardly they are plumed and buskined drum-majors, stepping out on a flower-strewn march-route to Destiny, beating time to the applause of a loving multitude. May they always beat true time, with never an unresolved dissonance in the Heavenly harmony—even when they transpose it for earthly rendition to the key of Jazz!"

The columnist, who may have been Natalie Scott, made the young women out to be paragons of virtue:

> It is interesting to observe how this group of 1922 is endowed with the flapper's facility for having a good time, but is innocent of the frailties and follies that made both the flapper and her good time questionable.... But their reasons for not indulging in any of these alleged privileges are not bred of smug self-righteousness, nor of any native or inherited fear of public opinion ... for these debutantes avoid the addictions allowed to men for the simple and old-fashioned reason that they find no pleasure in them. Their tastes are not expressed by cigarettes and cocktails.

Katty was identified as the daughter of Katherine Eustis Stewart in the article. There was no mention of her father.

> One of the beauties of her set. Finished school in New York. Rides and swims and dances as a girl should. Doesn't believe in any sort of pose. Declares the

debutantes of this year are a wholesome, unaffected, unselfconscious set, who do whatever they do because they want to, and not by suggestion or imitation. Thinks the flapper and all her works utterly passe, no more to be considered than an old-fashioned gown. As for herself, she is going to have her own good time in her own good way, and hopes nobody will find occasion for fault in any of the debutantes this year.[38]

As for Moosie:

Upon her own confession as reported by another, she attended every school in New Orleans, specializing in art at Newcomb, which school she will enter again, after her debut, for the study of languages and voice-culture. Reads avidly both French and English literature. Is a member of the Little Theatre, where she has appeared in small parts several times. Recites Creole monologues cleverly, that were written for her by Mrs. Christian Schertz. Adores music. Delights in developing her character by any sacrificial means not too spectacular.[39]

According to Moosie's nephew Maunsel White, she did not pursue a degree at Newcomb and, frankly, had no musical talent.

She was probably more interested in socializing than scholarship. Those years also coincided with my grandfather's financial reverses which also could have been a factor. The whole family were big opera and symphony lovers and fancied themselves as potential operatic singers, but there was *no* resident talent for that, to be sure. My mother [Sue Bryan White] recounted her first opera attendance with "the Whites" and was appalled that they all sang along in unison with each of the famous arias, all wildly out of tune.[40]

Meanwhile, Walker also had some excitement at the end of 1922. Princeton's Triangle Club came back to town, and newspapers reminded Orleanians about Walker's connection to the esteemed drama club. Years had passed since he had played Fi-Fi in the Fitzgerald play, and Walker had little to show for the years.

It spurred him to become involved again in the Little Theater. Walker appeared in Alfred Sutro's *The Man in the Stalls* on November 20 at the Le Petit Théâtre du Vieux Carré in its new location on St. Peter. "Mrs. Rhea Goldberg, Mr. A.J. Christodora and Mr. Walker Ellis were exceedingly clever."[41] Another newspaper called the play "[a] favorite with the audience…. It was so well set that the staging provoked a salvo of spontaneous applause; and it was so well acted by Mrs. Goldberg and Messrs. Walker Ellis and A.J. Christodora that one who did not know really could think it was being given by professional artists. There was an abandonment, a self-effacement, an enveloping of self in the roles on the part of the actors that is extraordinary in amateurs."[42]

Yet another society columnist echoed the kudos directed at Walker. "Praises heaped upon Walker Ellis, bereaved husband…. He did a splendid piece of work."[43] Natalie Scott chimed in: "Walker Ellis vanished completely, and presented in his stead, a whimsical, clever, mildly sophisticated but sound-hearted man of the world, with a warm fullness of voice tone that was a pleasure to hear.... All hail to the Princeton Triangle Club, and its former president."[44] Finally, Cay Saunders of the *New Orleans States* congratulated Walker and Rhea Goldberg: "It can be said without exaggeration that they entered into their parts with all the experience, dignity and eclat of professional performers."[45]

In 1922, Katty and Walker were more often than not at the same events. They crossed paths frequently. In fact, it'd be fair to say that Walker was now part of Katty and Moosie's clique.

In January 1923, Will Stewart hosted an "Oriental" dance for his daughter, "a lovely event of the month in younger smart circles."[46] The dance, one of Katty's last deb events, was held in the gold room of the Grunewald Hotel and was "one of the 'successes' socially of the winter."[47]

Natalie Scott credited Kittie for Katty's outfit. In a long passage that almost sounds like it was dictated by Kittie, Scott wrote:

> Katty's costume was magnificent marvels of rose color and gold. There was a gold undress that followed straight lines, for slenderness. About it was swirled, and caught, and hung, and draped, a piece of cloth that was a perfect full diapason of color, vivid rose and gold, and burning blue, that was swathed about a cloth of gold underdress intricately, caught with a bucket of fiery jewels, low on one hip, and then carried up somehow to the shoulders, and on up in a sweeping line to form a magnificent veil, held on each side of her piquant face by round capuchon plaques of glittering jewels. The cloth was a piece of magnificence to set you marvelling. No rest for me till I discovered where it came from—India!.... The costume looked like a creation of some inspired queen of modistes. Only a day or so ago did I learn the full story of it."

The full story makes Kittie into a hero for saving Katty from a disaster:

> The morning of the party came, and Katty woke at her usual luxuriously late hour, and, considering her day, was suddenly confronted that she costume for her own party.... Much agitation. Then mother to the rescue. You know the miraculous needle that is Mrs. Stewart's? You know how it can nonchalantly achieve the daintiest of bed coverings that is convertible instantly instantaneously into the most fascinating of negligees.... And the scissors snipped, and the needle plied, and the folds of the beautiful material were subdued, and directed, and manipulated with the innate skill of the artiste, and there was the gorgeous costume complete, and looking as though it had been the work of carefully planned weeks.[48]

Moosie's outfit also got the Natalie Scott treatment.

> Moussie White's was another strikingly lovely one that evening, and wonderfully becoming, with Turkish "trous" in quaint evidence, and a headdress of feathers that swept up very regally from the center of her turbonned brow. It

had some last-minute touches too, I hear, though there was nothing to indicate it in the least; but they say that the united efforts of the family centered in some eleventh hour pinnings and drapings in a general chorus of delighted ... comment and laughter."[49]

Walker was at the event, and his outfit also caught Natalie's eye. "Walker Ellis made the concession of a turban ... very advantageously. I was sly enough to intercept several masculine glances.... I say discreetly that if a man saw a girl with such an expression as I detected in those glances he would have diagnosed 'envy' without a moment's hesitation. It's quite striking—a turban with a full dress!"[50]

Walker turned 30 in 1923. He spent much of the year attending social events. Like Katty, he had many friends who were married or were marrying, but it's doubtful his purpose at these events was to find a wife. Week after week he attended parties, dances and other events, but apparently, he began to wonder what he was doing with his life. Indeed, former colleagues saw him as someone who had wasted his potential. Matthew Bruccoli, an expert on F. Scott Fitzgerald's life and work, described him as a

Kay Francis (right) appeared in 1932's *Trouble in Paradise*, arguably her best film, with Herbert Marshall (center) and New Orleans debutante Miriam Hopkins (author's collection).

failure. "Ellis served as a pilot in the war, but after 1918 failed to fulfill the promise of his college years."[51]

On January 18, Katty attended a debutante event in honor of Corinne Hopkins, daughter of Mr. and Mrs. Guy Hopkins. It was held at the Louisiane ballroom. Attendees numbered in the hundreds and included Moosie and two of Corinne's sisters, Miriam and Gladys.[52] Miriam ended up going to Hollywood and having a successful film career. She was Kay Francis' friend, and they appeared together in 1932's *Trouble in Paradise*, perhaps Kay's best film.

On February 11 in the *New Orleans States*, another ball was described in detail. This one had an Alice in Wonderland theme, and the writer carefully commented on the attractiveness of various young women. For example, Moosie was described as "sparklingly handsome"; and "[Katty's] features have a purity of outline that suggests Billie Burke."[53] In truth, Katty was more handsome than pretty and not nearly as delicate as Billie Burke. Katty resembled her father. (Her mother Kittie did resemble Billie Burke.)

Walter's life continued in a similar way into 1923. Along with the usual names, though, appeared Livingston Dickason, brother of the ill-fated Dorothy; he was now renting an apartment on Peters Street in New Orleans. He went to many of the same events as Walter and Walker and also hosted parties, including at least one that Moosie, Burdette and Walter attended.[54]

In addition to his social activities, Walter continued to stay active in the Bridle Club. Richard Orme had also joined the club. "Bridle Club days knew no more enthusiasm for horseback riding than holds sway just now, in the crisp days of spring's beginning. All the open spaces afford glimpses of riders. Dick Orme, Henry LeBlanc, Jack Audley and Roger de la Vasselais ride every Sunday morning. Walter Stauffer is another faithful rider."[55]

That spring, the Bridle Club became serious about polo. "Revival of polo in this city is the feature of a plan in which many prominent New Orleanians have been interested. A committee headed by Joe Gumbel and composed of Phil Williams, Allen Mehle, Walter Stauffer and Joe Onorati is going ahead with the organization of a Riding and Polo club and it is expected that the club will be a reality within another month."[56]

Katty was friendly with socialite Mrs. J. Cornelius Rathbone. According to a brief in a local newspaper, Mrs. Rathbone "will entertain this afternoon at a 'baseball' picnic at 'Refuge,' her plantation home on the Mississippi, complimentary to Miss Katharine Stewart and will have a number of the younger set as her guests."[57] Walker was a guest.[58] On April 15, readers were privy to more details about the party:

> Individuality was the note that was sounded in a party that was given for Katty Stewart last Sunday afternoon…. The place was Mrs. Rathbone's over-the-river home, one of the spots to which spring is shamelessly partial….

10. Debutantes 99

Knickerbockers were the order of the day, for the girls, and baseball was a further special feature. The girls played the men and the game went very "hot and heavy" and quite close. The men finally won by one run, or perhaps two. The day was marvelous, and nowhere more marvelous than it was under the big oak trees that shot out from their gnarled old massive trunks a dark-veined mass of sheltering green over the "diamond." There were various swings and trapezes attached here and there, and ... there was nothing wanting for perfect happiness.... It was a tempestuous afternoon that came to a tranquilizing end in a delicious tea,—the liquid and literal part of which was served in quaint little cups that were each one a different color,—like the flowers in the garden.[59]

In that same month, Walker and his father traveled to Europe together. The elder Ellis was probably counseling Walker to do something, *anything* with his life. "Walker Ellis is ... among those blest with the prospect of an early visit to Europe. [He and his father] will spend the greater part of their time in Paris. Probably there is some business involved.... An attitude which even Walker, masculine and business-like might condone, since he is a connoisseur of Paris and drinks the joy of it with the discrimination of one who knows!"[60]

On April 29, the *New Orleans States* provided insight into how Katty and Moosie spent their carefree days. "You phone Katty Stewart,—but if it's before noon she's not up, and if it's afternoon, she is just as likely to be in Biloxi, or Mandeville, or Brown's Wells as at home. In fact, more likely. The same with Moussie White."[61]

By this time, Katty, Moosie, Walker and Walter were socializing together, along with other friends they'd grown up with. Certainly one of the reasons they all became friends was because they lived near each other. Natalie Scott wrote using the Peggy Passe Partout moniker,

> You must remember the old neighborhood, between Jackson Avenue and Washington, the "Garden District" of the city, where we spent the happiest parts of our childish days, climbing over the Mays' fence, into the Farwells' back yard to steal the figs or hanging by our teeth or toes on Jane Scales' trapeze. Well, almost all of the bunch are still living down there; the Perkins, the Haynes, the Waldos, the Whites and a number of the others and ... they decided to organize themselves into the "Garden District Social Club" and have a real old-time banquet. The banquet was held in no other than the ever-faithful Commander's restaurant. The next day they were literally bubbling over with excitement all over the party. There was Kittie [she probably meant Katty], Jo LeBlanc, Becky Perkins, Moosie, Walter Stauffer, Bob Moore ... and several others.[62]

The *New Orleans States* seemed to be particularly interested in Katty's comings and goings and noticed her restlessness. "Speaking of people that flit back and forth, Katty Stewart left again Saturday, this time to visit Livingston Dickason and his mother and father [stepfather Dr. Frank Wall] in Saratoga. With her went Moosie White and Dick Orme. They are to be there at a lovely season, too, all during the yacht races!"[63]

In August, Walker attended a small dinner at Katty's house. The *New Orleans States* described a "delightful affair" that was "an informal dinner Wednesday evening with Miss Katharine Stewart as a very charming hostess. Miss Stewart had as her guests Misses Elizabeth White, Amelie May, Emily Hayne and Messrs. Edgar Bright, Walker Ellis, Gus Gibert, Jr., Robert Moore, Jr., and Chapman H. Hymes, Jr."[64]

In November, Katty was maid of honor at her cousin Josephine LeBlanc's wedding. Moosie was also in the wedding party.[65] LeBlanc married Leon Gustave (Gussie) Gibert, Jr., in her family home.[66] "And if you can imagine girls like Katty Stewart and Burdette Waldo and Virginia Claiborne and Elise Roussel to say nothing of Elizabeth White and Elizabeth Wood, lending themselves to be anybody's background, you can understand just how wonderful Jo was."[67]

One of the most intriguing newspaper entries for Katty was in the November 18 *Times-Picayune*. It suggested that she was pursuing a college degree in New York. Now finished with boarding school, Katty was perhaps tiring of society life and considering a career. "This is lovely—did you know that Katty Stewart had gone to New York to study journalism at Columbia?"[68] And then the December 25 *New Orleans States* reported, "Miss Katharine Stewart, who is spending the winter in New York and taking a course in Journalism, arrived the latter part of the past week to spend the Christmas holidays in New Orleans."[69] If Katty attended Columbia University, it was only for a short time. Perhaps she attended a few classes and realized it wasn't for her. Perhaps it interfered with her social life and frequent traveling.

In December, Moosie, always busy with social activities, returned to acting when she appeared in a workshop production of *The Real Thing* at the Le Petite Theatre. The futuristic play was written by John Kendrick Bangs. "The scene of this playlet is an employer's agency in 1950 ... and presents a very novel and interesting point of view on the problem of obtaining competent household servants."[70]

Walter was a regular at social events in December 1923 and frequently seen at the Country Club. "Peggy and Elise, Becky Perkins and Yvonne Dumont sauntered into the room, followed by Walter Stauffer, J.R. McCarthy, Jake Gillespie and Shine [Shermon Pardue]. The mere presence of these four always lends an athletic touch to any scene, or perhaps it is the bright, almost English ruddiness that golf and riding have given them that does the trick, but anyway, the effect is potent."[71]

Meanwhile, Walker again expressed interest in a career. His social events were far less frequent, and his name rarely appeared in the newspapers. It could not have pleased Dad that Walker wanted a career in the theater.

In February 1924, Walker was in New York, as was Katty. Natalie Scott ran into somebody who had seen Katty "in the post-examination interim between her Columbia courses. They confirm too the reports which have drifted down of the success of the play in which Walker Ellis is appearing, *The Beggar on Horseback*, which is being very favorably received."[72]

The Broadway play, written by George S. Kaufman and Marc Connelly, opened at the Broadhurst Theatre on February 12, 1924, and closed August 23. Walker played "A Guide." Other cast members included Richard Barbee, George W. Barbier, Spring Byington, George Mitchell, Osgood Perkins, Kay Johnson and Roland Young. It was Byington's Broadway debut. Although married in 1909, she was a lesbian. She and husband Roy Chandler divorced around 1920, after having two children. The play was also Kay Johnson's Broadway debut. A few years later, she would become an intimate friend of Kay Francis. Osgood Perkins was the father of Anthony Perkins. Roland Young, born in London, starred with Kay Francis in *Street of Women* in 1932.

⟨ 11 ⟩

1924

> It is a joy to let one's imagination play with the idea
> of the meeting of Katty and Moussie in Paris.

In February 1924, Natalie Scott revealed that Katty often started her sentences with "Well, dearie."¹ Around the same time, there was another newspaper report about Katty attending Columbia University: "Mrs. Katherine Eustis [by this time, Kittie occasionally dropped the Stewart] left recently for New York, to join her daughter, Miss Katharine Stewart, who has been a student this session at Columbia University. She has been a guest in New York at the Schuyler Hotel on Forty-fifth Street near Fifth Avenue."²

The *Times-Picayune* included more details: "[Mother and daughter] will probably be abroad for a long stay. They are planning to visit in Africa and elsewhere in the autumn, though their plans are not definitely settled."³

By April, Katty and mother Kittie had arrived in Europe. Moosie soon followed. Many in New Orleans recognized the closeness between Katty and Moosie. "Moussie White ... will join Katty and Kittie Stewart in Paris. It is a joy to let one's imagination play with the idea of the meeting of Katty and Moussie in Paris. Paris has tried all the novelties, but that will be strange even to Paris! Surely no two are more calculated to enjoy the many-sided life of that enchanting city.... They ... bubble with life, with humor, yet love beautiful things and thrill to them."⁴

It became clear in June that Kittie, Katty and Moosie were not returning to New Orleans any time soon when the three published their forwarding addresses in the *New Orleans States*. The women's mail was being sent to the Guaranty Trust Company, 3 Rue des Italiens, Paris.⁵

By the end of June, Katty and Kittie were visiting Mrs. John Douglas Little, formerly Stella Hayward, who lived in Ethandune, near Liverpool in England. Moosie was there, too. A columnist wrote that Moosie was visiting the Littles "at their beautiful country home. Mrs. Stewart and Miss White will return soon to Paris and later will visit in Italy."⁶

Also in June, Moosie appeared in a silent movie titled *The Message of Hope*, "a four-reel film pointing the way to health and happiness." It was filmed months earlier and then shown in the Knights of Columbus auditorium at a benefit for a local tuberculosis charity. "Miss Genevieve Murphy of the Charity Organization Society is the author of the play, which was filmed entirely in New Orleans and with an Orleans cast."[7]

Walker's father, Caswell Ellis, died on June 29, 1924, a week after having surgery for a burst appendix. According to his obituary, he was prominent and important. "Caswell P. Ellis, cotton broker and banker who died Sunday in Touro Infirmary, is widely mourned in business and social circles in New Orleans and the South. His funeral was set for 3:00 p.m. Monday at the residence, with many of the foremost men of New Orleans paying him honors at the last rites."[8] Among the many honorary pallbearers was Katty's father, William P. Stewart. Walter J. Stauffer was an active pallbearer.

Caswell's will was accurately described as "a remarkably brief and simple document." He left everything to wife Nellie, "except that to his son Caswell P. Ellis, Jr., he gave his membership in the New York Stock Exchange, and to his son, Richard M. Ellis, his stock in the New Orleans Stock Exchange."[9] Walker and his sisters were not included in the will.

Meanwhile, a local society columnist, probably Natalie Scott, gave insight into the antics of Katty and Moosie in Europe. The description suggests they were a New Orleans version of Emily Kimbrough and Cornelia Skinner, who wrote about their own comical adventures in many books, including *Our Hearts Were Young and Gay*. Or perhaps they were more like Lucy and Ethel:

> Everyone who has letters from that scintillating duo which is Katty Stewart and Mousie White ripples and chuckles, and passes on accounts of their doings which are as interesting as their sayings.... Sid White brought back accounts of their visit to Mrs. Little. He says that they went to spend a weekend, but the Britishers were so captivated by their bubbling spontaneity originality of the two that they insisted on keeping them for a week at least. They were the center of things all the while—dinner parties, tennis matches, long motor trips. Incidentally, they have ... seen royalty and hobnobbed with aristocrats....

It does not appear that any letters from Katty survive.

> Someone was reading a letter from Katty the other day, and I remember her account of discovering Mrs. Little in the suite which the Littles have at Claridge's.... Mrs. Little was involved with dressmakers and tea, but chatting all the while.... Katty struck one of her descriptive phrases speaking of her as an "attractive woman greyhound looking creature." There was something about the trip down, with much baggage and maids ... and motoring through Wales, when they all talked so much they that they forgot to look at the scenery.

"Everyone looks at Wales and says it's a pity the day isn't clearer," as Katty remarks.... Katty's letter enthused at length over the Littles' home, its beauty, the loveliness of its gardens ... daily the lawn was dotted with gay color and white flannels, while magnificent cars drove in and out, with beautiful children, carefully guarded by trim nurses. The picture sounds like a fastidiously aristocratic story-book, and I love to think of it!

Katty apparently had the talent and connections to become a published writer if she had pursued it. She was not the only wealthy, educated lesbian who failed to reach her potential in the 1920s. For example, Esther Murphy, Gerald's sister, received contracts to publish her writings. However, like Katty, she failed to produce much tangible work. Alcohol and mental illness may have been factors.

Of course, the travelers, as usual, ended up in Paris. "The girls have done a great deal of motoring in England, visited Kenilworth and Warwick Castles, among other places, and have ferreted out London's most interesting secrets before going back to Paris, which they did last week. Mrs. Stewart, Katty and Moussie are staying at a charming little place on the left bank, not far from the 'Rotonde.'"[10]

Walter was still interested in the Bridle Club and riding. In July it was reported that he "recently purchased a superior jumper in the North which has reached here and will create a new sport in Bridle club activities."[11] Compared to Walker, Walter was more socially engaged. He also was much more civically engaged and had become a respected part of New Orleans society.

Walter spent the inheritance from his late wife as quickly as he could. According to Maunsel White, "My parents always implied that he really lived the high life during the years. He went through all the money he inherited from the first wife."[12]

Following his father's death, Walker continued his pursuit of an acting career. Although he was left nothing in the will, no doubt Nellie Ellis opened up the purse strings for her favorite child. In August 1924, columnist Althee Bernard reported a fellow Orleanian's news about Walker: "She had a glorious time in New York, with not a theatre left unvisited.... Among the most interesting was one which vouchsafed her a view of Walker Ellis at work; she gives an enthusiastic account of that, and adds that she heard wholly unprejudiced praise of him in dramatic circles, where his future is painted in the gilt of fame. And we knew Walker! Let's not forget it, or let it be forgotten!"[13]

In September, the Stewart women and Moosie were in Italy. Once again, Natalie Scott's society column provided a delightful peek into Katty's life:

> As for the trio which is Kittie and Katty Stewart, and Moussie White, they are the most dizzying aggregate to follow.... One minute you see someone who

met them in France, a letter from Italy the next moment relates that someone has encountered them there.... For a while ... they visited Madame Paulet, whose name is familiar to many of us, through the Giberts, who were intimate friends of hers. Madame Paulet has a chalet on the Normandy coast, in a picturesque spot which has a wealth of allure in natural scenery, and abounds, besides, in legends of William the Conqueror, and various other historical personages.... It is quite certain that the Three in question revelled in all the romantic tales. They stayed at St. Jonin for awhile.... It is quite near Etretat ... a mere nothing from Havre and its over-the-bay elegant neighbors, Deauville and Trouville.... I remember hearing, too, that they visited another chateau later ... nearer to France. I have a feeling that Switzerland was next on their program, and that they went from there for a grand finale in Italy.

Scott also dropped news that they had become friendly with American painter Waldo Peirce:

Quite thrilling is the news that Katty's portrait is being painted by our distinguished artist friend, Waldo Peirce. Katty should be a very paintable subject, more particularly, a draw-able subject. She reminds me of some picture.... The rounding line from her forehead to her slightly, piquantly tilted nose; it is what one calls a "candid brow" I suppose—there is somehow a touching, child-like naivete about it.... Anyway, it will be interesting to see the portrait, if that is vouchsafed us.[14]

Waldo Peirce was "Rabelaisian, bawdy, witty, robust, wild, lusty, protean, lecherous, luscious, the kind of man Ernest Hemingway wished he could be. Waldo Peirce (1884–1970) is Maine's satyr prince of the art world. He devoured life."[15] Katty, Moosie, Kittie and Walker formed a friendship with Peirce and his wife Ivy Troutman in the early to mid–1920s when they made Paris their second home. How in the world did they meet him? "It was just the time in the '20s when well-connected 'artsy' people like Moosie and Katty sought out types like Waldo who were part of the American expat community in France. They were good at 'looking up' people to whom they had connections, no matter how tenuous those connections were."[16]

Another eccentric American ex-pat, Peirce was born into a wealthy Maine lumber family. He barely graduated from Harvard in 1909 and then got on a cattle boat with American Communist John Reed (Warren Beatty portrayed him in the movie *Reds*) to sail to England. Peirce changed his mind, jumped off the boat and swam back to shore. Unfortunately for Reed, he was then accused of Peirce's "murder." Peirce went to England to prevent Reed from being charged. There are many versions of this story, and some of them may have a kernel of truth.

Peirce was a gifted painter. "Living and painting in Paris off and on in the 1920s, Peirce became friends with many of the notables who defined this period in the arts: Gertrude Stein, James Joyce, Sylvia Beach, Berenice Abbott, Archibald MacLeish..., John Dos Passos—and Ernest Hemingway.... Both men were voracious readers. Both were remarkable presences in a room, regaling others with ribald tales, great stories, and vivid word pictures."[17]

Peirce married his second wife, Ivy, in August 1920. Described as "dark and lovely," Ivy lived with Waldo in Paris at 77 Rue de Lille.[18] Waldo and Ivy were celebrities in Europe and America, described as "The Kardashians of their day."[19] Ivy and Waldo hung out with Scott and Zelda Fitzgerald; Gertrude Stein; and, apparently, Katty, Kittie and Moosie.

While Ivy also painted, she had other duties. "Ivy ... was the youngest in the salon, so she always poured the tea." Ivy, born in 1884, was an actor who made more than 20 appearances on Broadway. It is said that Hemingway based a character in *The Sun Also Rises* on her. Katty stayed in touch with her in later decades. Ivy died at the age of 94 in 1979.

There is an unfinished painting that supports the report about Katty's portrait. Maunsel White inherited a Peirce painting that includes Moosie, Katty and Kittie. They are faceless, and Peirce has written, "For Katty, when her hair was human."[20] The painting also has an image of Peirce and an unidentified figure. According to William Gallagher, Peirce "enjoyed giving away paintings to friends and acquaintances,"[21] and Maunsel inherited two that belonged to Moosie.

The body language in the unfinished painting suggests an intimacy, a friendship between all of them. Other evidence suggests that the relationship between Peirce and Katty, Moosie and Walker was a close one. In addition to the paintings, Maunsel White inherited an undated letter fragment written by Moosie to her mother in which she describes a gossipy conversation she had with Waldo: He tattled that Walker had said horrible things about Katty.[22]

In early October, Katty, Kittie and Moosie returned to New York. While Moosie was traveling in Europe, her family moved to a new house. It was a newly built, lovely home on Second and Chester Streets.[23] Along with Moosie, Ellene was still living at home with her parents. Moosie, who appears to have been sheltered by her family, would remain living in her parents' house, even after her marriage to Walter Stauffer in 1929.

Meanwhile, Walker toured with an acting troupe and ended up in Chicago. "What a name Walker Ellis has made for himself in *The Beggar on Horseback*, which is now playing in Chicago." Reports came back of "glowing accounts of how splendidly Walker is and the hordes of admirers.... Walker is always a great favorite wherever he goes."[24]

Later that month, the *Times-Picayune* reported that Walker "is at present trying out in a play in Detroit, planning to bring it to New York

Waldo Peirce's unfinished portrait includes a dedication to Katty Stewart. Left to right, unidentified, Peirce, Moosie, Katty, Kittie (courtesy Maunsel White).

at an early date."[25] The next news came in December when Katty and Walker were, again, in New York at the same time. Near the end of 1924, Natalie Scott was also in New York and mentioned Orleanians she had seen. "Katty Stewart is but two blocks away, and Walker Ellis [is] coming to town in a new play."[26] The play was Philip Barry's *The Youngest*, which opened on December 22, 1924, and closed on March 23, 1925.

In 1924, Katty was 21, and Walker was 31. By now, the two were adults, friends and in contact.

12

A Surprise Marriage

> Claiming keen interest in exclusive fashionable circles was the wedding of Mrs. Katherine Eustis Stewart to Mr. Victor da Cunha.

While Katty and Kittie were in Europe, Laura Buckner Eustis died in Milwaukee on August 9, 1924. Neither Katty nor Kittie returned home for the funeral.

On November 28, 1924, the *Times-Picayune* provided insight into how Katty and Kittie could travel extensively in Europe for months. According to the article, the Eustis' estate totaled "$209,496.09, including advances made to her children in her lifetime."[1] The late Laura

> apportioned among her eight children and a grandchild, daughter of a deceased son. These are: Mrs. Ellen Dearborn, Havana, Cuba; Mrs. Laura Russell, Milwaukee; Mrs. Katherine Stewart, New Orleans; Cartwright and Allan Eustis, New Orleans; Herbert L. Eustis, Greenville, Miss.; Laurance Eustis, Memphis; Mrs. Maude Seaman, Milwaukee; and Elizabeth Eustis[2] [daughter of Alice and Richard Eustis], New Orleans. Each of the heirs received $20,846.83 [almost $330,000 in today's money], the inventory showed, besides $11,000 appropriated to them before the death of Mrs. Eustis.

The reason for the estrangement between Mumsie and Kittie soon became apparent. Around the same time of the news about Laura's estate, Kittie married Victor da Cunha in London on November 19, 1924.

Attractive, wavy-haired da Cunha worked in the New Orleans Brazilian consul. Born in Brazil in 1894, he had arrived in New Orleans some time around 1921 and made a quick impression:

> He's a romantic-looking personage from an Anglo-Saxon point of view, dark in coloring, with black hair and a bronzed skin that makes his eyes seem curiously light. I would have said he was quite young, in spite of the fact that he speaks with easy nonchalance of 12 years of diplomatic service, for he has, as a background for his contagiously spontaneous enjoyment of life, unusual poise. But then poise would be a natural result of an education such as his, which ranged from Switzerland, to Italy, and to France. With all this, he seems strangely American, somehow.[3]

Da Cunha played violin and golf and was popular with the ladies. His name often appeared in society columns, and Natalie Scott was friendly with him.

Da Cunha's official title was general consul for the United States of Brazil at New Orleans. The charming man spoke six languages fluently and could read and write in five. He had lived in New York, London, San Francisco and many other places.[4] He was also 15 years younger than Kittie.

It's unknown when he first met Kittie, but they were both socially active, so it's not surprising that they crossed paths. They first appeared in public together in 1921, and by 1922 they were regularly seen together. For example, in October 1922 they were together at the Country Club. "Forming a party ... for tea at the club were Mrs. William P. Stewart, the Italian Consul General and Mrs. William Silenzi, the Brazilian Counsel General Victor da Cunha, and a few others."[5]

By 1923, it was an open secret that Kittie and Victor were having an affair. One of their favorite places was the Orpheum. They also attended a Jerusalem Temple performance of *La Boheme*.[6] By May of that year, Kittie and Victor were behaving like a couple. "The roof garden at West End was most attractive Tuesday evening with any number of parties out.... The Brazilian consul general Mr. Victor da Cunha had a party of friends with him, including the French Consul General and Mrs. Maurice Simonin, Mrs. Katherine Eustis Stewart, the new Spanish consul general, Mr. Juan Vasquez Amor; the Italian General Consul and Mrs. William G. Silenzi and Mr. and Mrs. Maurice Goldstein."[7] Mumsie did not approve of the arrangement.

Shortly after the May event, the social sightings of Victor and Kittie diminished, as if someone had told Kittie to cool it. Perhaps it was Mumsie. But something changed. At least for a time.

In an undated letter, Moosie, who was in Europe with Katty, Kittie and Victor, gushed about the romance to her mother and showed she was definitely on Team Kittie-Victor. "Victor has been sick and hasn't been to Paris since I've been here—but they're crazy about each other—He really loves Kitty—I've seen the letters he writes every single day—They're trying to save up so that they can get married—Don't mention—Don't say anything—There's bound to be gossip—N.O. people have nothing else to do."[8]

Four months after Mumsie's death, the *New Orleans States* made a stunning announcement:

> Claiming keen interest in exclusive fashionable circles [I'll bet] was the wedding of Mrs. Katherine Eustis Stewart to Mr. Victor da Cunha, formerly Brazilian consul of this city, now serving in the consular service of Switzerland, which was quietly celebrated in London, November 19. Mrs. Da Cunha and her young daughter, Katharine Stewart who have been spending the past six

months touring Europe, have returned to New Orleans and are at home for a few weeks at the Eustis residence in St. Charles Avenue and later will leave for Zurich, Switzerland, where Mr. and Mrs. da Cunha will make their home for the next year or so. Mrs. da Cunha is a great belle and general favorite in the social world of this city and news of marriage will be of interest to many.[9] [That's an understatement.]

Additional information was reported in the *Times-Picayune*. "Mr. and Mrs. J.D. Little, formerly of New Orleans but now of Liverpool, England, were among the very few guests at the wedding. Mrs. Stewart [this reference to her previous marriage seems intentional] was very prominent in fashionable circles here and extremely popular and her departure to live abroad will be keenly regretted by her many friends."[10]

By the end of 1924, Katty and Walker were both in New York. Kay Francis was, too. Kay made two entries about Katty in December 1924. On December 17, she wrote, "Katty drunk! Put her to bed and then Paul [Abbott] and I slept together to be interrupted by her coming in! Hell! What a funny night!"[11] At the time, Kay was still in a bad marriage to Dwight Francis and having an affair with Abbott, who was also married.

While this entry does not bode well for Kay and Katty's relationship, Kay's final diary entry in 1924 suggested that Katty had become an important person in her life. "This has been an eventful year—D-P-Pisa-Katty-Fielding. What will the next one bring forth?"[12]

Katty was in New Orleans when 1925 started but suffering from sinus problems, probably from a cold she caught in New York.

> She has been having a difficult time with the intricate misbehaviours [*sic*] of various nasal passages; they seem capable of an astonish[ing] amount of annoying tricks.... Katty keeps strictly within the doors of the white-columned home on St. Charles Avenue, except when going down for the ministrations of the awesome arrays of pipes and tubes, and sprays, which are at the command of all nose and throat specialists. At home, she divides her time and interest between two absorbing occupations, one, of keeping herself at an even temperature, which involves a complexity of sweats combined with gorgeous Oriental versions of house-attire: the other, receiving the succession of visiting friends, who follow each other over her threshold.[13]

In the same column, the writer provided an update on Walker:

> I have been scanning the dramatic criticisms from New York for news of the first night of the play in which Walker Ellis is "doing Broadway" at present. It opened the Monday before Christmas, which is not the most propitious moment, but the criticisms were favorable, and predict a steady, if not brilliant success for the play.... I hear that Walker has an interesting part, but I was distressed when I was told that his role was that of an old man: why hide the light of those good looks under a bushel—of whiskers and lines? It is a tribute to his histrionic ability, at any rate.[14]

12. A Surprise Marriage

Walker, who turned 31 in 1925, likely appreciated the comments on his good looks.

In March, there was more news about Walker's stage career. He was appearing in Gertrude Purcell's *Tangletoes* as Tony Kemp:

> First-hand accounts of Walker Ellis' latest dramatic venture are available now. Mr. [Leon] Gibert went to see the play in which he appears.... He enjoyed the play and found Walker a noticeable feature of what good points it possesses. One of the important dramatic critics of New York—Stark Young, I believe ... speaks of Walker as a "worth-while acquisition to the New York stage...." Mr. Gibert met Walker after the performance and went with him to his apartment, where a number of Walker's friends came in and the evening went merrily. Walker is still living on East 54th Street.[15]

The play closed soon after.

Kay Francis and Katty stayed in contact in 1925, likely by telephone and telegram. Kay mentioned in a January 25 entry that Katty had helped her get out of some kind of mess.

* * *

In February, Katty and Moosie attended an interesting Country Club event: a costume dance in honor of debutante Audrey Butler:

> This affair represented "a touch of Greenwich Village" with the large lounge of the Club transformed into the well-known "Washington Square" and its various familiar haunts, such as "The Little Brown Jug," the "Black Cat," "The Basement Attic," "The Futuristic and Cubist Studies," all of which were pictured in miniature, and upon entering these corners, personages associated with these places greeted and entertained the guests.... All the guests came in costumes typical of Greenwich Village which invited a pleasing variety of clever attire.[16]

Katty was back in New York by March, this time with her mother. "Katty Stewart has not even waited for April to be announced but is in New York already and tasting the joy of spring in the East."[17] Kittie quickly departed for Europe again to rejoin her husband. "Miss Stewart will remain in the East until her mother sails and will then return to New Orleans."[18]

Meanwhile, Walter's name appeared in the credits for a couple of skits in the Junior League Revue benefit in March 1925 held at the Jerusalem Temple. He appeared in "Evening Promenade" and "Cafe des Apaches" with Peggy Mason Smith, Richard Orme, Edgar Bright and others.[19] "Walter Stauffer shone in ['Cafe des Apaches'] as an alert, imperturbable French 'garcon de restaurant,' with dextrously flicking napkin and many dartings to and fro."[20]

Moosie was also in the revue, appearing in "Popular Magazines." According to a columnist, "Elizabeth White was handsome in an elaborate evening costume as a *Cosmopolitan* cover."[21]

New Orleans was perhaps the only Southern city where Junior Leaguers and bohemians partied together. "The easy familiarity between uptown and downtown impressed young writer Oliver La Farge…. The two worlds rubbed along happily together. In any other Southern city a 'Junior League Bohemian' would have been something very odd indeed, but that combination seemed natural enough in New Orleans."[22]

In April, Walter hosted a party that included Moosie at the family's Pass Christian home.[23] It was around this time that Walter and Moosie began spending more time together and established themselves as a couple. Moosie's letters suggest that she and Walter had an on-again, off-again relationship. According to Maunsel White, "I get the feeling that Walter was a bit of a 'rounder' before he married Moosie. It was the Roaring Twenties; he was a good-looking and socially prominent widower with a fair inheritance from his first wife."[24]

Walter, still working at his father's hardware company, was often called upon to speak at events because of his relationship to President Zachary Taylor and General Dick Taylor. For example, in April 1925, he spoke at a Louisiana Daughters of the Confederacy convention.[25] He also was a guest that same month at an event honoring the Battle of Mansfield, a Confederate victory.

Natalie Scott described Katty's return to New Orleans in April:

> Opening of shutters and a general air of cheer about the roomy white house in St. Charles near Jackson Avenue betokens the agreeable fact that Katty Stewart is home again. She is quite her delectable, whole-hearted, amusing self, and looks wonderfully, though she declares the climate of New York anathema, and holds it responsible for the return of misbehavior on the part of her sinus [sic]. She expects New Orleans to set her right again, and in the meantime is instantly a center for a choice circle of intimates."

Once again, Walker Ellis' name came up:

> She has endless accounts of all the New Orleans-New Yorkers, of Walker Ellis among others. The press continued its praise of him during the run of the last play in which he appeared, where he won laurels, a generous allotment of individuality, though the play was not fortunate. His individual success meant all the more, for it is difficult to shine in a poor medium, as the critics frequently remarked. He goes on in something else in May, I believe, or early June.[26]

Katty returned to New Orleans, partly to attend the wedding of her cousin Edwa Stewart to Charles Farwell on April 13. Katty attended other social events, but it was likely that her mind was on New York and Europe. And Kay Francis.

In mid–May, Natalie Scott reported an incident involving the christening of William, Jo and Leon Gibert's baby:

12. A Surprise Marriage

I encountered Katty Stewart shortly after it happened, and found her weak and trembling and in a state of agitation.... It developed that she, as godmother, had had to hold the baby, and that he was a young Samson, a Hercules, and a guileful Achilles besides, for not only did he wiggle with unheard of strength, but he wiggled with wile, and Katty was palpitating nervously still with the terrible strain of holding him. Being a godmother has its responsibilities even at the outset![27]

Katty may have decided then and there that motherhood would never be in her future.

Around the same time, Moosie attended several "exuberant parties," including one at a new place, the Red Cockatoo on St. Peter,

> a moaning, lilting, joyous jazz made its way out from the broad doors that were flanked on either side by two red cockatoos, ... sounds of much laughter. Inside, Kingsley Black, and the Dupuys [Esther and Marie Elise], ... Moussie White and some dozen besides, were dancing away madly, to the sobbingly joyous music.... Others were busy with brushes, painting impromptu frescoes on the wall.... A ship in full sail careening over a maiden's bobbed hair, numerous initials, several dancing nymphs, wild cartoons, making a madly assorted ensemble. Double-arched iron doors in the back wall give out onto a cool courtyard filled with crowded tables, where a banana tree reigns in the center.... The crowd was very gay and the music crashed happily on into the midnight hours to an echoing tune of laughter and merriment from the dancers.[28]

13

1925

> Those two tempestuously willed happy souls decided with thunderbolt haste upon the trip.

Something happened in the summer of 1925, and Katty and Moosie were soon off on another of their adventures. They abruptly left for New York and then Paris. One article mentioned that the departure was "unexpected … having [been] decided only a few days before leaving."[1]

Natalie Scott shed light on the pair's impulsive decision:

> Those two tempestuously willed happy souls decided with thunderbolt haste upon the trip. A week before, and they were settled for a summer in New Orleans. Then, talk of Europe, talk to the Europe-bound, a sudden Europe-longing, such as assails those who have once been subject to its spell, and, presto! the decision. An emergency passport, emergency shopping, emergency farewells. Their first thought was to keep it a secret from all their friends; go down to the boat as though to say farewell to the departing; stay on when it pulled out and wave farewell dramatically over the rail. It would have been a tremendous stunt, but I am sure that several heart failures would have resulted.[2]

Here's a description of the ship sailing off:

> The *De La Salle* has sailed! … I stood upon the pier and watched the travelers with an interested eye—such flowers, such gigantic boxes of sweets, such adieus, and, be it recorded in a whisper, such tears! But after all that is the privilege that one has when one is leaving one's native land and what a joy and delight tears can be—an indulgence that is remarkably satisfying! But back to the frocks.… There was Moussie White in yellow and Katty Stewart in dark blue with a knobby little hat making her piquant face more interesting than ever.[3]

Perhaps it was a case of what we now call FOMO, fear of missing out. Or perhaps one or both of the young women was missing someone who lived in or was traveling to Europe. Intriguingly, Kay Francis was in Europe at this time getting divorced from Dwight Francis. Despite recording affairs with men and women, not to mention an abortion, Kay did not mention Katty in her diary. Still, it is possible that Kay and Katty saw each other in Europe in 1925.

Something led Katty and Moosie to make a dramatic, impulsive decision that, though rash, turned out fine. By the end of June, there was talk of Katty and Moosie cycling in Brittany with Olga Kaufman and Edith Loughborough.[4]

Many Americans were discovering France at this time.

Kay Francis passport photograph, circa 1925.

By 1925, 5000 Americans were arriving in Paris each week. They came on the *Ile de France* and the *Leviathan*, the *Majestic* and the *Mauretania*, the *Berengaria* and the *Aquitania*.... For some passengers the voyage was a time for shuffleboard and skeet-shooting and brisk walks on deck. For others it was a week-long cocktail party culminating in wild last-night revels and instructions to the steward to "pour me ashore" at Cherbourg or Le Havre in the morning. The liners were alive with what Thomas Wolfe called "the life, the hate, the love, the bitterness, the jealousy, the intrigue of six-day worlds."[5]

In July, Natalie Scott gave her readers an update on our travelers:

News drifts back from the numerous voyagers who went over on the *De la Salle* of the French line. They report a superb crossing and a qualm of seasickness from ever the most susceptible. And they made the passage in 14 days, decking at last on the 28th of June. A comparatively quick crossing of all those watery miles! ... The grand finale was a champagne party the evening before landing at Le Havre, a sort of preparation, I suppose, for sparkling Paris.[6]

Meanwhile, Walker, who had also traveled abroad when stage roles dwindled, returned from Europe in July 1925 and was living at New York City's Princeton Club. Located in midtown Manhattan, it is still a private club primarily used by Princeton faculty and alumni.

In August came word that Katty and Moosie had visited Cannes. It's now famous as the site of the film festival, but Cannes was relatively unknown in the mid–1920s. Scott described its wonders in one of her columns:

Moussie White and Katty Stewart have taken the road ... to Cannes, which seems to be becoming more popular as a summer resort. It is very tropical with a luxuriance of foliage set off by the bright colors of the villas that climb the roughly terraced hills: the sun is a burning blue; the light seems to vibrate with intensity, and the colors are strangely clear but swimmingly ardent, all pastel tones, it seems, but heightened vividly, somehow. It is wise to stay in the cool, closed interiors during the three midday hours, for the play of the sun is thrown back blindingly everywhere. But with that precaution, Cannes is idyllic in the summer, the air sweeping cooling in from the Mediterranean, or creeping in through the mountains cooled by the snows of the Alps. A number of New Orleans people have been there this year. The sea bathing is delightful. There are the usual big umbrellas along the sand; and there are the usual enthusiasts who scorn them, and lie flat on the beach, full in the sunlight, trying to burn themselves golden brown, or darker. And one may be served with ices from the Casino in between dips.[7]

… { 14 }

Oak Alley

> Miss Katharine Stewart ... is in New York where she is visiting Mrs. Katharine Francis.

Olga Kaufman, one of the young women who traveled to Europe with Katty, was inconsolable when a record she brought back was accidentally broken:

> However, we are not so inconsolable, for it is perfectly certain that Moussie White and Katty Stewart will be well fortified with all the popular musical favorites. Don't you remember how Katty and Moussie and their "gang" used to make the echoes ring in Livy [Livingston] Dickason's apartment with the whole score of "Phi-Phi" and "Ta Bouche" before them. Katty was the one, too, who brought over first that deliciously seductive "Violetera" of Raquel Meller's, guaranteed to haunt the brain for ages.[1]

Katty perhaps learned of Meller from Kay Francis, who worked as Meller's press agent for a time.

Katty and Moussie returned to the States in November. That same month, Katty, who likely wrote the words herself, had her name linked to Kay Francis for the first time in a society column: "Miss Katharine Stewart ... is in New York where she is visiting Mrs. Katharine Francis."[2]

Kay wrote in her diary that she had lunch with Katty on November 6. Kay was in the middle of rehearsals for a stage production of *Hamlet* and romantically involved with the man who would become her second husband, Bill Gaston. Kay lunched with Katty again on November 10, and then Katty spent the night with Kay on November 12.

Katty was back in New Orleans before the end of November. On December 13, Natalie Scott wrote about Katty's love for horseback riding: "The slender ranks of equestiennes ... are being increased this winter. Katty Stewart, for one, has taken up the ungentle but delightful art. She is never more emphatic than when proclaiming her inability to ride, but she was at the City Park track the other day, cantering around in a very capable fashion, and a few minutes later I saw her take two ditches—and that not inadvertently, as sometimes happens."³ Meanwhile, Walker was back in New Orleans in mid–December, living with his mother. By now, Walker had given up on his dream of being an actor, at least on Broadway.

As for Walter, his moustache commanded interest throughout his life. According to a social column, at least one young woman had trouble telling the wealthy mustachioed New Orleans men apart: "There were two flappers at a table next to us the other day at the Country Club and one of them glancing casually over towards the Club remarked, 'My! Hasn't Hennen Legendre changed a lot!' The other followed her glance to where the occasion of the remark strode towards the door of the Club. 'I don't know,' she retorted. 'But that's Walter Stauffer.'"⁴

Moosie occupied her time attending numerous social events and studying French. Moosie was proud of her Creole ancestors. A social club was formed and, among other things, its members studied the life and works of George Sand:

> This past Friday the same group met again, this time at the Albert Sidney Whites, and French once more received a violent stimulus, this time of a totally different kind, for the medium of the language was song, the soft sentimentality of "Violetera" and on through a range of very gay and idiomatic gems of late musical comedies that sent the audience into peals of laughter—when it did not send them into a daze of bewilderment with some intricate bit of "argot." The gatherings were very gay both times. Moussie White, Dorothy Spencer, Clarisse Claiborne and several others have tended the flame of their French heritage with reading and study.⁵

Moosie continued studying French in 1926. One of the more interesting things occupying her time was regular attendance at a French class "composed of several of the married and younger set in New Orleans.... At each meeting there are interesting talks given in French by the members."⁶ Jo Gibert and Maude White Farrar also frequently attended the classes with her.

Walter became active in the Arts and Crafts Club, which met on Royal Street. In April 1926, he was elected treasurer.

> Various committees reported, and it was found that more serious work is being done by students than ever before in the club's history.... It is particularly gratifying to see the interest in sculpture, especially modern sculpture.... Plans are underway for the gala event of the year—the Artists' Ball which will be held at the club Saturday night, with numerous smaller parties in the studios of individual artists in the vicinity.⁷

The Club had been around since the early 1920s. It was originally called the Artists' Guild, but officially became the Arts and Crafts Club in 1922 when George Westfeldt, a coffee importer, and his wife Martha made it an important part of the French Quarter. "Of all the institutions founded by the Famous Creoles' circle, the single most important one for setting the tone of the French Quarter scene was unquestionably the Arts and Crafts Club (and not just for its Bals des Artistes)."[8]

Eventually, the Club had its own building. "A few months after the Club was chartered, preservationist W.R. Irby gave it a new clubhouse, the huge slave quarters in the rear of the historic Seignouret-Brulatour house.... The building had space for a long exhibition room on the ground floor, as well as classrooms, studios and a salesroom, and its picturesque courtyard became probably the most often painted scene in New Orleans."[9]

Still, like virtually everything in New Orleans, it was segregated. "When the secretary of the Arts and Crafts Club pointed out proudly that the New Orleans Art School's classes were 'open to men, women and children, with no restrictions as to age, sex or previous training,' it went without saying that race was a different matter."[10]

The Arts and Crafts Club did allow Jews at a time when Jews were excluded from "the very top of New Orleans society." According to a Godchaux family member, "We were an extremely prominent family, but of course when it came to the social clubs and Mardi Gras itself, we were left out."[11]

In mid–February, during Carnival, Katty hosted a gathering at her home on St. Charles.

> Thursday night was Momus, and you would have thought that "the world and all her children" had turned out to see the parade—the exciting first parade! Ever fresh is the charm of watching those great wondrous floats, and the fun of jumping greedily for the beads and other favors thrown by the generous maskers; and what could be more fascinating than seeing the swaggering strut of the Ethiopian torchbears balancing their flaming lights dripping with grease. The houses on the "avenue" were of course crowded to overflowing.... Further down toward Jackson Avenue, Katty Stewart's porch steps and lawn held throngs of people.... Virginia Claiborne, Burdette Waldo, the Samuel Schwings, Natalie Scott, Elizabeth White, Norvin Harris, Walter Stauffer ... were some I saw.[12]

As for Walker, he may have given up dreams of Broadway, but he still enjoyed acting. He was cast in a one-act play, *Big Kate*, at the Little Theater. It opened on Monday, February 22, and received rave reviews. "Never before in the memory of this writer has the Little Theater scored such a triumph.... The audience refused to allow the curtain to remain down on *Big Kate* and were not satisfied until Helen Pitkin Schertz and Walker Ellis had given a curtain call.... Schertz ... scored a personal triumph along with Walker Ellis as Lord Ribbersdale."[13]

The *Times-Picayune* noted that Schertz "was given a tremendous ovation. Mrs. Schertz was called four times before the curtain, and up on her last appearance she drew Walker Ellis out with her, thus graciously sharing with him the honors of the performance. Mr. Ellis ... gave a splendid reading of his part."[14]

In February 1926, there was much buzz in New Orleans concerning Italy. Madame d'Ambricourt was in town and feted on several occasions, sometimes with Katty in attendance. Natalie Scott described Madame d'Ambricourt with flattering prose: "Her personality ... is the sort that makes any cause attractive; and she is likewise a Portia for logic and persuasion, with the dash of restrained eloquence with elegance which is a heightened Latin heritage."[15] She had many New Orleans fans, including Moosie's mother Ellen White. "Driving down St. Charles Avenue the other day.... I espied the svelte figure of Mrs. Sidney J. White, and happily inveigled her from walking to riding with me. Her words fairly waved Italian flags, the flag of Fascist Italy: She was still vibrant with the enthusiasm which the Contessa di Robilant had roused in her address at the Orleans Club that morning. Fascist flags have been rampant all week, conversationally as a result of her visit." Katty was learning Italian, along with many others in town, including Moosie and her mother, who "have been studying away diligently with various masters for many months."

At the end of April, Katty became a charter member of a new social group, the New Orleans branch of the Italy-America Society. Its purpose was to promote good relations between the two countries.[16] Obviously they weren't the only Americans fooled by fascists, but it's unsettling to see such a large group fall under the spell of attractive and eloquent speakers.

The biggest news in the Stewart family in 1926 was the purchase of the Oak Alley plantation, "their country place on the Mississippi,"[17] by her Uncle Andrew and Aunt Josephine. Members of the family, including Katty, often visited. "Oak Alley is a favorite destination. Every Sunday and most Saturdays find groups of motorists up there.... The old oaks, as fine an avenue of trees as the world can boast, and the beautiful old house are in themselves worth a far journey to see. The hospitality of the Andrew Stewarts is an additional joy."[18]

The former sugar plantation was built by slaves in Vacherie, Louisiana, on the banks of the Mississippi River. Completed in 1839, it's located between New Orleans and Baton Rouge. Of course it's haunted—apparitions, candles flying across the room, the smell of cigars, etc.—and was featured on an episode of the reality TV series *Ghost Hunters*. It's also been used several times as a movie and TV set, including for the films *Hush... Hush, Sweet Charlotte* and *Interview with the Vampire* as well as Beyonce's "Deja Vu" music video.

14. Oak Alley

Oak Alley, originally named Bon Sejour, was purchased in 1926 by Andrew and Josephine Stewart, Katty's aunt and uncle. The former plantation included a cottage named for Katty. She often entertained guests at Oak Alley, including Moosie, Walker and Walter (author's collection).

After the Stewarts bought the property, Josephine converted the plantation into a cattle farm. Richard Koch was hired to restore and modernize the home. Josephine died in 1972. Oak Alley is now open to the public.

Katty was 23 when Oak Alley was purchased. Aunt Josephine had a reputation for not liking children but she doted on Katty. William Gibert, the baby who Katty almost dropped at his christening, claimed that his great-aunt Josephine "wasn't particularly fond of children and it was only during afternoon tea—and while on his best behavior—that he was allowed to see her."[19]

Katty made Oak Alley a second home. It was also around this time that Katty, Moosie, Walker and Walter began spending more time together as a group, often congregating at Katty's cottage. "Several smaller houses, as large as the average city house, stand about in attendance on the large one, dwarfed in comparison, but actually roomy and comfortable. One of them has been alloted to Katty Stewart, who has not let the opportunity it offers for weekend parties be for a moment neglected."

Oak Alley provided a discreet getaway for Katty and her friends:

Last week, there was a capacity gathering…. Moussie White, Walker Ellis, Walter Stauffer, Tommy Farrar, and Laura and Chick Monrose, formed the party.... This particular party was scheduled to do its own cooking and housework but it casually let fall some remarks about a certain girl of dusky hue, which makes me suspect that the labors in question partook more of the nature of theory than of fact. The dusky maiden ... is Fidelia, and she is accompanied in all of her slow movements by a small object on four feet which does not [look] like a dog, but yet is more like one than like any other object of the animal kingdom.... The pair, Fidelia and her pet, may probably be listed among the resources for diversion in Katty's part of Oak Alley.[20]

Tommy Farrar was an interesting character. He worked with the legendary set designer Norman Bel Geddes, who called him "a brilliant young man."[21] He was also a good friend of Hollywood costume designer Miles White. Not only was Tommy a creative designer, he also was fluent in French and an able translator for Bel Geddes when he worked with French casts. In the 1940s, Tommy worked for the Barnum & Bailey Circus. John Murray Anderson, his boss, ironically nicknamed him "Economy" because he could be hard on a budget.[22]

Tommy married Beatrice Howard on May 31, 1933, in New York. According to writer Arthur Laurents, she too was a character. Bea grew up in Boston but ended up in Paris. "There she became the mistress of Marcel Duchamp and lived on absinthe and potatoes. When she was retired, she came home and married a man almost as jolly as Peaceful [Allen] and twice as gay. His name was Tommy Farrar, of 'the Virginia Farrars'; he was dying, he had run through all his money and Beatrice was his last friend on Fire Island. He shared her house at Cherry Grove, where, as Beatrice observed, 'each year, the boys get gayer and the girls get grimmer.'"[23] Tommy and Beatrice eventually divorced but they continued to live together

> despite the disapproval of some in their circle, claiming that this arrangement suited them much better. According to one narrator, although the Farrars lived together amicably, they did not speak to each other except at cocktails and dinner, even during the long winter of 1937 when they had Pa Case build Pride House. A white two-story New England–style cottage, Pride House still graces Beach Walk.[24]

Tommy died at the age of 50 on June 10, 1951, in New York.

The *Times-Picayune* got wind of Katty's frequent presence at Oak Alley:

> Katty Stewart, Elizabeth White, Burdette Waldo and Virginia Claiborne ... left Thursday for Oak Alley. A heavenly spot, Oak Alley, where wonderful old oak trees shade both the large rambling old house of the Andrew Stewarts and the charming little cottage that belongs to Katty.... Katty is an expert housekeeper and her house here runs with a clocklike precision and exactness that would make many a seasoned housewife turn green with envy.... Right at present the cottage is taking up a great deal of her time and thought.[25]

14. Oak Alley

On May 10, Natalie Scott provided a glimpse of the lives of Katty and Moosie. The two were again planning a trip to Europe, though in their own individual styles.

> Domesticity descended on Katty.... She launched upon a campaign of having things painted, renovated, decorated and stored, at the same time as she launched upon her final packing and arranging; and the resulting state of life was chaotic. She emerged, flushed, agitated, but triumphantly packed and ready and punctual at the station on Monday afternoon. Moussie had had her own perturbation. The last moments of departing are like a quart measure: so much can they hold and no more, and usually the measure is full up of hectic happenings; and one is as perturbed as possible.... It was a somewhat flustered, remarkably pretty and inevitably smiling pair that finally boarded the train, amid bursts of farewells and parting injunctions.[26]

Walker also left for Europe, aboard the *Carlton*, "impeccably groomed and good-looking, Walker the charming with his easy distinction, his brilliant mind, his reserve, and his sunny flashes of quiet humor.... They are to stop at several places probably in Sicily, certainly in Naples, and Genoa. Walker will eventually go to the south of France, where his fancy has fixed on Antibes."[27]

15

The Lost Generation

> Let's think only of today, and not worry about tomorrow.
> —Zelda Fitzgerald

In the 1920s, post-war Europe beckoned many Americans, especially artists, writers and those who wanted to be artists and writers. Walker probably met Gerald and Sara Murphy through his friend F. Scott Fitzgerald.

> When American artists flocked to Paris during the 1920s, many of them met and were inspired by Gerald and Sara Murphy, an American couple who embodied the imaginative flair of the era. F. Scott Fitzgerald captured that aura in *Tender Is the Night*, his novel modeled after Gerald and Sara and life on the French Riviera. As they sat "under the filtered sunlight" of the Murphys' beach umbrellas on the Garoupe beach, Fitzgerald and his American compatriots knew that "something went on amid the color and the murmur." Here was "the centre of the world," where "some memorable thing was sure to happen."[1]

Gerald and Sara Murphy, restless Americans born into wealth, never felt comfortable with the bourgeois lives their parents led. They moved to Europe in early 1921, finally settling, at least for a time, in France. "All the action was there, on the French Riviera and with the Murphys who, as the legend has it, knew how to throw a good party."[2]

Walker became part of their circle. Hollywood writer Donald Ogden Stewart, who, along with wife Beatrice, was a friend of Kay Francis, wrote, "[Gerald and Sara] were both rich; he was handsome, she was beautiful; they had three golden children. They loved each other, they enjoyed their own company, and they had the gift of making life enchantingly pleasurable for those who were fortunate enough to be their friends."[3]

Their friends included people like Walker, grown children of wealthy people with vague ideas of becoming a writer or perhaps an artist or actor. Something more glamorous than going into business with one's father. In the meantime, they wanted to be around other creative intellectuals and drink and party.

At Villa America, they [the Murphys, in this context, but it could also refer to Walker, Katty, Moosie and Walter] moved in a shimmering bubble that seemed to insulate them from ordinary cares. The late '20s passed there in a charmed blur of jazz and champagne and beaded dresses, of spats and white flannels, and sherry and biscuits on the seashore. A representative guest list: Picasso, Fitzgerald, John Dos Passos, Archibald MacLeish, Philip Barry, Robert Benchley, Dorothy Parker, Cole Porter, Monty Woolley, Igor Stravinsky, Fernand Leger and Ernest and consecutive Mrs. Hemingways."[4]

When Katty, Moosie and Walker traveled to Europe in the 1920s, they were part of a larger group of Americans who were called the Lost Generation. That term "came to convey the whole anonymous horde of young Americans abroad, particularly those with literary or artistic inclination."[5] Those who did not become writers or painters became material for creative Americans.

> The story of these artists and friends, as individuals and as a group, is the account of an era and its extraordinary art. Beyond Fitzgerald's *Tender Is the Night*, Gerald and Sara Murphy and life at Villa America would inspire poems by Archibald MacLeish, paintings by Pablo Picasso and Fernand Leger, plays by Philip Barry, and memoirs by John Dos Passos, Hemingway and others. To the great degree that the Murphys' lives embodied both the allure and the devastation of the era, they have emerged in later years as the decade's most compelling metaphor.[6]

Sara and Gerald Murphy had moved with their family to Antibes in the summer of 1925, "on the Riviera, then an unheard-of destination in warm weather. (The Murphys are credited with starting the Riviera's summer season.) They christened their house Villa America."[7]

Before Gerald, Sara and their children could occupy the former chalet, extensive renovations were required. But once the family moved in, Gerald described it as

> "our real home." The modest chalet had been transformed: it was now a sleek art deco variation on a Mediterranean theme. Its limestone walls had been stuccoed beige; a third story had been added; and the peaked chalet roof had been replaced by a flat Moroccan-style one that also functioned as a sundeck for luxurious and private basking. The dark little house had now been opened up with generous windows through which you could see the gardens and the glorious view; and striped awnings and yellow louvered shutters could be drawn against the midday Provencal sun.[8]

In May 1926, Natalie Scott explained to her readers that when Walker left New Orleans,

> [h]is plan was to have no plan, at least no very fixed one. The probability was that he would quit the ship at Genoa, if he was tired of the sea.... But Genoa found him in no such state of mind. He loved the sea, life on shipboard seemed vivid, sharply real, colorful ... and when the ship set out, he was with it, the

glory that was Greece ... directly before him.... Later, there was to come Alexandria, in Egypt, and whatever other ports the chances of shipping made advisable.... To Walker ... the experience will be particularly rich.⁹

Meanwhile, Walter, who probably would have loved to travel, was a full-time businessman with responsibilities. He stayed home in New Orleans and continued to be an avid horseman. "Walter Stauffer on his big black horse is a familiar figure on all of the few possible riding paths, as good a horseman as we have to show."¹⁰

On May 16, Natalie Scott again wrote about the zany couple, Katty and Moosie.

> What a sparkle vanishes when that clever, original, versatile pair of friends, Katty Stewart and Moussie White, get on the New York sleeper tomorrow, bound for New York and for Paris. They are part of the zest of life, those two, with a slant of their own, that gives novelty to old happenings; they have a sense of humor that finds unerringly the bit of funniness that lies in any situation and hales it out to make a conversational bright spot when things are dull. But ... they are bound for Paris.... Katty will meet her mother, Mrs. Victor da Cunha, in Paris, and will spend most of the summer with her.¹¹

Katty and Moosie planned a motor trip through Brittany with Kittie and then a stay in Zurich with the da Cunhas.

Katty and Walker partly enjoyed Europe because there was no Prohibition and more freedom for gay people than in America. Europe also afforded them the opportunity to live without scrutiny and indulge in whatever they desired. They could rebrand themselves in Europe. "In the 'anything goes' atmosphere of Paris, Americans tasted forbidden pleasures.... Paris was where you could do the things you could not do at home."¹²

Unlike the previous year, when Katty and Moosie took off for Europe with their hair on fire, this vacation was planned. "You remember they decided to go one day and two days afterward they were on their way. This one has been planned and talked about and even the date of their return has been decided upon.... Moosie will come back some time in August and Katty some time in October."¹³

Various reports throughout the summer had them on the Riviera, in Vichy, and then on to Brittany. On July 25, the *New Orleans States* reported, "News from Brittany tells of Katty Stewart, Moosie White, Virginia Claiborne, Burdette Waldo and Mrs. Victor da Cunha taking a cottage at some village for a few weeks."¹⁴ The village was Cap d'Antibes in southern France. On August 1, Scott wrote further about Katty and her traveling companions:

> A postcard with diverse intricate signatures gave the news, calculating to rouse the envy of all recipients, that Kittie da Cunha, her daughter, Katty Stewart,

Moussie White, and Count deWitte[15] had all met together in a party for dinner at Cannes. You know we love it even in the summertime with the sharp gleaming of its seductive pastels, with its rocky terraces, and vines and villas, and stone walls, its crowding, snow-packed mountains, and its intense infinity of blue, into which sea and sky melt, indistinguishable.[16]

News about Walker popped up in September. "He has been in Italy for some time and was in Venice when last heard from."[17] By the end of that month, he was headed home. "He recently sailed from Marseilles on the steamship *Roma* for New York. Mr. Ellis spent four months of his stay abroad on the French Riviera, occupying a villa at Cap d'Antibes, near Nice."[18]

Meanwhile, though Moosie had returned to New Orleans in August, Katty was still in Europe, but complaining about weight gain. "She writes that Swiss cooking is making her 'look like an old-fashioned automobile.' Figure that out. The capricious and captivating Katty is going to Vichy ... to see what can be done."[19]

Walker, perhaps after hanging out with the Murphys and other friends in Antibes, was thinking about a new career. In the same column on the same day, Walker

> was contemplating entering the field of journalism.... He breezed into New Orleans the other day after having been absent since last spring. It was then that he lived a long fancied dream and traveled through the Mediterranean on an outward bound cruise aboard a tramp steamer with a "bucking-beam sea roll" to spend the greater part of the summer in a villa at Cap d'Antibes. Whether Walker is to allow New Orleans to have the pleasure of seeing him act this year in the Little Theater is not yet known.[20]

Katty was in the news again when she left Europe on November 2 to return to New York aboard the *S.S. Leviathan*. "Miss Stewart will remain in New York for a fortnight, visiting Miss Katherine Francis, and will later come to New Orleans."[21]

Katty returned to New Orleans on Wednesday, November 17 to attend a concert by Shura Cherkassky, "the boy pianist."[22] Katty was back home earlier than planned, and Natalie Scott noticed:

> Quietly stealing into our midst last Sunday night was Katty Stewart. She was scheduled to spend several weeks in the great big city of New York but she seems not to have been able to withstand the appeal that is New Orleans.... She has shut herself up and refuses to see anyone. A large number of swains are reported to be gnashing their teeth. Katty says that she has a cold and that her dog is sick. She brought a Kerry terrier back from Europe with her, which is supposed to turn blue after it has gotten a little older.[23]

It's likely that at least one of Katty's problems was Kay Francis. Kay did not mention Katty in her diary in November and may have been avoiding her. She was preoccupied with boyfriend McKay Morris and perhaps rebuffed Katty, who left New York in the dumps.

The only entries in Kay's 1926 diary concerning Katty are at the end of the year. On December 28, Kay wrote, "Spent night with Katty at Stafford house."[24] And on the next day, December 29, she wrote that she and Katty went sailing. That December, Kay was still obsessed with Morris. It was a difficult relationship, largely due to the fact that Morris was gay.

At the end of the year, one of the society columnists commented on Katty:

> Why is it, my dear, that we are not fortunate enough to keep Katty Stewart here with us for a good long while? Away she sailed last summer, you remember, and stayed away well into the fall, then hopping into our city again unannounced. Once again, she "opens up the house," takes hold of the running of the servants and all seems well. That's not to last, my dear, although we had thought it might. This evening, about five o'clock, to be exact, she sails off again. You know, of course, that Fanny Craig Ventadour has been here with her family for about six weeks. Well, she is leaving today, and Katty is going with her. It is quite an opportunity, the chance to sail with someone you know and someone as fascinating as Fanny. So we can hardly blame her for not wanting to wait and go alone.[25]

Fanny Craig Ventadour is yet another interesting woman who ran in the same New Orleans circles with Katty and Moosie. The daughter of a Mississippi cotton broker, she survived three husbands and lived to be 104. She was also rumored to have had an affair with the notorious Weeks Hall. Unlike others who grew up in the South and never changed their racist, conservative views, Fanny was a radical woman who was still protesting war and inequality and fighting for women's rights into her nineties and beyond.

At the end of 1926, William Faulkner and William Spratling were living together on St. Peter Street, collaborating on a book, *Sherwood Anderson and Other Famous Creoles: A Gallery of Contemporary New Orleans*. It was published by the Pelican Bookshop Press, which was housed on Royal Street. The small printing sold out and the book is now a collector's item. Among the people profiled (and illustrated by Spratling) were Grace King, Meigs Frost, Genevieve Pitot, Marion Draper, Joseph Woodson "Pops" Whitesell, Richard Koch, Helen Pitkin Schertz, Lyle Saxon, Charles Bein, Natalie Scott, Oliver La Farge and Fanny Craig Ventadour. Decades later, Spratling wrote, "It may now be considered a sort of mirror of our scene in New Orleans."[26] These "famous Creoles" were the friends and acquaintances of Katty, Moosie, Walker and Walter.

By the way, "Pops" Whitesell, a popular photographer of the time, photographed Katty several times. "His bread and butter work was portraits of Mardi Gras royalty, brides and socialites like the Junior League officers he photographed for Junior League Review programs in the mid-1920s. 'He could carve 30 pounds of heft off a Mardi Gras queen effortlessly and imperceptibly.'"[27] Although best known for his high society portraits, he also "photographed nearly nude, oil-slicked male models for muscle magazines, the closest thing to gay pornography at the time."[28]

Whitesell, who lived in a French Quarter studio, "had a charming demeanor and impish appearance [that] made him a universally popular figure among his neighbors in the French Quarter, high society clientele, celebrities from the fields of arts and letters, and fellow photographers." According to historian Frank Perez, Whitesell remained in the French Quarter and later became friendly with lesbian photographer Frances Benjamin Johnston when she moved to New Orleans in the 1940s. By that time,

> Whitesell was the last man standing, a holdover from the glory days of the 1920s. The two became fast friends and lived out their last years in the Quarter—Johnston died in 1952, Whitesell in 1958—and one imagines these two queer photographers passing their days in Johnston's courtyard or perhaps having cocktails at Café Lafitte, the *de facto* gay bar of the era, located in what is now Lafitte's Blacksmith Shop."[29]

16

1927

> People have now started to crowd onto our beach,— discouragingly undeterred by our natural wish to have it alone.

Few newspaper articles mentioned Katty Stewart in 1927. That's not surprising, but what is surprising is that as early as January 11, a newspaper reported that she had already left for Europe.[1] Perhaps it was disappointment with her ill-fated romance with Kay Francis, but for some reason Katty left far earlier for Europe than she had before.

In February, the Minneapolis Symphony Orchestra performed at the Athenaeum to a huge crowd, a "great number of people ... literally every nook and corner.... [A]lmost all of New Orleans had turned out in full force."[2] The crowd was treated to a special performance on the second night: "200 voices which had been trained to a finish ... were heard in the ninth symphony of Beethoven." Among the voices were Richard Orme and Moosie White, "who have been going religiously to rehearsals every Thursday night since many months back and it was for this very event that they so enthusiastically threw themselves into the seriousness of those Thursday nights of training."

On March 17, the *Times-Picayune* provided an update on Katty. "In Paris just now with friends is Miss Katharine Stewart of New Orleans, who has been spending much of her time abroad for the last few years. She was joined in Paris for a part of the late winter and just after her arrival abroad by her mother, Mrs. Victor da Cunha, now of Switzerland."[3] On March 20, the *New Orleans States*, again used "Mrs." in front of Walker's name. "Mrs. Walker Ellis left Sunday for Galveston, Texas, from where he will sail on the S.S. *Niagara* for France, to be gone for several months."[4]

Despite the restlessness and yearning for Europe, there were advantages to living in New Orleans. For example, Walter and Moosie were lucky enough to be invited to dinner parties at the Walter Keiffers' beautiful house. Known for their delightful dinner parties, they were also known as smart art collectors:

One room is converted into a Chinese den with nothing but Chinese furniture, tapestries, lights, rugs and fascinating show cases indirectly illuminated containing some of the rarest pieces of jade, in white, green, pink and opaque, each piece either signed or with its history written somewhere about it.... Mr. Keiffer is an ardent motion picture camera enthusiast and showed some very interesting reels of his trip to Mexico, the races and Mardi Gras. Guests always envy their ease at entertaining so delightfully.[5]

On another night, Moosie and Walter were at Eileen Slidell's for a dinner party. Other guests included Richard Orme, Virginia Claiborne, Ellis Moore and Harold Barthel, who may have been Orme's boyfriend at the time. "There had been talk during supper of this famous Hindu doctor and philosopher who is in town, so supper finished up and it was decided to get the Hindu up and spend the evening in the throes of Yogi philosophy." The handsome Dr. Mahinder gave them tips on diet and breathing, and also threw in a few magic tricks. "Time flew and the evening was over. And this ... proved one of the most delightful entertainments a hostess could give to her guests."

On June 22, the *Times-Picayune* reported that the Giberts were traveling in Europe with their niece Moosie. Of course, Moosie's plan was to meet up with Katty. "Miss Katharine Stewart, who has been abroad since the winter, will join Mrs. Gibert and Miss White for a time during their stay in Europe."[6]

Maunsel White says, "As for the trips to Europe by both Ellene and Moosie, I think they were subsidized by my grandmother's sister, Maude Tobin Gibert, whose husband was a very successful cotton broker. They lived in a big house on the corner of St. Charles and Washington. My grandmother [Moosie's mother Ellen White] and Maude Gibert were always very close."[7]

That summer, Moosie also traveled to Holland, visiting

all the fascinating "cheese factories," though not the kind of factories we would imagine, but picturesque, colorful places which look more like spick-and-span houses we would love to live in. Can't you well imagine Moosie's golden-haired loveliness, vying successfully with all the plump little Dutch maidens' exquisite coloring? After Holland, there will be a trip to Switzerland and then all the Italian lakes. Isn't Moosie a lucky person? But let's get back to her doings in Paris. She had an unusually delightful time and was entertained in a round of dinners and suppers, for she made such an impression on the admiring French and Americans she met that they couldn't do enough for the "vivacious, clever New Orleans girl."[8]

Katty and Moosie appear to have stayed most often in Paris when they traveled to Europe. "Paris was simply fun. It was the international capital of pleasure, the city where the art of living had been raised to its highest point…. And in the '20s the hectic animation of its night life reached perhaps its wildest limits."⁹ American writer Hart Crane, and friend of Black Sun Press founders Harry and Caresse Crosby, once described Paris in the early 1920s as "a test for an American. Dinners, soirees, poets, erratic millionaires, painters, translations, lobsters, absinthe, music, promenades, oysters, sherry, aspirins, pictures, Sapphic heiresses, editors, books, sailors and how!"¹⁰ Unlike Walker, who preferred Antibes and the Murphy crowd, the two women likely enjoyed the cafés and salons of Paris.

Esther Murphy, Gerald's lesbian sister, also preferred Paris to Antibes. Esther's crowd included Natalie Barney and women interested in and active in literature and art.

The summer of 1927 found the French beaches crowded. Sara Murphy complained about it in a letter to Zelda Fitzgerald:

> People have now started to crowd onto our beach,—discouragingly undeterred by our natural wish to have it alone—However, by means of teaching the children to throw wet sand a good deal, & by bringing several disagreeable barking dogs & staking them around—we manage to keep space open for sunbaths—It will go on no doubt, until Sept—when we leave ourselves.¹¹

In the same letter, written from the Murphys' Riviera home, Sara also mentioned that they had seen Walker that summer, and he had an expensive new toy. "The Old Guard of last year has changed, giving place to a new lot of American Writers & Mothers—The [Charles] Bracketts are back, also Wymans—the Barrys [Ellen and Philip] in Cannes,—and Walker Ellis who has bought an awfully nice boat—upon which we (with les Barrys), went on a trip to St. Tropez the other day & and had a lovely time."¹² Philip Barry was a Broadway playwright best-known for his comedies making fun of the rich, such as *The Philadelphia Story*. He died in 1949.

By August, Katty was staying near Nice and entertaining Moosie and brother Buddy.

> Miss Katharine Stewart, who has been abroad for the last several months, has been at Villa Franche, in the vicinity of Nice for the last several weeks, having taken a cottage there for a part of the summer season. Miss Stewart's brother … joined her there recently and her mother … runs down frequently from her home in Zurich, Switzerland, to be with her for short visits. Also with Miss Stewart at Villefranche just now is Miss Elizabeth White, who went there from Vichy for a fortnight's stay.¹³

Natalie Scott wrote again about Moosie and Katty in October:

> Moussie White … has had a perfect summer, it appears. A chief point of its perfection was a two-week visit to Katty Stewart, who has a villa at Villa Franche and is reveling in the *sans souci* of the Riviera. The Riviera is

becoming increasingly popular.... Time was when it was almost deserted in the warm season, but with the weather sending chills almost consistently ... in Deauville, Etretat, Biarritz, Dinard and all the other west coast places all summer long this year, the warmth of the Riviera seemed an asset instead of a drawback.[14]

Moosie and her aunt and uncle sailed on the *S.S. Aquitania* to New York in October, and Moosie soon arrived back in New Orleans. "Moosie White, always the fascinating, lovely Moosie is ... home again after five months abroad.... Since Moosie's return everyone has kept her busy repeating the amusing and thoroughly interesting occurrences of her trip.... She is a born storyteller."[15]

In November 1927, Walter and Moosie were seen at the recently opened supper club Baroness Pontalba, housed in the Vieux Carré. It became a popular place for the smart set to gather. Joining them were Richard Orme, Harold Barthel, Frank Hemingway and others. According to one society columnist, "Moosie looked beautiful in a flowered chiffon, a stunning white shawl about her shoulders."[16]

According to a November issue of the *Times-Picayune,*

> A true surprise was the arrival of Fanny Ventadour and Katty Stewart in New Orleans from Paris.... [N]o one had been informed.... Katty is always an adorable looking person, with her soft curls, her delicious bright manner and delightful unexpected way of doing and saying things. She's spent nearly a whole year away on this last trip and has any number of things to tell about. Don't think for one moment that Katty is settled here for the winter, because she is not; indeed, far from it, because on December 7 she will leave again with Fanny. Can't say how long she will be away this time but I did hear that she would like to go to Africa for a little while this winter.[17]

Katty did not, in fact, leave December 7 with Fanny. She (and her mother) would not leave for Europe until the following month. Before she left, however, a remarkable story was published in a late November *New Orleans States.* The headline was "New Orleans Girls Save Parisian from Suicide." The story detailed how Natalie Scott (hardly a girl) and Katty "prevented a derelict of the street from committing suicide by jumping off the Pont Neuf into the Seine."[18] According to the awkwardly written report, Katty and Natalie "were coming from the Comedie Francaise on foot to their hotel on the Left Bank when they noticed a shabbily dressed man, who had been walking in front of them, stop and throw one leg over the rail of that bridge over the river.... Miss Scott ... ran to his side, seized him by the arm and pulled him back. The man started to struggle with Miss Scott.... But Miss Stewart joined in the scuffle and the two New Orleans girls held the man until the arrival of a gendarme." The man explained that he was down on his luck, and his wife had left him. The young women listened to his story and made him promise he'd pull himself together, find a job, and not attempt any such thing again. The story ended with a hint of who supplied the newspaper with the story. "Miss Stewart recently returned to New Orleans after practically a year's absence abroad."

This is an odd story. Natalie was indeed in Europe that summer and stayed through most of December, but the story is not mentioned in Natalie's lengthy biography written by her great-nephew, *Natalie Scott: A Magnificent Life*.

Still, it was flattering news to the Stewart family in a year in which there had been an ongoing family scandal. This time it had nothing to do with Kittie da Cunha. On September 27, the *Times-Picayune* reported,

> Suit for $65,628.65 was filed Monday ... against Andrew Stewart, Jr., and his father of 2228 St. Charles Avenue by Mr. and Mrs. Louis Teissier, whose nine-year-old daughter, Lois Teissier, is said to have suffered the loss of her right eye as the result of injuries suffered when the automobile in which she was riding ... the night of December 26 is said to have been struck by a machine driven by young Stewart. The parents charged that Stewart was driving his father's automobile up Prytania Street at an excessive rate of speed and on the wrong side of the street. It was further alleged that the father had permitted his son to operate the automobile without a driver's certificate and was liable ... for damages.... The little girl's right eye had to be removed and a glass eye substituted, the petition alleges. The parents say the child has been permanently disfigured as the result of the accident.[19]

That same weekend, Katty took off for Oak Alley with her closest friends, perhaps hoping to lie low until the story died down. "Oak Alley is beautiful this time of the year. The trees and plants are still as green as in the springtime. A delightful place to spend the weekend, with the Andrew Stewarts as hosts and so Katty Stewart, Virginia Claiborne, Moosie White and Burdette Waldo motored there Saturday morning to be away until Monday."[20]

On Christmas Day 1927, Katty hosted a party at the St. Charles Avenue address. "Up the broad long steps to Katty Stewart's house—for Katty is having a small and informal eggnog party this morning. All of her friends will be there, so you know that Moosie White, Burdette Waldo, Eileen Slidell, Walter Stauffer, Virginia Claiborne and Dick Orme will be among those there."[21]

Before the end of 1927, Kittie returned to New Orleans. This was one of the first hints that her marriage to da Cunha was in trouble. She appeared at a New Year's Eve party at the Country Club. "At another table Kittie da Cunha, in a most becoming frock of violet color, was with Katty Stewart, Dick Orme, Harold Barthel, Burdette Waldo, Allen Huggins [Burdette's first husband] and one or two others."[22]

17

Illusions

> Walker Ellis was on the Riviera at the time Scott was. We all knew him—and his discomforting habits.

In late January 1928, Katty and her mother left to travel overseas yet again. They had quite a group to see them off:

> Mrs. Allen Eustis, Mrs. Sam Clark, Buddy Stewart, Moosie White, Dick Orme, Virginia Claiborne and other friends and family were at the train … on Tuesday when they left for New York on their way to France. It was really quite sad having to bid these two *au revoir* again: the beautiful blonde Kittie and the attractive Katty. Katty had been here since the early winter and Kittie paid us a visit of a month or so, much to our delight. But they are off again, both of them.[1]

In March came news that Kittie had not gone back to Switzerland to be with her husband. "Mrs. Victor da Cunha and her daughter, Miss Katharine Stewart, have returned to France after spending several weeks on a tour in Northern Africa. They will visit in Paris for a part of the spring."[2]

Walker, who had been missing from the society columns, finally received a mention in May.

> Right now Walker Ellis, who usually treats us shamefully, is here for a visit of undetermined duration after having spent last winter on the French Riviera where he was one of the most sought after figures, and where his yacht with its name so reminiscent of New Orleans was the haven of many intellectual and delightful people and the center of gay parties. He cruised up and down the coast, even going over to Africa for a glimpse of Moorish architecture and Arabic life; writing, entertaining, visiting, always a welcome and attractive personage. His stay here will cause the twirl it always does, with the literary intelligentsia and his many friends entertaining for him.[3]

In truth, Walker's glamorous life was a charade. Former friends wondered about him and openly gossiped about his behavior. Gerald Murphy, who was friendly with F. Scott Fitzgerald and Walker, told a Fitzgerald biographer, "Walker Ellis was on the Riviera at the time Scott was. We all knew him—and his discomforting habits. Scott was struck by the contrast between his spectacularly 'successful' career at Princeton and his later life of dissipation.... It would seem that the wild character [Francis Melarky in *Tender Is the Night*] ... was drawn from Ellis, as he was much on Scott's mind. He spoke often of him to me."[4]

This is the same Walker Ellis once described as the "effortless embodiment of all the qualities of elegance and superiority, which were the Princeton ideal."[5] Fitzgerald idolized Walker. Until he didn't.

> At every stage of his career, [Fitzgerald] made a hero out of the most representative and brilliant man he knew, out of Reuben Warner, the leader of his little set in St. Paul; out of Walker Ellis, during the early years in college when his dream was to make Cottage Club and the Triangle.... "When I like men," he wrote in his Notebooks, "I want to be like them—I want to lose the outer qualities that give me my individuality and be like them. I don't want the man[;] I want to absorb into myself all the qualities that make him attractive.... I cling to my own Innards."[6]

Like *Tender Is the Night*'s Francis Melarky, Walker "was a Southerner and seems to have had a difficult relationship with his mother.... It would appear likely that Ellis joined [Theodore] Chanley as a model for Francis Melarky."[7]

Critics have suggested that Dick Diver, another *Tender Is the Night* character, was based on Walker as well; many others think Diver was mostly patterned on Gerald Murphy. "Like most writers, Fitzgerald created composite characters.... Dick Diver in *Tender Is the Night* is drawn from Gerald Murphy, Walker Ellis, Theodore Chanley and himself."[8]

Fitzgerald, who had his own demons, was puzzled about Walker's fall from grace. How could someone who'd been so promising, so successful when young, blow up his life?

Katty returned to New Orleans in August with plans to visit her mother in Paris in the winter. "Mrs. da Cunha now makes her home in Paris," a society column tersely announced.[9] Like Walker, Kittie's "happy" life was an illusion. She was no longer living in Switzerland, and very soon she'd stop referring to herself as Mrs. da Cunha.

Kay Francis included only one mention of Katty in 1928 in her diary. It was on December 4, and she simply said that they'd had a long talk. At this time, Kay was *still* obsessed with McKay and also Allan Ryan, Jr., the grandson of multimillionaire Thomas Fortune Ryan.

Interestingly, Kay also mentioned Tommy Farrar in December. "Saw 'Perfect Alibi'—Tommy Farrar at 3 a.m. to quiet me—stayed til 7."[10] Kay and Tommy were friends, and perhaps had met through Katty.

In addition to her usual social activities, Katty also attended an Andres Segovia concert at the Athenaeum with her father, future husband

Walker Ellis. and Walker's mother Nellie. This was one of the rare occasions where Katty and Nellie attended the same event.[11]

Perhaps Nellie Ellis simply did not like Katty, or perhaps the Kittie Stewart–Victor da Cunha scandal soured her on the Stewarts. Maybe no one would have been good enough for Walker, but Katty and Nellie did not have a warm relationship.

Speaking of Victor da Cunha, by 1929, the marriage was over, and Kittie returned to New Orleans for good. On February 4, the *Times-Picayune* reported, "Mrs. Katherine Eustis, who reached New Orleans earlier in the winter from Europe, is at home now in an apartment at the Pontchartrain hotel."[12]

Believe it or not, a remarried da Cunha returned to New Orleans in 1953 to serve as consul general. In January 1955, he died of a heart attack at the age of 61 in Rome where he was vacationing with his wife.[13]

18

Kay and Katty in Hollywood

Slept with Katty only because she wanted me to—Damn!

In the spring of 1929, Kay and Katty enjoyed their Los Angeles affair. Kay had departed New York on the 20th Century train on April 11, and then met Katty in Chicago. They spent the night at the Ambassador in Chicago.

At the time, Kay was having a typical crazy, passionate love affair. This time it was with Millard Webb, her director on *Gentleman of the Press*. Still, Kay wanted to see her old school friend. One of her diary entries on April 12 read: "Slept with Katty only because she wanted me to—Damn!"[1]

This photograph shows Kay Francis as she looked around the time that she and Katty Stewart traveled to Hollywood together in 1929 (author's collection).

Katty and Kay were back on a train the following day, on their way to Los Angeles where Kay's film career would take off. Their comings and goings suggest a delightful Kay Francis pre–Code romantic picture. While Katty was focused on Kay, the soon-to-be movie star was again involved in many flirtations and several love affairs. Yet the two women were together so often that rumors swirled that Paramount's new contractee was a lesbian.

The two arrived in Hollywood on Monday, April 15, were met by studio brass at the train station, went to the studio, and ended up "dead tired"[2] at the Roosevelt

Hotel at eight p.m. The rest of the week was crammed with errands, going to the movies to see Jeanne Eagels in *The Letter*, driving lessons, minor car accidents, publicity stunts, working on *Dangerous Curves* with Clara Bow, fittings, telephone calls and more. Katty was along for most of it, along with Kay's assistant-maid-confidante Ida Perry, a 29-year-old divorced West Indian woman, who had a drinking problem.

Not surprisingly, on Saturday, April 20, Kay wrote in her diary that she'd slept all day. She then went to the studio with Katty at six p.m. and didn't return home until 11 p.m. The next day, Kay went alone to Kay Johnson's house. "Told me she would always love me!" Kay wrote in her diary.[3] The two were intimate friends who talked frequently.

Kay Francis appeared in many films released in 1930, including *Passion Flower*. This was the same year Kay visited Katty Stewart in New Orleans (author's collection).

They would later appear together in *Passion Flower*, a 1930 film directed by William C. de Mille. Johnson was newly married to director John Cromwell, but they were already having marital problems. Kay Francis enjoyed female attention—and received lots of it.

The next week in Hollywood was, again, busy. Kay was often at the studio, going in early and staying late. But on Saturday, April 27, Kay took Katty to a party at Basil and Ouida Rathbone's house.

Either that weekend or early the next week, Kay bought a puppy and had drinks with character actor Walter Catlett and Hal Skelly (she was working with Skelly and William Powell on *Behind the Make-Up*). She also attended the premiere of *The Dance of Life*, a film directed by John Cromwell, and starring Skelly and Nancy Carroll.

On Sunday, May 5, Kay went to a party at Richard Arlen's and drove to the Santa Monica Beach with Katty. The good times went on and on. This was the rhythm of Kay Francis' new life, and Katty was able to keep up.

As the weeks progressed, the two shopped, partied, dined and met an interesting group of people. In her diary, Kay mentions Ruth Chatterton, Edmund Goulding, Joan Bennett and more.

They saw Francine Larrimore on stage as Kitty Brown in Rachel Crothers' *Let Us Be Gay*, traveled to San Francisco, got drunk with Richard Arlen and Gary Cooper, and drove to Yosemite. As the time grew closer for Katty to return to New Orleans, they saw *Innocents of Paris* starring Maurice Chevalier (who would later become one of Kay's lovers). Kay commented in her diary about Katty and herself: "Public appearance by we!"[4]

They weren't done. They hung out with Clara Bow at Malibu and spent the night with Kay's *Gentlemen of the Press* co-star Walter Huston ("Walter Huston for dinner—followed by a little light drinking—all got plastered."[5]). Huston ended up sleeping between them. Then Kay and Katty had the heart-to-heart conversation on June 1 where they talked until 5:30 in the morning. Kay wrote: "I really adore her—and I guess she really loves me!"[6]

Katty's train left the next day, Sunday, June 2, at ten a.m. She wasn't on it. She'd missed it and didn't leave until three p.m. Still, Katty departed, feeling somewhat confident that Kay was her girlfriend. She'd finally had the nerve to tell Kay how she felt.

Kay carried on as usual. That night she went back to Clara Bow's, had a makeout session with Walter Huston (despite writing in her diary, "That is the last person I want to have an affair with"[7]) and then spent more time with Kay Johnson.

Back in New Orleans, Walker attended several society functions. In April, he gave a reading at the home he shared with his mother. "Mrs. Caswell P. Ellis entertained a group of friends informally though very charmingly for tea in the afternoon Tuesday at her home in Audubon Place.... During the afternoon, Mrs. Ellis' son, Mr. Walker Ellis, gave a delightful reading of several of the works of Ruth McEnery Stuart."[8] Stuart was a popular Louisiana writer who often wrote about African Americans living in the South.

While Katty was cavorting with Kay, the real drama in New Orleans involved Moosie. She was in a different movie than Kay and Katty. Hers was more of a melodrama.

Perhaps while in the middle of a meltdown or temper tantrum, Moosie made a surprise announcement on May 5. "There is an engagement announced today in which the fashionable will be most interested. That of Elizabeth White and Walter J. Stauffer, two delightful personalities and great favorites in younger circles of the social world of New Orleans."[9] While Katty was out of town with Kay, Moosie, likely jealous and angry, made her move, and it probably surprised and even shocked Katty. And maybe Walter.

It probably took New Orleans society by surprise, too. "No engagement announcement of the season claims more attention than that of lovely Elizabeth White and Walter Stauffer.... Miss White is a decided beauty and has been a belle in younger circles since her debut a few seasons ago when she received several Carnival honors."[10]

Another society columnist implied that she'd known for some time. "I almost feel as though I shouldn't tell it, I have been on the verge so many times and hushed up on the brink of disclosure but now ... no one is talking about anything else.... It is a perfect match of two fascinating people, way above the average in clever personality and charming appeal."[11]

The newspapers made it clear what was important about Moosie and Walter:

> The wedding will unite members of two of the oldest and best known families in fashionable circles here.... She was a member of the courts at several of the most exclusive of the Carnival balls the winter of her debut, and since then has traveled extensively in Europe at different times. Mr. Stauffer is a graduate of Yale and in the World War was a captain in the American Expeditionary Force. He is prominent in both the social and financial world here.[12]

The wedding was much smaller than the typical society marriage.

> They are to be married at the Whites' on the 8th of June at a very quiet ceremony with only the two immediate families present and no reception afterwards, even the bridal party will be a family one. When one says just family that means ... the most prominent names, Albert Sidney Johnston, Zachary Taylor, the Rodds, the O'Kelleys, the Schwartzes, the Tobins, the Provostys, the Farrars and so on ... all the backbone of historical and financial New Orleans.

One of the guests was Walter's sister, who had married John McIlhenny. The rich son of the inventor of Tabasco sauce, Edmund McIlhenny, John was a longtime friend of Teddy Roosevelt and one of his Rough Riders. They lived in Key West and on an estate near Charlottesville, Virginia.

Not surprisingly, Walter and Moosie were related. It's complicated, through marriage and not blood, but Moosie's great-grandmother was Amanda Davis Bradford, the sister of Confederate president and American traitor Jefferson Davis. Davis' first wife was Sarah Taylor, known as Knoxie, and the daughter of President Zachary Taylor, Walter's great-grandfather, making her Walter's great-aunt. Davis and Knoxie were married for only three months before she died at the age of 21. But that makes Walter and Moosie cousins of a sort.

The announced attendants for the wedding suggested a rift between Katty and Moosie. "Miss White will have as her only attendants her sisters, Mrs. Stamps Farrar and Ellene White, as matron and maid of honor."[13] However, by the time the wedding took place, Katty was a member of the wedding party.

Moosie was on the verge of turning 27, and Walter was 36, when they married on June 8 at five o'clock in her parents' home on Second and Chestnut Streets. A recap of the wedding appeared in a newspaper:

> There was a feeling of nearness, of deep friendship, and understanding happiness. Just before five, people started streaming into the Whites' lovely old cottage on Second Street, exquisitely decorated with colorful spring flowers. The rear drawing room, in which the ceremony took place, was entirely in gold and white, the slightly raised dais placed before a wall panel of cloth of gold. In front of this stood a long altar covered with cloth of gold and holding in the center, a huge gold bowl of calla lilies, and on either end heavy gold candelabra. The sides of the dais were enclosed by branched gold candelabra and banked palms and the aisle leading up to it was of heavy twisted gold cord entwined with asparagus fern, strung between tall baskets of white gladioli and calla lilies.

Much was made of the members of the wedding:

> The stairway down which the wedding party came made an appropriate vista for the loveliness of the girls with its railing completely intertwined with smilax and covered with waxy white magnolia blossoms and as one saw first Katty Stewart, then Ellene, Maudie, little Maudie and Pierre Gibert, one was impressed by the style and chic of the wedding party. The children were picturesque and cunning in their Kate Greenaway costumes, Maudie's of yellow organdie that blended admirably with her golden red curls, Pierre's of white silk worn with a bright gold sash. Katty, Ellene and Maudie wore gowns made alike, soft, flattering, summery and chiffons of green with long, fluttering skirts and they carried big bouquets of magnolias; the white of the blossoms, the dark green of the leaves and the lighter green of their dresses standing out in high relief against the white and gold of the room. The three were so different, Katty with her piquant face and brunette coloring, Maudie and Ellene's blonde waves glinting in the light of the candles.

Of course, the society columnist saved her most effusive writing for the bride:

> And then came Moussie, a Moussie so ravishing in her loveliness that the gold and white of the room faded into insignificance before the rich sheen of her ivory satin gown, the golden curls waving out below her veil, the brilliance of her smile and the blue of her eyes. She was a dream bride in her beauty, her statuesque height enhanced by the long line of her gown, the distinguished contours of her features outlined by her veil. Her gown was made with a low-cut waist, fashioned in point d'Alençon lace and filled in with tulle. The skirt was long and full at the bottom and over this fell four trains, one at each side and two in the back. The veil of illusion was caught by a single spray of orange blossoms and she carried a bouquet of gardenias and lilies of the valley.

Walter also received compliments. "Though grooms are usually overlooked in the description of bridal finery, Walter could not be eclipsed in

18. Kay and Katty in Hollywood

Elizabeth (Moosie) White married Walter J. Stauffer on June 8, 1929. Here she's featured in her wedding gown in a jewelry store ad (courtesy Maunsel White).

Mrs. Walter J. Stauffer

chose her wedding silver in this beautiful new Princess Patricia pattern.

CHARM—distinction—beauty—all that the world could wish for a bride of her important position is the rich possession of Mrs. Walter J. Stauffer.

She assumes her new rôle of hostess under most auspicious circumstances - not the least of which is her discerning choice of silver.

She decided upon Gorham Sterling, she tells us, because she so admired its distinction of design, its exquisitely rich finish.

We were proud that this choice should have been made in our store.

We will be glad to show you our many other designs by the inspired Gorham artists. Flat silver in many patterns, with hollow ware to match, may be purchased at surprisingly low cost. Six teaspoons in this Princess Patricia pattern, for instance, cost but $11.50.

Mrs. Walter J. Stauffer, the former Miss Elizabeth White of New Orleans, whose marriage took place on June 8th at the home of her parents

"In the beautifully designed Princess Patricia pattern I found the silver I have always wanted," Mrs. Stauffer says

Coleman E. Adler
Manufacturing Jeweler
722 Canal Street

This jewelry advertisement also celebrates Moosie's wedding to Walter Stauffer in 1929 (courtesy Maunsel White).

any surrounding for by his vivid personality, charm and wit he will always share honors with Moussie, and as they turned around to accept the congratulations of their friends we reiterated our thought that New Orleans is indeed lucky to possess such a couple."[14] By the way, Walter was considered one of the city's best-dressed men and was once described as having "the best cut clothes in town."[15]

Later that month, a short blurb reported that Moosie and Walter "are honeymooning in the summer home of Mr. and Mrs. Stamps Farrar on East Beach."[16] Walker does not appear to have attended the wedding. Perhaps he disapproved. Perhaps a rift had developed between Walker and Walter and Moosie.

Another interesting detail about the union between Moosie and Walter is that she was an early version of an influencer, according to an ad placed in the June 14 edition of the *Times-Picayune*. Not sure how she did it, but Moosie apparently convinced local jeweler Coleman E. Adler to at least partially sponsor her wedding. Moosie is described as a "[f]oremost bride of a brilliant Southern season."[17]

Another ad, appearing on June 18, included a different photo as well as quotes. "'In the beautifully designed Princess Patricia pattern I found the silver I have always wanted,' Mrs. Stauffer says." Another part of the ad states,

> Mrs. Walter J. Stauffer chose her wedding silver in this beautiful new Princess Patricia pattern. She assumes her new role of hostess under most auspicious circumstances, not the least of which is her discerning choice of silver. She decided upon Gorham Sterling, she tells us, because she so admired its distinction of design, its exquisitely rich finish. We were proud that this choice should have been made in our store.[18]

The ad also mentions the low cost. "Flat silver in many patterns, with hollow ware to match, may be purchased at surprisingly low cost. Six teaspoons in this Princess Patricia pattern, for instance, cost but $11.50."

When Walter and Moosie returned from their honeymoon, they lived with Moosie's mother—and paid rent. According to Maunsel White, they did it to help out Ellen White. "They rented a house in the first block of First Street after selling the Esplanade Avenue home. It wasn't until about 1920 or so that they bought the 1304 Second Street home, probably with my grandmother's small inheritance. The only way they were able to keep the Second Street house during the Depression was by cutting it up into apartments and renting it out to strangers. Moosie and Walter moved in and paid rent too."[19]

19

The Beginning of the End

> Life itself has stepped in now and blundered, scarred and destroyed.

After Walter and Moosie married, Katty hurried out of New Orleans, aware that something important had changed, and almost immediately left for Europe. "Miss Stewart [and her mother] may also visit in Europe … but her plans are not yet decided on. She reached New Orleans only recently from Hollywood, Cal., where she visited Mrs. Katherine Gibbs Francis, a former classmate at school in Garden City, Long Island...."[1] By September, Katty and her mother were renting a Paris apartment. "They were recently traveling in the south of France, spending a great part of their time at Villefranche-sur-Mer."[2]

In November, the *Times-Picayune* noted that most New Orleansians had returned from Europe but not Katty and Kittie. "They are now in Paris in an apartment on the Boulevard Raspail, and have not yet fixed a date for returning. They had a number of New Orleans friends as their guests for tea at their apartment just about a fortnight ago."[3]

Meanwhile, in November, Walker Ellis appeared in another Little Theater production, the George Bernard Shaw play *Devil's Disciple*. According to a newspaper blurb, "Walker Ellis and Adam Lorch, Jr., are the devil's disciple and the Presbyterian minister, about whose clashing personalities the play revolves."[4]

Katty finally returned home from Europe in December 1929. Kittie Eustis returned to New Orleans by the end of December.[5]

For the rest of 1929 and into 1930, Walter and Moosie attended social functions. They remained active in the Arts and Crafts Club and were members of the reception committee, which also included Natalie Scott, Elizabeth Gilmer (Dorothy Dix) and many other socially connected citizens.[6] Moosie was now mostly known as Mrs. Walter Stauffer, Jr. In fact, one society columnist in 1932 claimed that she honestly could not remember Mrs. Stauffer's given first name.[7]

By January 1930, it was usual for Katty to attend events with the

19. The Beginning of the End

Walker Ellis, shown here with a noose around his neck, was the star of George Bernard Shaw's *The Devil's Disciple* in 1929 (The Historic New Orleans Collection, Gift of Le Petit Théâtre du Vieux Carré, MSS 620.5).

Stauffers. For example, Katty hosted a dinner at her father's house, and the guests included Moosie and Walter. "Miss Katherine Stewart ... entertained a few evenings ago ... in honor of Mr. and Mrs. Sidney Legendre. The table was pretty with a cluster of yellow roses held in a large silver bowl."[8] When Walker socialized, it was usually in the company of his mother. There was no evidence that he was on the verge of getting married to anyone, let alone Katty.

Katty turned 27 in 1930. In 1920 and 1930, the median age for a first marriage for American women was, respectively, 21.2 and 21.3.[9] There were no broken engagements or any sign that Katty was interested in marriage. Somehow she'd resisted for years what had to be considerable pressure from her family and peers to marry. But something changed in 1930. Perhaps it was Moosie's surprise marriage. Maybe it was Kay's heartbreaking visit to New Orleans in the spring of 1930. But someone decided Katty should marry Walker Ellis, a childhood friend and lifelong bachelor, a man ten years older than her.

In March 1930, shortly before Kay Francis arrived in New Orleans, Katty, Kittie and Moosie traveled to Havana, Cuba,[10] a popular destination for rich Americans in the 1920s and 1930s. Perhaps Katty was nervously killing time before Kay arrived.

Later that month, a society columnist reported on opening night of *The Silver Cord* at the Le Petit Théâtre du Vieux Carré. "Katty Stewart had on a cunning soft blue crepe frock with the short ruffled epaulette sleeves, lingerie collar and high waist line, and the beauty of Moussie Stauffer's exquisite skin and golden wavy hair impressed me anew as she stood chatting in the soft light of the Patio."[11] Interestingly, the play was about the disastrous effects of "mother-love" gone haywire between a widowed mother and her adult son.

Kay Francis, filming *Raffles* with Ronald Colman, made plans to visit Katty later that month. The year had already been a busy one for Kay. She was regularly seeing Kenneth MacKenna, the man who would eventually become her third husband, and her film career was busy, even hectic. She also spent the early part of January comforting Mary Astor, whose husband, Kenneth Hawks, died with nine others in a plane crash while he was directing the film *Such Men Are Dangerous*. During that month, Kay perused real estate listings, suggesting that she planned to stay in Hollywood. And why wouldn't she? She was successful, and the studio was putting her in film after film.

Kay appeared in nine films in 1930. Many of her diary entries during that time simply said things like, "Working," "Working all day and night," and so on. In her January 25, 1930, entry, Kay wrote, "Worked at United Artists all day and Paramount at night."[12] She also socialized frequently, enjoying dinners, cocktails and parties with celebrities, including Ina Claire and John Gilbert, Ouida and Basil Rathbone, Jean Harlow and others.

The film Kay made right before visiting Katty, *Raffles*, is surprisingly old-fashioned, especially in comparison to the lives actual women were living. The women in *Raffles* are prim, proper and from an era that probably never existed. Also, the film is male-focused. If filmed today, the much more interesting story would be if it delved into the lives of the women in *Raffles*, not the gentlemen thief. Or, even *more* interesting, a story that would focus on Kay Francis' life at the time, or Katty's, or Moosie's. But that was not Hollywood in 1930.

After Kay's visit to New Orleans in the spring of 1930, Katty was never again mentioned in Kay's diary. While it's likely there may have been letters, phone calls and other communication, the intense relationship between them was over.

Most of the news about Katty after 1930 is vastly different from previous decades. She becomes more diminished as the years pass. A woman who'd once had thousands of mentions in the society columns slowly disappeared from the newspapers.

In fact, the entire world was changing in 1930. Sara and Gerald Murphy had closed up Villa America for good in late 1929. Many of Katty and Walker's friends were leaving Europe and returning to America. The relatively carefree travel to Europe and other lands would become more difficult.

Many friends also faced setbacks and tragedies. Two of Sara and Gerald Murphy's three children died of illness in the 1930s. Two sons of Stella and John Little were killed in World War II. F. Scott Fitzgerald died in 1940 of alcoholism. Zelda Fitzgerald, a former Southern debutante like Katty and Moosie, spent much of the 1930s in a mental institution and then died in a fire in 1948. In a letter to Ernest Hemingway, Gerald Murphy wrote, "Life itself has stepped in now and blundered, scarred and destroyed."[13]

After Kay left New Orleans, Katty continued with her society activities, though probably with a broken heart. She and Moosie attended the Arts and Crafts ball in late April. "Mrs. Walter Stauffer was striking in a costume of black, with a headdress of orange color. Miss Katharine Stewart was piquant in a Moroccan costume—shoes, fez and coat."[14]

Walker and Walter also attended the costume event. In fact, Walker, Elizabeth Werlein, Natalie Scott and a few others were on the committee that helped put on the elaborate ball. "Mr. Walker Ellis wore a Moroccan costume.... Mr. Walter Stauffer went as a French sailor."[15]

The Arts and Crafts balls, first held in the early 1920s, were wild events that included a mix of bohemians and the smart set. "Arts and Crafts Club balls were still being held as late as 1930 and 1931 ... but they seem to have run out of steam about that time. The Depression put a damper on all sorts of frivolity ... [and] changes in the French Quarter may also have reduced the market for ... 'imitation Greenwich Village parties.'"[16]

Katty was back in the swing of the social world in June, though it was clear that she and her contemporaries were gradually moving aside so that the next generation could take their place.

> The younger social set met Monday and Tuesday at the Junior League Theatre for the presentation of *Beauty and the Beast*, and the mothers, though a delightful group, had to take second place in the importance of these young people. They watched the drama, round-eyed with wonder, and if imagination and feeling count for anything, we should have a group of brilliant and clever people in a few years.... Maude Ellen Farrar wore a cunning brown and white dotted swiss that went well with her red hair and dark brown eyes and she was accompanied by her mother and Katty Stewart.[17]

A July 1930 newspaper described an incident that involved the antics of a different madcap wealthy young woman:

> What do you think our friend Joel Lawrence will do next? Certainly an operation would have calmed down anyone else, and the ambulance ride home would have been an ordeal got through as quickly as possible. Did it affect Joel that way? Of course not! Riding up the avenue, looking from right to left, she saw some cars in front of Katty Stewart's and immediately made the driver turn the corner and pull up in front of the house. With a long screech of a siren she called everyone out and thereupon had tea served to her in the ambulance, the others sitting around highly entertained. Katty avers she felt exactly as though she were toasting the King of the Carnival, and Joel is positive the tea party was the nicest part of the operation.[18]

20

The Wedding

> An important engagement announced today of interest in exclusive circles is that of Miss Katharine Stewart to Mr. Walker Ellis.

Kittie traveled to Paris in June 1930. Katty soon followed. Then brother Buddy. Earlier, in May, a notice about Walker suggested that a plan was afoot. "Mr. Walker Ellis will leave early in June for New York to sail for the Continent where he will be for an indefinite period."[1]

However, Walker did not leave in June, because he visited his mother at her summer home in August. "Mr. Walker M. Ellis left last evening for Rosecraggon, N.C., where he will join his mother ... at her summer home for a few weeks."[2] Perhaps he went to break the news of his upcoming nuptials to Katty. Oh, to be a fly on the wall for *that* visit.

On September 5, the *New Orleans States* announced that Walker "sailed Wednesday [September 3] on the *Dixie* and after a short visit in New York will go abroad to spend the winter in travel."[3] No other announcements appeared until October when the big news hit: "An important engagement announced today of interest in exclusive circles is that of Miss Katharine Stewart to Mr. Walker Ellis. ... The ceremony will be performed in Paris, *very quietly* [emphasis added], on October 11."[4]

On October 7, the *Times-Picayune* echoed that announcement and added, "Miss Stewart is a delightful personality in younger fashionable circles here and has been in Europe since early in the summer, having spent much of her time abroad for the last few years."[5]

> On the same day, another newspaper published a slightly different announcement: Mr. William P. Stewart announces the engagement of his daughter, Miss Katharine Stewart, to Mr. Walker Ellis.... Both Miss Stewart and Mr. Ellis are well known in the social circles of New Orleans as charming and talented members of the younger set, and their wedding will be one of the most interesting of the year. The ceremony will be performed in the presence of Miss Stewart's mother, Mrs. Katherine Eustis, and a few close friends.[6]

20. The Wedding

The October 12 *New Orleans Item* published a photo of "Mrs. Walker M. Ellis."[7] It is a flattering shot of Katty, looking adult and attractive. Attributed to photographer Louis Valentine Schaff, it was likely taken in New Orleans before Katty left for Europe. Schaff also photographed Le Petit Théâtre productions, including some with Walker in the cast. A gifted artist, Schaff drowned in a hunting accident in Mississippi in January 1933, along with two other men, when their boat capsized during a storm.

On October 15, a few days after the wedding, it was reported that Katty and Walker "will spend their honeymoon in the southern part of France, visiting there for several weeks. They will return to New Orleans sometime in the winter.... Mrs. Katherine Eustis ... was among the very few relatives or friends attending the wedding."[8]

While Katty and Walker were marrying on Saturday, October 11, Buddy and his father were in the middle of a family emergency in Baltimore: Buddy was hospitalized with a serious liver ailment. In September, after visiting with Katty and Kittie, he returned to New York. Strangely, Buddy, who spent the summer months with his mother and sister in Europe, decided to return to America a short time *before* the wedding.

Buddy became ill on the ship. His father met the ship and immediately had him admitted to Johns Hopkins Hospital.

> After having been ill for more than a month following a physical collapse on shipboard while returning from Europe, only son of William P. Stewart, president of Stewart Brothers, cotton merchants, was reported Tuesday to be recovering.... Mr. Stewart has had private telegraph wires in operation from his suite in Belvidere Hotel, Baltimore, through which he has kept in touch with the New Orleans Cotton Exchange and the New York Cotton Exchange as well as Liverpool movements. He also kept constantly in touch with physicians at the bedside of his son, who is known to hundreds of Orleanians as "Buddy" Stewart. Every moment he could spare from his business he was sitting by Buddy's bed. Buddy Stewart, because of deafness, went annually to Europe for treatment by German doctors. He had completed this year's treatment and was returning home when his liver was infected.[9]

Along with the article, the newspaper published a photo of Will Stewart under the heading "Boss by Wire." This article was published four days before Katty's marriage to Walker.

There was no mention in the article of Katty or Kittie. Admittedly, Buddy rarely played a big part in the lives of his sister or mother. The article, frankly, was more about Will Stewart and how he was behaving like a good father than about poor Buddy. Still, one has to admire Will Stewart for balancing his fatherly duties. While running between his hotel and his son's bedside, Stewart was also able to get a marriage announcement out for his daughter.

If you've ever seen the wonderful Jean Vigo film *L'Atalante* (1934), you'll recall the wedding scene. The shot of bride Dita Parlo is how I imagine Katty, and perhaps Walker, too, looked during the ceremony: grim, not like a bride or groom, but more like someone at a funeral.

Katty and Walker returned from their European honeymoon in November. "Mr. and Mrs. Walker M. Ellis ... reached New Orleans recently from Europe and are at home here at their residence, 2228 St. Charles Avenue. ...Mr. William P. Stewart is at home for the winter at the Roosevelt."[10] Katty quickly began using her husband's name. For example, they were listed as "Mr. and Mrs. Walker Ellis" in a blurb about their attendance at the Philharmonic performance of "La Argentina" at the Municipal auditorium.[11]

By November 10, Kittie Eustis had also returned to New Orleans. "She is at home here with her son-in-law and daughter, Mr. and Mrs. Walker Ellis...."[12] This insistence that Walker was living at the St. Charles residence does not ring true. Likely, Walker returned to the house he shared with his mother on Audubon.

For the remainder of 1930, Katty continued to use her married name, and she and Walker were seen at various social functions, including attendance at the Tulane theater to see the movie *Strange Interlude*. Among the cast members in this film was Alexander Kirkland, a former colleague and friend of Walker.[13]

Katty and Walker also attended a reception at the new French consulate building and a Christmas Eve party hosted by the John Stewarts at their home. Walter and Moosie were also there. For at least a short time, the two successfully pretended to be a happily married couple, and the society columns were used as the tool.

Katty standing behind and embracing an unidentified woman on the deck of a ship (courtesy Maunsel White).

20. The Wedding

Lavender marriages were nothing new. It was a way to use society's rules against it. Lots of people did it. Esther Murphy did it twice. Esther Newton described a Cherry Grove couple she knew: "Laura and Jack, both gay, got married but only pretended to live together to give themselves cover and to please their upper-crust families."[14] New Orleans had something called an "uptown marriage." John Shelton Reed explained it like this:

> When an artistic and socially well-connected young man is described in a document as the "intimate friend" of another, for instance, are they just *close* friends? Both were husbands and fathers, but was this code for what some New Orleanians call an "uptown marriage"? [Kenneth] Holditch describes that "not-uncommon union" as one in which "a gay man, born into New Orleans society, marries an appropriate debutante from his own class and fathers children by her but keeps an apartment in the Quarter for liaisons with male companions."[15]

The marriage between Katty and Walker was obviously a cover marriage, but whose idea was it? Kittie Eustis might have orchestrated it, telling Katty that it was time to marry. But why then? Perhaps Katty and Walker came up with the idea on their own. They may have decided, why not? The marriage would get people off their backs and provide cover for both. Maybe Moosie and Walter talked them into it. Whatever the reason, Katty and Walker decided to marry. It turned out to be a bad decision that made no one happy.

Katty and Walker left New Orleans for Europe in the spring of 1931. "Mr. and Mrs. Walker M. Ellis will sail from here this morning aboard the steamer *De la Salle* for France. They will motor first to Paris, where they will spend a few days, and will then motor to Villefranche, on the Riviera, in southern France, where they have taken a villa for an indefinite stay."[16] Among those who came to say goodbye were Kittie, Nellie Ellis and Moosie.

While Katty and Walker vacationed, a family tragedy struck the Ellis family. Walker's 38-year-old brother Richard, a cotton broker, died in a yachting incident on May 26 that may have been suicide. Richard, who was said to be an excellent swimmer, was first said to have fallen off the yacht. But it was later revealed that he jumped, perhaps after an argument with his wife. Alcohol may have been involved.[17] Walker and Katty did not return for the funeral.

While Katty and Walker were in Europe, Kittie Eustis managed to get her name and photo in the newspaper. Now 52, she struggled to be relevant. On May 31, the following blurb appeared: "Mrs. Katherine Eustis snapped on the roof of the Jackson apartments where she lives, by an *Item-Tribune* photographer. Mrs. Eustis is a charming matron of New Orleans' exclusive set."[18] The photo was not flattering: Kittie looked, yes, matronly.

Self-portrait of Elizabeth (Moosie) White. Moosie enjoyed art and took many classes (courtesy Maunsel White).

By all appearances, Moosie, or "Mrs. Walter Stauffer," enjoyed marriage and life in New Orleans in the early 1930s. Along with Dorothy Spencer and Mrs. Monte Samuel, she was responsible for a new tea place. "Quite the most delightful place to drop in for tea is the colorful little 'studio' maintained jointly by Miss Dorothy Spencer, Mrs. Monte Samuel and Mrs. Walter Stauffer, in the Vieux Carre. Tucked in among the apartments of the Pontalba building overlooking Jackson Square, it offers a cozy retreat from the noise and hubbub of our busy city."[19] Moosie was also pursuing her interest in painting. "The walls are splashes of color mostly blue and gold, and upon them are hung the masterpieces of those anything but amateur 'daubers.' On Monday, the young artists entertained at a large tea at which the belles of yesterday exchanged ideas over a cup of very fragrant tea, with the belles of today.... A very good likeness of the pretty and clever Mrs. Allen Huggins [Burdette Waldo], painted by Mrs. Walter Stauffer, 'smacked one in the eye' where it reposed on an easel."

21

The Marriage

The "house was filled mostly with moonlight and sunshine," explained Mrs. Ellis.

Katty and Walker were back in New Orleans by December 1931, still pretending to be a happily married couple. "Mr. and Mrs. Walker Ellis reached New Orleans last week after spending several months in France, at Villefranche for the greater part of the time. They are at home here for the winter in an apartment at the Jackson Apartments, on Jackson Avenue."[1] Again, it is likely that Walker returned to the home he shared with his mother. Katty may have been staying with her mother at the apartment or may have returned to the St. Charles Avenue house.

A couple days later, there was a lengthier article in which Katty talked about her stay in Europe and made it sound like a dream come true:

> Following an idyllic year 'living in the ocean'—her house was actually built in the warm waters of the Mediterranean—Mrs. Walker Mallam Ellis ... finds shopping in the local groceries very tame after the flower-filled markets of Villefranche-sur-Mer. ...While in southern France, [she and Walker] leased a villa owned by an artist friend of Mrs. Ellis, Ramonde Heubert. The lobster boats unloaded near the villa each day and when a squall came up the salty waves dashed into the house. They came very near missing their dinner one day when Marie Jeanne, their treasured cook, fell out of the window into the sea. The "house was filled mostly with moonlight and sunshine," explained Mrs. Ellis. Paul Mcrand, the French writer, came to call and proclaimed that "writing is the only profitable business." Mr. Ellis wrote short stories, while Mrs. Ellis mostly swam. And when parting time came the whole of the lovely little village where she had spent several summers rushed out to the dock near their house and toasted them with champagne. The Italian boat that they took from their house carried them straight to New York. Mrs. Ellis is looking about for a shantyboat upon which she will live in the spring in lieu of the villa over the sea at Villa Franche.[2]

This last sentence is a hint of what would become of Katty. She was approaching a time in her life when she became reclusive, often living alone on houseboats.

21. The Marriage

Katty, like her mother, tried to remain relevant in New Orleans society. She got her name in the newspaper for attending a social event: "Mrs. Walker M. Ellis ... was seen in a Vionnet model of Maron, heavy crepe material fitting snugly to the knees.... The slightly flaring flounce was stitched in points. She carried a Maron tweet coat with trimming of beaver on the collar."[3]

Katty probably started off with the best intentions in the ill-advised pretend marriage. However, she could not keep it up for long before she ended the pretense that she was a straight, married woman. Perhaps she resented being talked into the marriage. Or perhaps she and Walker simply weren't compatible.

In an undated letter to her mother, Moosie complained about Walker's treatment of Katty. "I'm quite worried about Katty. I saw Waldo [Peirce] and he told me all sorts of dreadful things that Walker had said to him about Katty—She's so pathetic and unhappy."[4] The letter was written in France, so it was probably written between 1925 and 1927, well before the 1930 marriage. Again, it's puzzling why Walker and Katty decided to marry if they already had serious conflicts.

While Moosie and Walter genuinely seemed to enjoy each other's company, this does not seem to be the case for Katty and Walker. Moosie and Walter appear to have actually lived together, and Moosie's nephew is certain they shared a bed. However, Katty and Walker, despite efforts to pretend they shared the same address, didn't keep the pretense up for long. Also, while Moosie and Walter often attended the same events and were listed as Mr. and Mrs. Walter Stauffer, Katty increasingly went her way, and Walker went his. It would have been clear to anyone who paid the least bit of attention that the marriage was rocky.

Walker got his name in the newspaper on January 7, 1932. Perhaps he too was trying to remain relevant. "Eleven years after he had his feet on the controls of an airplane, Walker Ellis, wartime flyer, stepped into a sky wagon at Menefee field and found that he still could fly."[5] The column made no mention of Katty.

In 1932, Katty and Moosie often attended events together again. The difference was that they were no longer Katty and Moosie, they were now Mrs. Walker Ellis and Mrs. Walter Stauffer. In February, Walker appeared as Duke in the Little Theatre's production of Frederick Lonsdale's comedy *On Approval* with Elizabeth Werlein, Lois Wurtele and Denis Burke-Roche.[6] Ironically, according to the *New Orleans States*, "the theme of the play is that folks ought to live together a month before they get married."[7]

The reviews were flattering. "Delightful as a morning ride in the sunshine of Mayfair, and as crisp as the snowy air of Scotland, is *On Approval*.... Monday night.... It was given a fine performance by the four who made up the cast.... If at any time Monday night any in the audience remembered that the Duke of Bristol was Walker Ellis playing a part—well, we just don't believe any did. He was superb."[8] The *Times-Picayune* added, "Walker Ellis made the Duke as attractive as he could be made."[9] In in the audience were Katty, Moosie, Walter Stauffer and Katty's Uncle Andrew and Aunt Josephine Stewart.[10]

The Little Theatre was beloved and an important part of the community. "A play at Theatre Petit du Vieux Carre is always of general interest socially ... for the gatherings at the little playhouse mean that one always meets many congenial friends or acquaintances and the intermissions are much like any larger reception."[11]

The play made Walker a local celebrity, and he and Katty briefly pretended to be a happy couple again. In March, they were invited to a George Gallup party at "his attractive apartment in St. Ann Street ... for tea."[12] Interior designer Gallup was best-known for his work with architect Moise Goldstein on the Samuel and Sarah Zemurray property. Zemurray was the president of the United Fruit Company.

That same week Walker did a reading of three short stories at the Little Theatre's weekly reception.[13] Katty attended the event with dozens of others.[14]

At the end of the month, the Stauffers and Ellises attended the Philharmonic concert together.[15] And in April, there was some name-dropping in the *New Orleans Item*: "Alex Waugh, the English novelist, who lived in the French Quarter during his recent visit here, writes Mr. and Mrs. Walker Mallam Ellis that he is safely back in London now."[16] Alexander Waugh, better known as Alec, was the older brother of Evelyn Waugh and son of writer and critic Arthur Waugh. He was expelled from a British private school, Sherborne, in 1915 for homosexual behavior. Meanwhile, Moosie continued painting, her favorite hobby:

> There is no group of artists in the city that work ... more than that little coterie of women who have a studio in the lower Pontalba building. Any day you should see them in paint-smeared smocks painting and discussing the whys and wherefores of art. They are Mrs. Walter Stauffer, Dorothy Spencer, Mrs. Leon Gibert, Mrs. Rudolph Hecht, Miss Elise Whitney and Mrs. Helene Samuel. They have live models pose for them daily and talks by artists as often as they can get them."[17]

On Saturday, July 30, 1932, at 11:45 a.m., Walter's father Walter Robinson Stauffer, 78, died in his home. The announcement made the front pages of the local newspapers. He had not only been president of the company that bore his name, but was also president of the Eye, Ear, Nose and Throat Hospital and a member of the city board of liquidation. He'd also been an original member appointed to the Tulane Educational Fund's board by Paul Tulane.[18]

21. The Marriage

Walter took on some of his father's duties at the company and the hospital. He also became more politically active. In August 1932, Walter and Katty's father Will were part of a group of "49 leading business and professional men [who] issued an appeal to the city's white Democratic voters to join them in a non-partisan movement to insure a fair primary election on September 13."[19] Interested voters were requested to send their name and contact information "and advise as to whether you are registered and have paid your poll taxes for 1930 and 1931." The Democratic Party was segregated at the time, and poll taxes were one way to prevent black citizens from voting.

The group represented an intra-party conflict that stemmed from a belief that Governor Huey P. Long and Mayor T. Semmes Walmsley were less than honest politicians. Mayor Walmsley vigorously defended himself and "charged that ten of the 49 business and professional men ... cannot vote, six having failed to register and the other four being without poll tax. 'All of these six are friends of mine.... Some of them are my boyhood friends.'"[20] Two of the people he called out were William Stewart and Walter Stauffer.

22

The Houseboat

> Right down there next to the dream banks of Bayou St. John, Katty has her houseboat all tied up as well as all primped up.

By 1932, Katty was sometimes referred to in the local press as Katty Stewart Ellis. She apparently missed being a Stewart. She was also spending more time on her houseboat. In August, the *New Orleans States* reported on her housing and marital status:

> Edna Ferber may have given literature and the stage *Show Boat* and some musical composer may have given "Just a Shanty in Old Shanty Town" to the music lovers, but it has taken Katty Stewart Ellis to give the first society houseboat to the world.... Right down there next to the dream banks of Bayou St. John, Katty has her houseboat all tied up as well as all primped up.... It's something to see ... natty classy ... and she lives on it all alone with the exception of her Negro maid who tends to her wants.... There was once a time when Katty rented a villa in southern France and decided to live there ... but now it's just a houseboat on the banks of the Bayou St. John, as far as the young society matron is concerned.[1]

In fact, it was less than a year since Katty had talked about her life with Walker in a French villa. She no longer had allies at every New Orleans newspaper. The blurb made it clear she was estranged from her husband. And there was innuendo about her newest companion, who remained nameless.

John Shelton Reed points out that, despite segregation, "there was a great deal of contact between the races, and black people were always nearby, sometimes *very* nearby."[2] But "[a]ll interaction between black and white was ritualized, rigidly structured by law and custom to keep blacks and whites from interacting as equals."

The *Times-Picayune* also picked up this story, though it did not have quite the nasty tone. "Mrs. Katty Stewart Ellis is ensconced quite comfortably for the summer on a houseboat in Bayou St. John. It is a ducky little affair, painted white and slapping against the shore just a little beyond the

'Black Bridge.'³ Scrim curtains are at the windows, and a screened porch aft affords the 'skipper' a beautiful view of lavender hyacinths and their waxy leaves meeting a tranquil sky. That's the life."⁴ There was no mention of Walker.

By the fall of 1932, though Walker and Katty spent little time together, Katty and Moosie were once again close. This included occasionally staying together at the Farrar cottage in Biloxi.⁵

In November, Walker appeared in the Little Theatre's production of *The Cherry Orchard*. Reviews were good but not effusive for the challenging play. "Remembered will be Walker Ellis, Stanford J. Levy, Maria Ann Tusson...."⁶ The *Times-Picayune* wrote, "Stanford J. Levy as the landowner and Walker Mallam Ellis as the brother of Mme. Ranevsky share with A.J. Hollander some of the best male lines."⁷

The Stauffers must have had friends in the newspaper business because their names often appeared in newspapers in 1933. One time it was because of Walter's coin collection. He'd put out a call that he was searching for an 1893 (his birth year) penny. The response was overwhelming. "[B]efore 11:30 this morning four people called me up to offer 1893 pennies and two others brought them to me. It is now 4 p.m. and since I returned from lunch I have had five other calls. This gives me an idea. Why not mention that I am collecting coins of a much larger denomination? My collection is now complete and I have applied for membership in the leading numismatic societies. ...Mrs. Stauffer (Moussie White) complained bitterly about having to answer the telephone about pennies until 10 p.m."⁸

At least one person thought Walter looked like boxer John L. Sullivan. *Punch* was the publication of the New Orleans Athletic Club, and in February 1933 its editor opined, "The big husky man with the black, curly mustache ... reminds us of one of the many poses we have seen of the famous John L. Sullivan, and his arm is every bit as powerful as that of the famous John L."⁹

A mean-spirited mention of Katty, now 30, appeared in July 1933. The writer of the *Times-Picayune*'s "Society" column was no friend of hers. "As the disappointed hostess, Mrs. Katty Stewart Ellis takes the dinner! When some guests phoned her at a very late hour that they'd be unable to enjoy the delectable dinner that she'd painstakingly prepared in her little houseboat on Bayou St. John, Mrs. Stewart simply sat down and had a royal feast herself."¹⁰ It's inconceivable that Katty self-reported this humiliating incident. No woman would want it published that not only had her friends no-showed for dinner, but that she then gorged herself on the food.

Moosie started working on the *Item* society column some time in the early 1930s when her friend Burdette Waldo Huggins was the editor. Maunsel White's mother, Sue Bryan, was an assistant. According to

Maunsel, Moosie was on the *Item* society column staff for years and thoroughly enjoyed it. In fact, it was a perfect fit for her: "I'm pretty sure Moosie was at the *Item* before my mom started there around 1931. I don't know when she stopped working there, but well into the 1930s or early 1940s, I think. She always did talk about it and of being a 'newspaperwoman.' I

Walter Stauffer and Jo Stewart Gibert relax at the Giberts' Mon Repos property in Covington. The country home often hosted Walter, Moosie, Katty, Walker and many other friends. This photograph probably dates from the late 1940s or the early 1950s (courtesy Maunsel White).

seem to recall vaguely that she may have also worked for *The States* for a time."[11]

In August, Walker Ellis reviewed *South Wind* by Norman Douglas for the Le Petit Salon. Moosie's mother, Ellen White, was chairman of the committee. According to Maunsel White, Ellen, his grandmother, along with her friend writer Grace King, were co-founders of the Salon.

Grace King is a complicated person. While she did much to help preserve the French Quarter, she was also a full-throated Confederacy lover who was "anxious to defend the South ... when it was represented so badly in literature."[12] She did a lot to help local writers, and her salons brought in famous writers and literary figures. Yet she believed that stories about cruelty to slaves and African Americans should be "suppressed."[13]

The popular Quartier Club ended up closing in 1924 not long after the liquor raid,

> but it was the precursor of another, longer-lived organization, Le Petit Salon, founded later that year, which met only three blocks away. That group involved many of the same women (Helen Pitkin Schertz and Dorothy Dix were officers), and its purposes were much the same—although it seems to have been a bit stuffier. Its first president was the eminent lady of letters Grace King, and the free-spirited Elizabeth Werlein is not mentioned in the organization's history. Miss King described the new organization as 'a circle of distinguished ladies, animated with the desire to maintain the social prestige of the old Creole quarters and preserve its social traditions.'"[14]

They eventually moved from St. Peter Street and moved into an older mansion next to Le Petit Théâtre.

At this event, Walker was a hit.

> Walker Ellis, whose attractive voice and smooth acting charmed audiences last winter in *The Cherry Orchard*, had just as appreciative an audience Thursday morning. He held his mother, Mrs. Caswell P. Ellis, and the other members of the Le Petit Salon a whole interested hour while he told them in an informal way of the unique style of Norman Douglas and took them to that island of unusual tourists created by Douglas in *South Wind*.[15]

The *Times-Picayune* columnist also enjoyed the event. "Mr. Ellis delighted his listeners, who were most enthusiastic over the review."[16] One person who wasn't listed in attendance was Katty. Nor was Moosie, despite the fact that her mother organized it.

Katty was still close to her cousin, Josephine Stewart Gibert. During Jo's final years, Katty and Moosie often stayed with Jo and her family in Covington. "Katty Stewart Ellis spent last week with the Gustave Giberts at their summer home in Covington. She returned with them and their four children Sunday."[17] The *New Orleans Item* provided more details:

Sunday is a big day for the little clique living in Covington this summer. Instead of monotonous dinners in the middle of the day at home, all the couples and their young children assemble on the sandy beaches of Boguefalaya river and partake of fried chicken and sandwiches, taking occasional dips in the icy water. Not long ago, the Gussie Giberts gave a grand party on the spacious lawn of their summer cottage, in honor of a houseful of guests. There were tubs of beer and large boxes of sandwiches and, of course, cocktails. The Giberts' guests were, besides the Philip Notts, who relinquished their farming at Bayou Liberty for a day, Mr. and Mrs. Walter Stauffer, Dr. Emile Neaf, Mrs. Walker Ellis, Mrs. Katherine Eustis and Myra Loker, Buddy Kearny, Corinne Grima, Olga Kaufman, Captain and Mrs. Crabbe, and Mr. and Mrs. Carroll Bobb.[18]

In early November, there was a brief, intriguing blurb about Walker: "Walker Ellis suffered slight injuries recently in an automobile accident."[19] The *New Orleans Item* reported, "Ellis, 33, of No. 8 Audubon Place, well known in social circles here, received a gash on one hand early this morning when his car skidded into a curb at Lowerline and Belfast streets. Driving down Lowerline, he was turning into Belfast and swerved his car to avoid another automobile when the accident occurred, breaking a wheel on his machine. He cut his hand on glass which had previously been broken in his car. Treatment was given by a private physician."[20] A couple of things. One, Walker was not 33. He was 40. Two, it was further proof that he lived on Audubon with his mother.

Walker quickly recovered, and he appeared on November 21 in an "all-star cast"[21] in *The Man in the Stalls*, a one-act play sponsored by the Orleans Club. It also featured Val Winter and Rhea Loeb Deutsch.[22]

In November, columnist Elizabeth Kell provided more details on Katty's life on the houseboat. "Flapjacks on Sunday morning are the attraction on Katty Stewart Ellis' houseboat, anchored in Bayou St. John. Katty spends a great deal of time on it now. So do her friends."[23] Elizabeth Kell, society columnist for the *New Orleans States*, seemed particularly interested in Katty's life and dropped nuggets like the following: "Katty Stewart Ellis and her father, Mr. W.P. Stewart, are fond of hunting together. She wears khaki trousers and sweater."[24]

At the end of December, Walker gave a Christmas reading at the Le Petit Salon. The work was by Dorothy Dix (also known as Elizabeth M. Gilmer[25]), president of the Salon. She was born Elizabeth Meriwether Gilmer and became a popular columnist and journalist. Neither Katty nor Moosie attended.

{ 23 }

Restless

> Mrs. Walker M. Ellis (Katty) writes often of the big time she is having in New York with all her talented friends.

In January 1934, columnist William Wiegand mentioned Katty, Moosie and a friend of theirs in a nostalgic look back at their carefree life in Europe in the 1920s:

> Before the dollar and the playboys and girls became deflated, there was an amusing figure capering about the American colony on the French Riviera. His particular hangout was Cap d'Antibes. His name, John Chapin Mosher. Mr. Mosher was, and is, a writer by profession. His opi have appeared in the principal magazines of America. Orleanians summering in France met and were convulsed by him. Just ask Katty Stewart Ellis and Moosie White Stauffer. They will recite with glee some of the stunts this writer pulled off in France.[1]

Mosher, born in 1892, wrote short stories and film reviews for the *New Yorker*. He was gay and active in the Greenwich Village theater community. And, yes, he was a character. When he died in 1942, he was described as "witty, perceptive … and one of the most delightful companions we have ever known."[2]

Moosie was noted in February for being a fashion trend setter: "[She] wore a smart white and gold creation. The skirt, which was straight and very long, was of white heavy crepe, and the bodice, in blouse effect, was white embroidered in gold. The sleeves were full, and with it she wore gold sandals."[3] Not only did this show that Moosie was still relevant but also that her husband was wealthy and successful enough to buy expensive clothing. The point was to show off beauty, taste and, of course, wealth.

Walter's new hobby was yachting, including sailing and racing. In March 1934, he planned to travel with Commander Garner H. Tullis and his schooner, *Windjammer*, from Biloxi to St. Petersburg to compete in the fifth annual St. Petersburg-to-Havana marathon.[4] However, "Walter Stauffer didn't go because his wife is recuperating in the hospital."[5] There was no indication as to why Moosie was admitted to Touro. However, according to her nephew Maunsel White, she "had a tubal pregnancy after her marriage that left her unable to have children, a cruel fate for her, because she *loved* children."[6]

Tullis, born in Louisiana in 1893, was a world-renowned yachtsman. A cotton trader who owned his own brokerage firm and eventually partnered with E.F. Hutton, he died in 1966 while aboard his beloved yacht.

Walter's mustache got him a mention in the newspaper in 1934 when he was mistaken, for at least the second time, for Hennen Legendre. This time a man rushed up to him and told him that his tennis racket would soon be ready. "Now Mr. Stauffer is not a habitue of the courts; he cares not a whit for the hectic sport. Nevertheless, always the perfect gentleman, he answered calmly, 'Have you, really?' 'Yes, Mr. Legendre, we're hurrying the job for you.' The gentleman for whom Mr. Stauffer was so abruptly mistaken was Hennen Legendre, who also wears one of those puzzling, fascinating, twisting moustaches."[7]

That same spring, Katty decided to travel to New York with a friend. "Noted for her sudden impulses, [she] left this Tuesday when she couldn't resist leaving with Fanny Craig Ventadour for New York. A wire from a group of old friends she had known in Paris proved more than she could stand, so she boarded the train with little notice."[8] She planned to stay for a few weeks.

She stayed longer but kept in touch with New Orleans, bragging about her friends:

> [Katty] writes often of the big time she is having in New York with all her talented friends. She is the guest now of Mrs. Ivy Troutman, divorced wife of Waldo Peirce, the painter. Also a guest of Mrs. Troutman is Maimie Sze, daughter of the Chinese Ambassador, who is pursuing an artistic career in New York. Miss Sze's picture, taken in slacks and a nautical sweater, appears in the latest edition of *Vogue*. She is a graduate of Wellesley.[9]

Sze, captain of the Wellesley crew team and a Schiaparelli model, was also a painter.

> In May, the *Times-Picayune* called Katty someone who knew just about everyone. "[She] is another one of the local gals improving her education in New York—but not at school, of course. Incidentally, it's who she doesn't know that is stumping New Yorkers. They bring forth a peer from England, an opera singer from Rome, or, maybe, just a missionary from Africa, and somehow, somewhere, Katty has met the man before.[10]

Also in April, Katty and brother Buddy had a financial setback when they lost a court case against the Canal Bank and Trust Company. They were listed as the intervenors, and the other party was the liquidators.[11] According to a court document, Will Stewart had opened a trust for Katty and Buddy on June 22, 1922. The details are murky, but the Stewart children accused the Canal Bank and Trust of negligence, causing a loss of almost $42,000.[12] The court decision likely left a bad taste.

Elizabeth Kell further reported on Katty's travels in June 1934:

> Katty Stewart Ellis returned yesterday from visiting her aunt, Mrs. Andrew Stewart, at beautiful Oak Alley Plantation. She spent all spring in New York surrounded by a group of old friends, all of them celebrities, whom she had known in France. Because she hadn't been on the sea for three years and was homesick for it, she caught a boat and sailed as far as Savannah, where she got off and visited Mrs. Ben Archibald, who was formerly of New Orleans. Kattie reached New Orleans last Friday.[13]

Katty and Moosie participated in an artistic jaunt that same June. "The magnificent stretch of the sanded beach along the Mexican Gulf and the quaint fishing scenes of Grand Isle will furnish inspiration and material for the brushes of a group of New Orleans artists this week. The group … will motor to the island on Monday and spend seven days there in the old home formerly belonging to Dr. Engelbach."[14] Ellene White was also part of the group.

Katty and Moosie returned several times to the location. "Four New Orleans artists gathered their sketching material during the past week and journeyed to Grand Isle for inspiration…. [A] few sketches were made, but the artists found it so pleasant to be out of the city for a few days they couldn't keep their minds entirely on sketching. The four were Mrs. Helen Samuel, Mrs. Walter Stauffer, Mrs. Walker Ellis and Miss Ellene White."[15]

Elizabeth Kell reported another Katty sighting in July. This time it was at a Biloxi cottage belonging to Sidonie Provosty Scott. "Katty Stewart skipped about over there in a short gingham sunsuit that looked like a pair of rompers and revealed her perfect, brown back."[16] The flattering comment suggests a warm friendship between Kell and Katty. Sidonie Scott was Natalie Scott's sister-in-law.

In November, Katty attended an event featuring poet Edna St. Vincent Millay. Hosted by the Poetry Society of Louisiana, it was held at the Holy Name auditorium.[17] Katty perhaps reflected on Millay's famous poem about burning the candle at both ends. Millay was one of many in her generation who had lived a hard, fast life.

On Christmas Day 1934, a Tuesday, Moosie's father, Albert Sidney Johnston White, 67, died at his home at 1304 Second Street. He had been ill for some time. White was born on the Deer Range Plantation to Maunsel White, Jr., and Elizabeth Porter Bradford. He was the grandson of Colonel Maunsel White, Sr., who fought with Andrew Jackson at the Battle of New Orleans. His grandmother was Amanda Davis Bradford, Jefferson Davis' sister. A charter member of the New Orleans Country Club, he was described in his obituary as a "descendant of famous Southern families, and prominent in business and socially."[18]

According to Maunsel White, the family had been facing financial difficulties for years and were "merely keeping up appearances.... When my grandfather died in 1934, he was relegated to selling the old family wine sauce that he bottled by hand. The cause of his death was uremic poisoning that resulted from a rupture he suffered while manhandling barrels of sauce under the house."[19]

Walker made a rare public appearance when he attended a February 1935 Ted Shawn dance recital. Katherine Eustis also attended the recital; Katty did not.[20] By this time, when Walker was mentioned in newspapers, it was often for family functions that included his mother or other relatives.[21] Katty's social mentions decreased in 1935, though in March she attended a Mardi Gras party at a relative's home. "At the John C. Stewart home on St. Charles Avenue there was a bevy of children and grownups. Katty Stewart Ellis was in a peasant cape and was taking pictures of the crowds."[22]

Later that month, Katty was hospitalized after an automobile accident. "Kattie Stewart was suddenly catapulted into the air and thence into Touro Infirmary Sunday night. She was getting into her automobile in front of her home ... when it was suddenly struck by another car. She is still at Touro Infirmary recuperating from bruises."[23]

Katty's condition improved quickly and by the end of March she was again in Biloxi, visiting Tommy Farrar and wife Beatrice, who were visiting family.[24] She saw them again in May. "Mr. and Mrs. Thomas Farrar of New York ...came to New Orleans yesterday on a short visit to the former's brother and sister-in-law, Mr. and Mrs. Stamps Farrar. Mr. and Mrs. Farrar motored today in a party with Mrs. Walker Ellis to Oak Alley plantation to spend the day."[25]

The Stauffers were also traveling in April. "Mr. and Mrs. Walter J. Stauffer will leave Thursday for Biloxi, Mississippi, joining Mr. and Mrs. John Wood there and with them will motor to Miami, Florida, on a several days' trip. Mr. Stauffer and Mr. Wood will attend a convention to be held in Miami next week. En route they will stop in Mobile to view the azaleas."[26]

In June, Moosie and her female friends were part of the "'swankiest' picnic that has ever been heard of" at the City Park:

> After a few hours of dabbing their brushes on their paint palettes, their minds were on their own palates. Mrs. Hecht's chauffeur arrived with four tables, each covered with cellophane and tied with a big bow. A table was placed before each artist, and a feast—chicken, stuffed artichokes, bread and butter, olives and pickles and wine, fit for a king, was glued to the table so the wind would blow it off.[27]

Walter Stauffer developed a love for yachting and often sailed with his friend Garner H. Tullis. This photograph was probably taken in the 1940s (courtesy Maunsel White).

Meanwhile, Walter was off sailing with his *Windjammer* friends. This time they raced from Biloxi to Pensacola. His colleague William "Son" Hughes claimed, "We're no softies; we never burn, we're so used to the sun and water."[28]

An interesting article describing the geography of the Bayou St. John area where Katty kept her houseboat appeared in August:

> The seawall is divided into three parts, in its glistening run from the West End lighthouse to the hydroplane base at Shushan airport, each part neatly separated from the other by the absence of a bridge. Each of these three sections of seawall is especially adapted to the swimming needs of the great population of New Orleans that has wearied of pool routine. From the West End lighthouse to Spanish Fort, i.e., Bayou St. John, there is mostly shallow water.... From Bayou St. John to the London Avenue canal to Shushan airport there is more shallow water—this for residents of Milneberg, Gentilly and perhaps a few in-city residents who desire their recreation the hard way. With the deep water strip from Bayou St. John to the London Avenue canal we are most concerned. It is practically impossible to reach without dislocation of several automobile springs on the rocky road which follows the bayou, therefore it is more private. And the depth of its water makes it more fun.... Among those who take advantage of this short strip of sea bathing [are] Mr. and Mrs. Walter Stauffer ... and Mrs. Walker M. Ellis (whose houseboat in Bayou St. John is not far way)."[29]

Also in August, Walker visited the popular fun couple Tommy and Bea Farrar in Biloxi.[30] Walker returned to visit the Farrars in September.

In October, Mrs. Caresse Crosby of New York and Paris was entertained by Katty during her stay in New Orleans.[31] Born Mary Phelps Jacob in 1892, she renamed herself Caresse with the help of her second husband, Harry Crosby. She is credited with the first patent for the first commercially made bra. She was bisexual and defied social conventions. Oh, and she also had a dog she named Clytoris.

Caresse and Harry moved to Paris where they enjoyed a decadent lifestyle and hobnobbed with other members of the Lost Generation. According to Tony Allen,

> The couple were always eager to make new friends.... Among their acquaintances was a group of architecture students, who repaid their hospitality by inviting them to the famous Quartz Arts Ball.... Inside the ballroom, Caresse, naked to the waist and wearing a long blue wig, was the principal ornament of the students' dragon float. Harry wore a collar of dead pigeons, and carried a bagful of live snakes. The night ended as riotously as it had begun. Caresse ... returned home to find her husband sharing their sunken marble bath with three pretty girls. Their bed held seven people that night—the seventh being a total stranger who found his way to the bedroom dressed only in a loincloth.... The bedroom ... played an unusually important part in their lives.... Promptly at eight o'clock each evening, Caresse and he would undress and get

beneath the sheets. Guests were then invited in to sit at small tables around the bedside.[32]

The Crosbys started Black Sun Press in 1927 and published works by Hart Crane, James Joyce and Ernest Hemingway. Harry died in 1929 in a suicide pact with a woman. The fact that Katty knew Caresse well enough to have her stay at her home suggests that she and Moosie were hanging out with an unconventional crowd when they traveled to Paris. Many of their friends were famous, and some were infamous.

Katty spent the winter of 1935 in New York, "[where she] has many friends there and always has a gay whirl."[33] One has to wonder why Katty didn't move to New York. Richard Orme lived there for a while, as did Kingsley Black. Tommy Farrar moved there permanently. For some reason, Katty always returned to New Orleans.

Around this same time, there was an incident at Ellen White's home: "A 32-caliber bullet was fired into the living room into which a number of guests were sitting Friday night in the home of A. Sidney White, 1304 Second Street."[34] Besides Walter and Moosie, also present were Burdette and Allen Huggins, Ellene White and Katherine Eustis. Ellen was not feeling well and had retired to her bedroom. "Guests said that there was a cracking noise which they at first thought was caused by the fire on the hearth. Investigation showed that there was a small hole in the window glass and a 32-caliber bullet was found on the floor. Apparently it missed Mr. Huggins' head by a very short distance."

Where was Katty? Perhaps the newspaper was mistaken, and they meant Katharine Stewart was at the party, not Katherine Eustis. Maunsel White believes it *was* Kittie who was at the gathering. "She was an old friend of my grandparents. They all lived for years in the same small area of the Garden District, mere stones-throws away from each other. My dad always referred to Kittie as Kittie Eustis and never Kittie Stewart. Katty was always Katty Stewart."[35]

Katty left for New York a week later, so she probably was in New Orleans at the time. And if it was her mother and not her at the house, why wasn't she there? Was she not invited? Was the shooting accidental? Was someone in the group targeted? Was it a random attack? There was no follow-up in the newspaper, so this incident will remain a mystery.

Moosie was still getting her name in the newspaper due to her family's special sauce in February 1936:

> We noticed Mrs. Walter Stauffer with what looked like pride as she read Mary Frost Mabon's column in "Town and Country" on delectables. Inspection revealed that Miss Mabon was saying some very nice things about the White family's pride and joy, "1812 Sauce," first served by Colonel Maunsel White on his Deer Range plantation at a dinner for his friend Andrew Jackson. Miss

Mabon says in part, "It is called '1812 Sauce' to commemorate the Battle of New Orleans, but after tasting it you realize that those Southern colonels, with all their smooth talk, were still fire-eaters."[36]

Katty was still in New York in February 1936. "News from Katty Stewart Ellis is that she feels very much at home in New York, considering that her neighbors in the metropolis are much the same as they once were here. She says Elise Whitney, Anna Farrar Goldsborough, the Bill Labrots and herself all live within pebble throwing distance."[37]

The *New Orleans Item* published an article about Kay Francis in April 1936 that mentioned Katty and *Let's Not and Say We Did*, the high school play they'd collaborated on in 1921. "Kay Francis, sleek and poised lady of the screen, was aided and abetted by a New Orleans girl when she made her first adolescent excursion behind the footlights.... The New Orleans girl was Katharine (Katty) Stewart, now Mrs. Walker Ellis, who still lives in New Orleans, as do her parents, W.P. Stewart and Mrs. Katherine Eustis." According to the article, Kay and Katty

> saw each other frequently, once went to Paris together. A few years ago Miss Francis slipped out of Hollywood in the full blush of her success and visited her childhood friend here. They had two weeks together in New Orleans, Oak Alley, the Stewart plantation, and Grand Isle. Miss Stewart did not take the road to the stage. She chose New Orleans society, marriage and travel. She has been in New York since November.[38]

After Katty got back to New Orleans in early May, she hosted an interesting group at Oak Alley that again included Ivy Troutman. "Among prominent visitors in New Orleans stopping at the St. Charles Hotel are Mrs. John Oliver of Pembroke Lodge, Richmond Park, Sursey [sic], England; Mrs. Ivy Troutman of New York and Paris; and Prince Sergie Belliofsky, New York. The party is en route to Taos, New Mexico, where they will join Mrs. Mabel Dodge Luhan. The party motored with Mrs. Walker Ellis yesterday to Oak Alley plantation, where they were guests of Mrs. Ellis' uncle and aunt, Mrs. and Mrs. Andrew Stewart, for the day."[39]

Katty hosted several parties on her houseboat in May. "Members of the social and artistic whirl in New Orleans usually find themselves Elsa Maxwelled into parties of delightful originality when Katty Stewart Ellis is in town. A group of gaily clad swimmers on the lakefront drive these May mornings is not a party ending but the start of one of those Dutch treat breakfasts aboard her houseboat."[40]

At the end of the month, Katty, Kittie, the Stauffers, Kingsley Black and many others attended a Richard Orme event at the Vieux Carré. It was a party for Allen Prescott, who was visiting from New York.[41] Prescott was a closeted gay radio star who also hosted several early TV shows in the 1940s. He was best known for a show called *The Wife Saver*. Prescott,

23. Restless

like Tommy Farrar, ended up living in Cherry Grove with his partner Ray Mann.

In December 1936, it was revealed that Walker's nickname was Wally and that he'd recently traveled to Europe again. "Walker Ellis ... [is] an intimate friend of.... Herman L. Rogers, at whose villa in Cannes Wally has taken refuge.... Walker went through college with Mr. Rogers."[42] Herman Livingston Rogers was yet another eccentric character in the lives of Katty and Walker. An American industrialist, he was a friend of the Duke and Duchess of Windsor and a witness at their 1937 wedding. Rogers died in 1957 in Cannes.

In April 1937, Kay Francis was interviewed by Mel Washburn on the set of *One Hour of Romance* (the title was later changed to *Confession*). Washburn told Kay he'd interviewed her before. "I reminded her that we had met years before, in the *Item-Tribune* offices, while she was here visiting her former school friend, Katty Stewart." Kay was not in the mood to discuss Katty. "'Oh, yes ... that was several years ago,' she replied, and that finished that much of the interview."[43] Brrr.

In fact, Kay and Katty's lives were quite different in 1937. Kay, though no longer at her career peak, was still a popular movie star, wealthy and successful. Katty was still wealthy, though it's likely the family fortunes were no longer as robust as they once had been. Katty, however, was no longer the popular New Orleans society woman who Kay visited in 1930. Her name rarely appeared in newspapers.

Columnist Hildegarde Lyons shared an unusual anecdote about Katty and Kittie in June, one that probably would not have been published in the 1920s:

> Lyle Saxon was having a quiet train trip home when who should come aboard at Oak Alley but Katty Ellis and her mother, Kittie Stewart ... and were they from the country! Twelve pounds of fresh butter wrapped in heavy brown paper, a dainty little washtub with the neatest covering of a big woolly bath towel, a huge straw picnic basket, all the latest fads in smart luggage, to say the least. They left the train at Gretna, and Lyle hailed three little darkies to carry the load and follow them to the ferry and the procession proceeded in great dignity, chatting un-self-consciously all the while ... it wasn't until they were on the ferry that they turned around and took a look at themselves and dissolved into gales of laughter at the perfect hick picture they made.[44]

Walker stayed out of the spotlight in 1937. A rare mention had him spending time with his relatives. "The mouth of Bayou Lacombe, Howze's Beach, was the spot where the fish were biting the best yesterday, and that's where those old veterans, Peggy Ellis and Jo Woodward, Jr., and Walker Ellis hunt their poles."[45]

At some point, Katty's alcoholism reached a point where it caused problems for herself and others. This was hinted at in a July 1937 newspaper: "Lyle Saxon was awakened at two a.m. by a telegram and the hour being what it was he had frightening visions of murder and sudden death and tore it open with trembling fingers.... 'Book fine. Should make good movie....' were the consoling contents. Speaks well for the book if Katty Stewart Ellis sat up at Oak Alley and read till that late...."[46] Drunkgramming?

The book that Katty "reviewed" was probably *Children of Strangers*. Saxon, who died in 1946, knew Katty for many years and likely was an eyewitness to her alcoholism.

That August found Katty improbably ensconced in Fort Walton, Florida, pursuing a different kind of life than the one she was born into.

> If Katty Stewart Ellis were a man, she would probably be a skipper aboard a deep water boat.... But being a doll, the nearest she can get to shipboard authority is running a floating hotel.... She writes, "I am on a huge boat anchored off Fort Walton, Florida. The truth is that an old man and his wife couldn't make it pay and I have the entire place to myself. He's an old-time old man and I'd like to help him; besides, this is the only type of work I'll ever do. Please don't make any wisecracks on account of my family. There's a lot of deck space on the boat and nice staterooms and a grand bar. You can walk across the sand dunes to the Gulf for swimming, or swim and fish off my boat, *The Pirate Ship*."[47]

Society columnist Hildegarde Lyons also reported on Katty's new life. "Katty Stewart Ellis writes from Fort Walton that in spite of all the people fighting to get rooms there, she is the sole boarder on the *Pirate Ship* ... nobody else seems to have discovered it. It was built for a gambling house and night club, but when the authorities stopped all that, the owner turned it into a floating inn and Katty is delighted...."[48] Katty returned to New Orleans the first week of September, after spending at least a month in Florida.[49]

Walter and Moosie traveled with Moosie's mother in the fall to Virginia. "The mountains of Virginia are their loveliest now with leaves turning gold and brown, all ready for the trip [that] Mrs. Albert Sidney White and her son-in-law and daughter Mr. and Mrs. Walter Stauffer will take. They leave in their automobile today and will pause longest in old Williamsburg."[50]

24

Walter Stauffer and New Orleans

"Arms Plot" Here May Bring on Some International Chuckles

Walter Stauffer was in the middle of a strange story about an "FBI gun-running coup"[1] near the end of 1937. The story's title was "'Arms Plot' Here May Bring on Some International Chuckles." Yes, chuckles.

Walter, described as "the socially prominent member of the firm of Stauffer-Eshleman," was arrested along with Israel Slobotsky (owner of Star Furniture company) and Stauffer-Eshleman employees Lewis Hardie and James F. Ferry. Stauffer and Slobotsky were quickly released on $5000 bond, and Hardie (Walter's brother-in-law) and Ferry were released on $2000 bond. They were charged with conspiracy to smuggle weapons and birdshot shells.

Their excuse was that, no, they were not participating in a military coup in Honduras, but in a hunting expedition. "According to some members of the Latin American colony, this is no unusual practice because of the very high price such ammunition brings in Honduras, where the hunting is excellent. One of the principal items of game is a large wild duck, similar in respects to the Muscovy duck, but so large that seven of them are about all a mounted huntsman can bring back with him."

According to a different newspaper report, "The charges were based on some shells which had been loaded into a taxicab by a returning employee of the United Fruit company [J.S. West], and so taken aboard the steamship *Sixaola* for transportation to Honduras."[2] West was returned to the U.S. on December 2 and released on $2000 bond.[3]

All the men claimed no knowledge of the crime. Stamps Farrar, Moosie's brother-in-law, represented Walter and his two employees. According to Farrar, "the outcome of the case will show that somebody is making a mountain out of a molehill."[4]

The Star Furniture store and Stauffer-Eshleman business were searched. By the way, Slobotsky was, like Walter, an old friend of former New Orleans police superintendent Guy Moloney. Moloney, who'd also served in the Washington Artillery, was now a "soldier of fortune" living in Honduras. Many thought he was involved with the plot, and that it had nothing to do with hunting.

None of this curtailed Walter's social schedule. His name continued to appear in society columns. He obviously knew he had nothing to worry about. He was right. On Tuesday, December 14, a grand jury refused to indict the five subjects. "The grand jury devoted four sessions to hearing witnesses in the case.... Its action closes as far as criminal prosecution is concerned." However, U.S. Attorney Rene A. Viosca announced that civil penalties and fines would be levied against the "parties responsible for failure to declare this shipment and others."[5] And that was the end of that.

There are a few takeaways from this. One, the grand jury decision was unanimous, which indicates how much they thought of Walter. He was very much a part of the New Orleans establishment. Two, the verdict points to anti-government sentiment, still present in New Orleans, a vestige of hurt feelings about losing the Civil War.

In 1938, Moosie attended "a party that Mr. and Mrs. Monte Samuel [Helene] gave at their red brick house behind its moss-draped trees in Metairie Tuesday evening for Abel Green, of New York City, editor of *Variety*, and his smart-looking brunette wife [Grace Fenn]."[6] Moosie attended. "There were plenty of interesting people there, several artists, including Mrs. Walter Stauffer, several writers, including Sidney Field, numbers of newspaper people and plenty of interesting folks interested in the motion picture industry. Champagne cocktails added to the liveliness."

That same month, Moosie became involved with the Reinike Academy of Art on Toulouse Street. Her friend Helene Samuel was chairman of the artists' group, and Moosie served on a committee.[7] A blurb in May 1938 revealed that Katty still occasionally traveled with Moosie. "Mrs. Walter J. Stauffer, her sister Ellene White, and Mrs. Walker M. Ellis return tomorrow from Biloxi, Miss., where they have been occupying the Stamps Farrar cottage for a few days."[8] Katty's life had become a series of short trips here and there, often to visit family and old friends. She was 35 and still restless.

A lengthy *New Orleans Item* article profiled Walter in January 1939. This again illustrates Walter's social prominence, especially compared to Katty and Walker. The focus was his complaints about the decline of New Orleans gourmet food. He was described as "secretary-treasurer of the Stauffer Eshleman wholesale hardware firm."[9] According to the article, Stauffer was "known as a gourmet and bon vivant, and the proprietor of one of the most traditional mustaches in New Orleans."

According to Walter. "Domestic and professional cuisine definitely are in a decline.... Perhaps the old Negro cooks are dying out, and the young ones are like the white people, unwilling to take the trouble. That would explain the domestic situation, if not the degeneration of some of our restaurants." Walter admitted he was not much of a cook. "I can't cook and don't know anything about cooking.... Eating is my metier, and I like it."

He particularly enjoyed eating good French bread, and during the interview two loaves were delivered.

> Bread is important.... Every Frenchman must have his bread, if he has nothing else, and it must be the best French bread.... The trouble is that this bakery is the only one in the city today that bakes the true French bread, thin, long and crusty. And he won't deliver out of the business district. So, every day, I have him bring two loaves to my office and I carry them home with me. It's no trouble and the satisfaction it brings is more than worth it.

Walter worried about the future of restaurants. "I know that a good bowl of gumbo is the hardest thing to find in New Orleans nowadays. I go to dinner at the homes of friends and they serve me something weak and watery, without the true gumbo stringiness, and then drop a little rice into it. Gumbo, I have found, is best when you have a hambone to cook in with it, or a chicken carcass."[10] One has to wonder if dinner invitations decreased for the Stauffers after the article.

Walter did name several New Orleans restaurants that still met with his approval, including Kolb's, Galatoire's and Antoine's. Moosie, to whom he'd been married for almost ten years, was also mentioned. "With Mrs. Stauffer, the former 'Moosie' White, herself the representative of a family that has treasured its escargot sauce recipe since 1812, the gourmet spent last summer in Mexico, and was enthusiastic about his gastronomic experiences there. 'There were three good French restaurants and one good Italian restaurant, Paoli's.'"[11] This was a marked difference from his experience with French food during World War I. "Mr. Stauffer remembered only the horse meat.... It ... had a flavor like beef, but with a peculiar, not unpleasant additional savor."

Walter also recalled a feast at Arnaud's with Natalie Scott on one of her trips back from Mexico. He called it "the gastronomic experience of my whole lifetime.... We ate for three hours. I have forgotten everything but the main dish, a turkey stuffed with snipe. I shall never forget the count carving that turkey, reaching in and pulling out the snipe. I don't suppose this was an article in the regular cuisine at all, possibly the count was showing off, but I shall never forget it."

Walter also talked about his deep love for snails and the best way to prepare them and mentioned brown rice:

Rice is one of Mr. Stauffer's major gastronomic interests, and he told with pleasure of a friend in Crowley who sends him, from time to time, a sack of "brown rice," not the unpolished rice, but the rice just after the hull has been knocked off. The manufacturers do not like to stop their machinery to produce this, Mr. Stauffer said, but it is rice at perfection, with all the grain flavor intact.

On Thursday, November 9, Katty and Walker surprisingly appeared at the same event. It happened in the French Quarter. "Last evening there was a dinner made gay by good company and good food, with all gathered around a candlelit table in a Vieux Carre center. Mrs. Therese Kohn, who makes her home now at the Pontchartrain hotel, entertained."[12] Besides Katty and Walker (their names were not listed together), attendees included Moosie and Walter, Kittie Eustis and many others.

25

1940s

> Mrs. Walker Ellis was wearing black lace, and a crimson wrap and was looking strikingly pretty.

In the 1940 census, Katherine Eustis was 60 and divorced. Katty, 35, who resided with her, was described as married. Sort of. The "M" for married is crossed out, and a question mark appears next to it. In the column marked "Income, Other Sources," the answer is "yes." Also, for the highest grade completed, the response is "High School, 2nd year." And in the column "Attended school or college," the answer is "no." So that casts doubt on the Columbia University claim.

Their apartment is listed as 938 Royal, and Kittie is described as a renter. The building was constructed in 1845 and eventually became apartments and is now condos. It's unknown why Katty was not listed at the St. Charles Avenue address.

Katty attended the Atlanteans Ball in the early winter of 1940. Hyperbole was still in force. "New Orleans has seldom seen a richer or more beautiful ball than that given Tuesday evening by the Atlanteans and in celebration of the golden anniversary of the organization."[1] The society columnist also complimented Katty's black lace and crimson wrap outfit.

In April, Walker finally got an opportunity to perform again, though for a small audience. "Mrs. Donald Maginnis had been visiting her mother, Mrs. John B. Hobson, for several days but motored back to her country place, Mulberry Grove, yesterday morning. Walker Ellis went there, too, to give a reading of [the George S. Kaufman–Moss Hart play] *The Man Who Came to Dinner*, current Broadway success."[2] Despite the small crowd, the event was a hit, and Walker was asked to do an encore. "Walker Ellis created so much interest ... that he has been asked to read it Wednesday at the weekly literary gathering at Mrs. Gustaf Westfeldt's on Prytania Street."[3]

This added some juice to Walker's acting career. He had another gig in June. "Le Petit Salon announced that at its weekly morning gathering

Thursday, the program will include a reading of one of Somerset Maugham's plays to be given by Mr. Walker Ellis."[4]

Katty and Moosie were still traveling together in 1941. Their friend Burdette Huggins wrote: "[They] have just returned from Covington, where they spent a delightful visit with Mrs. Josephine Gibert at her lovely home. Mrs. Ellis, after a short stay there, was joined by Mrs. Stauffer and the two motored home together."[5] By now, their friendship was at least three decades old.

That July, Katty and Moosie posed together for a flattering photograph. "Mrs. Walter J. Stauffer ... and Mrs. Katherine Stewart Ellis are in relaxed mood. They were photographed on the spacious lawn of the Gibert home in Covington. Mrs. Stauffer is the active chairman of publicity for the France Forever organization."[6] The two look like society matrons. Katty is wearing pearls and a sleeveless dress. Her hair is leaning towards a bouffant, and she has lost weight. Moosie looks happy and, yes, relaxed.

Meanwhile, Walter volunteered with the draft board. In July, he shared what he thought was a humorous anecdote. "Walter Stauffer, prominent businessman and member of Draft Board No. 11, tells a story he says is true about a Negro who was called before a local board."[7] If you have a bad feeling about how this will go, your intuition is correct:

> There was some question about this man's mentality, so he went before a psychiatrist. Queried the psychiatrist, "Do you ever hear voices you don't know where they come from or whose they are?" "Yas, suh, doctor. Ah does!" retorted the young man. The psychiatrist figured he had a real nut. He followed up with "And when do you hear the voices?" A minute later he was deflated when the boy replied: "When ah answers da telephone, suh."

Big news for Walker came in September with the announcement that he would play the lead in *The Man Who Came to Dinner*.[8] On October 12, the *Times-Picayune* featured him in a photograph, in costume, as Sheridan Whiteside, the character loosely based on Alexander Woollcott.[9] Reviewer Cleveland Sessums declared the play—and Walker—a hit.

> Le Petit Theatre du Vieux Carre opened its 25th season Wednesday night with an excellent production of *The Man Who Came to Dinner*, the Kaufman-Hart clinic on the whimsy and insult school of professional wits. Walker Ellis, returning to the Little Theater's boards after an absence of ten years gave a superlative performance as Sheridan Whiteside, the leader of the cult, and a capacity audience acknowledged the achievements of Mr. Ellis and his colleagues with enthusiastic applause.... Mr. Ellis succeeded admirably in conveying the mood of pontifical remoteness.... His relish over a quip, his petulance, his sudden frenzies were achieved with revealing success. His performance was a complete portrait of a spoiled genius at bay.... The comedy belongs to Whiteside and Mr. Ellis never forgot his responsibilities. He derived

every implication and innuendo from his lines, his acting was never too bold and, altogether, the evening was definitely his.[10]

Walker, now 48, must have been thrilled with his comeback.

In March, Le Petit Théâtre du Vieux Carré announced Walker as lead, along with Laurence M. Williams, "both very special favorites among the active members,"[11] in a play titled *Fashion*, written by Anna Cora Moffatt. On March 25, 1942, the *Times-Picayune* published a photo of Walker and co-star Margaret Williams. "The play ... is a satire on society of 1845.... Miss Moffatt appeared as a star in the old St. Charles Theater here in the 1840s."[12] Critic Cleveland Sessums was not wowed this time. "*Fashion* lacked even the interest normally evoked by a period piece.... Walker Ellis was properly distraught as the frantic Mr. Tiffany. The whole cast ... did excellent work, but their efforts did not result in an amusing evening in the theater."[13]

In April, Walker played Uncle Stanley in another Kaufman-Hart play, *George Washington Slept Here*, again at the Le Petit Théâtre du Vieux Carré. Walker was among a group who "gave excellent performances." The play was described as "an entertainment tonic which kept the opening audience ... in almost continuous chuckles or guffaws."[14]

Walker completed a draft registration card in 1942. He was 49 years old and listed his address as 479 Audubon Street (street numbers appear

Walker Ellis gave his final stage performance in 1942 when he played Uncle Stanley in *George Washington Slept Here*. In this photograph, he is second from the right (The Historic New Orleans Collection, Gift of Le Petit Théâtre du Vieux Carré, MSS 620.18).

to have changed on Walker's block). Under the section headed "Name and Address of Person Who Will Always Know Your Address," he did not list Katty. Instead, he named brother C.P. Ellis, Jr.

Katty was largely missing from the society columns in 1943. However, in January, along with Walter and Moosie, she appeared at a cocktail party honoring Richard Orme, "who has returned from Nevada where he served for several months with the U.S. Marine Corps Reserve."[15] This was one of the last times Katty and Moosie were at the same public event. Photographs from Moosie's collection, however, show her, Katty, and others partying privately. The photos have a boozy feel to them.

Walker had a new medium for his acting career in 1943. Now appearing on radio, he was featured in an ad in a January *Time-Picayune* newspaper, along with Val Winter, Aline Stevens and Mary Nell Ivey. They appeared in a show titled *Old New Orleans* on WWL. Sponsored by Regal Beer, it was broadcast on Sundays at 7 p.m. "Life as New Orleanians lived it, more than 100 years ago, is vividly portrayed … in 'The Road to Yesterday.'"[16] Mary Nell Ivey later became a legendary actor and teacher in

This Weegee-ish photograph appears to date from the 1940s. Left to right, Walter Stauffer, Burdette Waldo Huggins Westfeldt, Moosie White Stauffer, unknown, unknown, Katty Stewart Ellis (courtesy Maunsel White).

Atlanta theater, where she performed and taught as Mary Nell Santacroche. She died in 1999.

In the fall of 1943, Walker was a narrator on the twice-weekly radio program *We Cover the Battlefront*. At one point, he was temporarily replaced by Val Winter. According to the blurb, Walker was "recovering from an accident."[17]

Walker appeared on yet another radio show in the fall of 1944. "*Testing* at 5:15 p.m. from WWL will present a drama called 'Grin and Bear It.' Participating in the show will be Walker Ellis, Aline Richter Stevens, Betty Miller and Nick Kreegar. Script was written by Virginia Camp."[18]

Meanwhile, Walter was elected vice-president of the Eye, Ear, Nose and Throat Hospital in 1944. "Mr. Stauffer's election was regarded as appropriate ... inasmuch as his father ... was founder of the hospital and for about 30 years its president."[19] Walter was also active as entertainment director for an American Legion baseball league. And believe it or not, considering the ruckus he and Walker caused in 1920, he became first vice-commander of the Crescent City Post No. 125 American Legion.[20]

Walker again appeared on the radio in January 1945. "*On the Job*, at 5:15 p.m. from WWL will be a dramatic presentation.... Virginia Freret has written the script. Participants include Nick Kreegar, Walker Ellis and John Kent."[21] This was Walker's last credit.

Walker's beloved mother died on July 18, 1945. "Mrs. Caswell Prewitt Ellis, Sr., widow of one of the city's leading bankers and cotton men, died Wednesday morning at her residence ... after an illness of several months. Mrs. Ellis, who was Miss Nellie Mallam, was a native of New Orleans, and was widely identified with social and charitable activities of the community. She was one of the leaders of the local Red Cross chapter during World War I. She was a lifelong communicant of Trinity Episcopal church and was closely associated with much of its work."[22] Katty's name was not mentioned in the obituary.

Nellie's death was a blow to Walker, one from which he never recovered. His sister Hazel had died in 1938, and the loss of these close female relatives made his life unbearable. He became a recluse and was dead within three years.

Katty's brother Buddy Stewart married Mattie Kemp in 1947. This was Buddy's first marriage. He was 43. His wife, who also had not previously married, was 30. There was a brief mention by Burdette Huggins in her *New Orleans Item* society column. "Mrs. Charles A. Farwell will entertain at an informal cocktail party Sunday at 5 o'clock at her home in Webster St., in honor of her cousin, Andrew Eustis Stewart, and Miss Mattie Kemp, whose marriage will be celebrated on April 6."[23] There are few mentions of Mattie Kemp in newspapers. Little is known about her relationship with Buddy.

She was the daughter of Walter Kemp and Blanche Cook Kemp. Her father, a factory worker, died in 1935, and her mother took boarders into the home she shared with Mattie and an older daughter, Audrey. According to the 1940 census, Mattie worked as a bookkeeper and earned $700 a year. She had attended college for one year.

This may have been an act of rebellion by Buddy. Both parents were still living. Unlike Katty, Buddy did not choose a spouse from a wealthy, prominent family. Katty's name does not appear on the marriage license. Mattie's sister Audrey was a witness, as were Buddy's cousins Henry LeBlanc and Allen Eustis, Jr. The couple were married by the pastor of the First Methodist Church.

Moosie's picture was in the newspaper as one of the attendees at the opera on May 9, 1947. Smiling, she is well-dressed and still quite attractive.[24] A different newspaper article commented, "Mr. and Mrs. Walter Stauffer were there … she … in a black crepe model, and in her hair she wore a becoming coronet of cornflower blue roses."[25]

26

Everything Ends

Members of the family knew no reason for the shooting.

Katty Stewart faced a year of loss in 1948. On March 6, three days after her 45th birthday, her father died at the age of 71. His death was announced on the front page of the *Times-Picayune*. He was described as the "former president of the board of port commissioners and of the New Orleans Cotton Exchange."[1] His biography was impressive:

> Mr. Stewart, who resided at 2228 St. Charles, was a native of New Orleans. He was a graduate of Andover Academy.... He graduated from Yale University in 1896. Mr. Stewart headed the dock board under the late governor Luther Hall. He had also served as president of the Cotton Exchange, the Metairie Land Company, and the Stewart Realty Company. Active in social circles, he was a former president of the Metairie Golf Club, and a member of the Boston Club and the New Orleans Country Club. He had been active in Carnival groups in past years.

Walker Ellis was listed as an honorary pallbearer. "Surviving are a son, Andrew E. Eustis, and a daughter, Mrs. Walker M. Ellis."

Then, at around 6 p.m. on Monday, December 6, Walker, alone in his home on Audubon, put a gun to his head and pulled the trigger. He didn't die immediately. About an hour later, an unidentified person found him injured, and he was taken to the Touro Infirmary. He then "lived another hour and 23 minutes before he expired at 8:25 p.m." Coroner C. Grenes Cole ruled his death a suicide. "Members of the family knew no reason for the shooting."

The death certificate lists Katty as his widow. She is also listed as the informant, but she likely provided the information over the phone because her name was signed by the funeral director.

News of Walker's suicide appeared on page one of the *Times-Picayune* the following day. According to the obituary, Walker was "a member of a New Orleans family prominent in cotton circles."[2] The funeral was held the following day, Tuesday, December 7. Walker was interred in the Ellis family crypt in Metairie Cemetery.

Walker's alma mater, Princeton, acknowledged his death in an alumni newsletter:

> The class of 1915 will be shocked to learn of the sudden death of our classmate, Walker Mallam Ellis, at Touro Infirmary.... Following a brilliant undergraduate career at Princeton in which he served as president of the Triangle Club, a member of the Senior Council, Commencement Ivy Orator, and graduated with Phi Beta Kappa scholastic honors, Walker received his legal degree from Harvard Law School. Immediately upon the United States' entrance in World War I, he enlisted as a private in the Air Corps in May 1917, served with distinction as combat pilot on the Western Front, and was discharged with the rank of captain. Returning to civilian life, he briefly engaged in the cotton business and the practice of law in New Orleans. His Triangle Club career, however, eventually took him back to the theater; and many of his New York classmates will recall seeing him on Broadway stages when he played in *Beggar on Horseback* and *The Youngest* during the 1923–1925 seasons. Finally, deciding to devote his life to travel, study and literature, he went abroad in the late '20s and resided for many years on the French Riviera.... In Paris he married Miss Katharine Stewart of New Orleans and after long-continued residence on the Continent, they eventually returned to their native Louisiana home. Walker died, survived by his widow, a brother, Caswell P. Ellis, Jr., and a sister, Mrs. John Reed Murchison. To all of them the class sends its deepest sympathy in our mutual bereavement.[3]

There was no mention of Walker's suicide. It's not known who wrote that not-entirely-true summary of Walker's life.

Walter and Moosie Stauffer left New Orleans for a fishing trip in the Grand Isles either before or soon after Walker's death. "Spending a couple days in Grand Isle this week were Mr. and Mrs. Walter Stauffer."[4] The timing seems odd.

A Princeton newsletter printed a short blurb about how Antoine's, the legendary New Orleans restaurant, once named a seafood dish after him. "*Gourmet* magazine recently gave away one of the secrets of Antoine's (New Orleans). It was the recipe for 'Oysters *à la* Ellis' and stated that it was named in honor of the late Walker M. Ellis, artist and 'bon vivant.'"[5]

Walker died without a will. The house ended up being sold in September 1949, and Katty was one of 11 beneficiaries. It was sold to J. Norcom Jackson and his wife Abby Orme, sister of Richard, for $22,500.

The Stauffers were in Florida during the winter of 1949. "Mr. and Mrs. Garner H. Tullis will leave today for Fort Lauderdale, Fla., where they will spend a few days before boarding their yacht, the *Windjammer II*, for a trip to Nassau and a cruise through the British and French West Indies. They will be joined in Fort Lauderdale for the trip by Mr. and Mrs. Arthur C. Waters and Mr. and Mrs. George Griswold, and at Nassau, for the remainder of the trip, by Mr. and Mrs. Walter Stauffer."[6]

26. Everything Ends

On November 25, 1952, Katty's doctor admitted her to the Touro Infirmary. Her symptoms likely included shortness of breath, vomiting and pain. It's not known who visited her in the 11 days she lingered before finally dying on December 6 at 9:40 p.m. It was exactly four years to the day (and almost the hour) since Walker's death. She was 48.

The cause of death was congestive heart failure due to cirrhosis of the liver. The informant for the death certificate was Mrs. A. Stewart. This was probably not Mattie Stewart, Buddy's wife, but more likely her aunt Josephine, the owner of Oak Alley.

Despite hundreds of society column mentions throughout her relatively short life, only a terse death notice appeared in the Sunday, December 7, edition of the local New Orleans newspaper. Katty was described as "wife of the late Walker M. Ellis; sister of Andrew Stewart; daughter of Katharine Eustis and the late W.P. Stewart." The funeral took place Sunday afternoon at 2:30 p.m. at the 2228 St. Charles Avenue house. She was interred at the Metairie Cemetery in the Eustis section, not with husband Walker Ellis in the Ellis section, nor with her father in the Stewart section.

This Christmas photograph was sent to John White, Moosie's brother, when he was overseas during World War II. First row, from left: Burdette Waldo Huggins Westfeldt, Walter Stauffer, unknown, Moosie White Stauffer, unknown, unknown; second row, from left: unknown, Katty Stewart, Kittie Eustis, Wallace Westfeldt (Burdette's second husband), Elizabeth Lyons (John White's first wife) (courtesy Maunsel White).

There's no list of people who attended her funeral. Kittie and Buddy were likely present. Perhaps Moosie and Walter, Burdette, Jo Gibert and Josephine Stewart (Uncle Andrew had died in October 1946). It was a sad end to a life that had started with such promise and potential.

Katty, like Walker, died without a will. Kittie and Andrew ended up inheriting her estate.

Walter was named chairman of the board of commissioners of Liberty Place at a meeting at Antoine's on September 15, 1953. "The 79th anniversary of the end of carpetbag rule in Louisiana was commemorated…. Members … held an observance to mark the date, September 14, 1874, when members of the White League waged a pitched battle to drive carpetbaggers from New Orleans. The ceremony was held at the monument on Canal Street near the river."[7] Walter stayed active with the organization until his death.

The White League is exactly what it sounds like. Composed of white supremacists, it was a violent anti-government organization that resulted in the deaths of 13 police officers before federal troops ended it. Walter's father, Walter Robinson Stauffer, was one of the insurrectionists. So was society photographer Anthony H. Hitchler and many other wealthy pro–Confederate New Orleans citizens. It was a badge of honor among certain New Orleans citizens.

In 1993, the monument was moved to "an out-of-the-way corner next to train tracks and a parking lot at the edge of the Quarter." The Vieux Carré Commission voted 5–0 to remove it permanently in 2015, despite strong opposition. At the time, K. Brad Ott, a sociology professor, said he'd like to see the Liberty Place monument, once adorned with a plaque celebrating the end of the Reconstruction government, destroyed. "Hopefully, it ends up as ballast in a ship or destined for the construction of a Jim Crow cemetery."[8] The monument was removed for good in 2017 and placed in storage.

Ellen Virginia Tobin White, Moosie's mother, died at the age of 80 on December 12, 1954. Her obituary stated that she was "a member of one of New Orleans' older families" and that she "was one of the founders of Le Petit Salon and a member of the Colonial Dames of America."[9]

The Stauffers continued living the wealthy lifestyle they'd been accustomed to, attending the symphony and other concerts, often in the company of Moosie's sisters Maude Farrar and Ellene White. In addition, they often traveled, including frequent visits to Jo Gibert's home, Mon Repos, in Covington.

The public lives of Walter and Moosie Stauffer came to an end in the late 1950s. Walter stepped back from Eye, Ear, Nose and Throat Hospital, though he remained on the board. In an April 1958 newspaper photograph, he looked very much the distinguished older gentleman that he was, now bespectacled and balding.[10]

… 27 …

The End

> She was really up or *waaaay* down.

In the 1950s, years after Katty's death, family members still congregated at the Stewart's St. Charles Avenue house to watch the parades. According to Maunsel White, "We watched all parades there in the 1950s. I was born in 1950, so I don't have any memories of Katty. I only overheard her name mentioned a lot."[1]

White explained that when family members discussed Katty, they often used one word:

> Ironically, the phrase most often used by my family to describe Katty's personality was that she was always "so gay." They frequently used that description in the old sense and were actually much perturbed when the connotation changed. My parents said resentfully that a very useful word had been rendered unusable.[2]
>
> I do remember seeing Kittie a number of times. She was pretty old at the time and maybe an invalid. She was always sweet and kind to me. She gave me a neat army truck, all metal, which I kept for years. I only remember seeing Buddy a couple of times. Since he was deaf, there wasn't much said. I don't think little kids like me resonated much with him. I have no memory of Mattie. Buddy lived in the house, but his part was different from where Kittie lived on the main floor. It was like a finished basement where he lived with its own entrance.[3]

Thomas Griffin's society column on January 25, 1961, reported that Walter was "on the road back to his chipper self after surgery at Touro."[4] In fact, Walter was terminally ill.

Walter and Moosie celebrated their 32nd anniversary that June with a buffet luncheon at their Metairie home. Guests included "a group of their close relatives and friends."[5]

According to Maunsel White,

> Moosie and Walter drank a lot socially and often probably to excess, but I wouldn't classify them as total alcoholics. Everything revolved around the social swirl. It's the kind of thing that slowly creeps up on you. Years go by,

and next thing you know you have a dependency. In later years, Moosie would have a few cocktails and then call up distant cousins she hadn't seen for years to catch up. They told me later that they could tell she'd been drinking. But she never showed the ravages of serious alcoholism and remained an attractive lady until the end. Walter was much more controlled until he got sick. A former employee of his once told me he'd seen him drinking straight from a bottle in his office. That was toward the end when the pain from the cancer was setting in.[6]

Walter Stauffer died at the age of 69 in his home, 314 Atherton Drive in Metairie, of lung cancer (he and Moosie were heavy smokers) on July 16, 1962. He'd been ill since his diagnosis almost two and a half years before. His funeral was the following day at St. Catherine of Sienna Church.

Walter's obituary was published in the *Times-Picayune* on July 18, 1962. He was described as a "wholesale hardware executive and a former president of the Eye, Ear, Nose and Throat Hospital." It was once again pointed out that he was the great-grandson of former U.S. President Zachary Taylor and the grandson of Confederate General Richard Taylor.

Moosie did not do well following Walter's "long, lingering death from lung cancer."[7] She made half-hearted attempts to socialize. She traveled with her sister-in-law, Sue Bryan White to Seagrove, Florida, in September 1962 and stayed in the Tobins' Gulf Coast cottage.[8] In 1963, she spent Easter weekend with Jo Gibert and Jo's daughter Titine at Mon Repos in Covington.[9]

On June 7, 1963, a little before 3 p.m., Moosie, 60, walked out of the home she'd shared with Walter. Once she reached the street, she turned and walked a bit further until she reached the Southern Railway train tracks not far from her house. She waited until she heard the train, laid her head on the tracks, and was decapitated by a 42-car freight train. It had been less than a year since Walter had died. She was the last of the four New Orleans friends to die.

According to Maunsel White, "My mother [Sue White] always felt responsible for this because she took Moosie (recently out of De Paul's Hospital) to see a re-screening of her favorite old movie, *Anna Karenina* with Greta Garbo and Fredric March. In the final scene Anna kneels down and puts her head under the wheels of a moving train, *exactly* how Moosie ended her life one week later."[10]

Moosie had been admitted to De Paul's, at one time called the Louisiana Retreat for the Feeble Minded, several times over the years. According to White, "The supposedly famous head psychiatrist there predicted coldly that she would be suicidal after her last stay there. And he was right."[11]

Although it's not known when Moosie was diagnosed with bipolar disease, she struggled with it for decades. According to White, "It probably went pretty far back. My mom, who knew her way before she knew my dad, always said she had wild mood swings. She was really up or *waaaay* down."[12]

Moosie was survived by her sisters, Ellene White and Maude Farrar, and brothers, Albert Sidney White, Jr., and John Tobin White. Private services were held on Saturday, June 8, at St. Martin's Episcopal Church. Her body was interred in the Stauffer section of the Metairie Cemetery.

One by one, remaining friends and relatives died. Kay Francis made a half-hearted attempt at suicide in January 1948 when she overdosed on sleeping pills in Columbus, Ohio, while on the road performing in *State of the Union*. She was hospitalized after she passed out and severely burned her legs on a radiator. She recovered after lengthy treatment and continued to act into the 1950s. Kay, a heavy smoker and drinker, died of cancer in New York at the age of 63 on August 26, 1968.

Kittie Eustis lived to the age of 90 and died on July 7, 1969. "If the booze or the mental illness doesn't get you, you're probably in it for the long haul."[13] There was no obituary for her. Her death notice made no mention of her daughter, though Andrew was listed as her son.[14] In addition, mentions were made of her deceased parents and siblings. Kittie, like Katty, is interred in the Eustis section at Metairie Cemetery. Katty and Kittie share a gravestone. Although interred less than 17 years apart, Katty's inscription, compared to Kittie's, is already quite faded.

Elizabeth Werlein, another heavy smoker, died of lung cancer on April 24, 1946, at age 63.

Jo Gibert died November 13, 1970. She was 67.

Kingsley Black married Cornelius Abbott in 1939. They had no children, and she died at the age of 68 in 1975.

Kittie Eustis Stewart died in 1969 at the age of 90. Her death notice did not mention Katty (courtesy Maunsel White).

Ellene (Tita) White died October 22, 1979, at the age of 79. According to Maunsel White, she was committed to the Louisiana State Hospital in the late 1950s after a suicide attempt. She remained there until she died. Ellene never married, which White attributed to being "jilted as a young woman." He also said, "She was kind and sweet but suffered from bouts of catatonia…. She had a bad episode of the illness in the 1920s and was sent to a sanitarium, I believe paid for by the Giberts (who remained 'in the chips' much longer than did my grandparents), which seems to have been successful in stabilizing her."[15]

Burdette Waldo Huggins Westfeldt died on February 21, 1983. She was 80.

Richard Orme died in New Orleans in 1983 at the age of 83.

Buddy Stewart died on April 1, 1990, at the age of 85. He is buried with his father in the Stewart family plot at Metairie Cemetery. His wife Mattie inherited the 2228 St. Charles Avenue property.[16]

Maude White Farrar died at the age of 95 on January 28, 1993.

Mattie Kemp Stewart died on November 9, 1997. Her burial place is not known.

Epilogue

I solved the mystery of what happened to Katty Stewart and also learned a great deal about her friends Moosie White Stauffer, Walker Ellis and Walter Stauffer. All four have largely been forgotten in their New Orleans hometown despite being celebrities, at least for a time. They were flawed, socially connected people who used society columns to craft an image of themselves that was not a complete picture. Their real lives were messy, complicated and full of secrets.

While writing this book, I grew fond of all four as they faced success and adversity. They lived full, complex lives and collectively knew some of the most famous (and infamous) people of their era: F. Scott Fitzgerald, Kay Francis, Waldo Peirce, Gerald and Sara Murphy, etc. They ended up influencing some of these notables, perhaps even becoming characters in novels and films, subjects in paintings.

Maunsel White's recollections and his aunt Moosie's papers gave me important insight into the lives of Moosie and Walter. A truer picture would have resulted if I'd had access to manuscripts, journals, photographs, etc., that belonged to Katty and Walker. These materials were likely disposed of upon their deaths.

As I end this, I encourage readers to donate materials to research archives. Future researchers will be thrilled with you and eagerly devour material you think unimportant.

Thank goodness Kay Francis donated her papers to the Wesleyan University Cinema Archives. I have now used that material for three books. Because of my rewarding experiences using archives, my papers will be donated to the Georgia State University Research on Women Archives. I urge you to consider donations of materials, money, etc., to archives around the world as a final legacy for yourself and those you love.

When I started this book, I knew little about New Orleans. Building on the work of others, I discovered new information about New Orleans and its citizens. I only scratched the surface. There's plenty more to be written about. For writers who are looking for a subject, I encourage you to dig further into New Orleans and its colorful citizens. There's a lot there.

Finally, I encourage more research on gay and lesbian people who lived in eras where much of their lives was intentionally hidden. While it was challenging, I am glad that I took on this project and introduced Katty Stewart and Walker Ellis to those eager to learn more about gay history.

Chapter Notes

Prologue

1. Lynn Kear and John Rossman, *Kay Francis: A Passionate Life and Career* (Jefferson, NC: McFarland, 2006).
2. Kear and Rossman, *Kay Francis*.
3. "Movie Star Visits N.O," *New Orleans Item*, 23 March 1930, 2. Kay did not record the Yellowstone visit in her diary.
4. Kear and Rossman, *Kay Francis*.
5. Kear and Rossman, *Kay Francis*.
6. Kear and Rossman, *Kay Francis*.
7. Kear and Rossman, *Kay Francis*.
8. Kay Francis, diary, 21 March 1930, Kay Francis Collection, Ogden and Mary Louise Reed Cinema Archives, Wesleyan University, Middleton, CT.
9. Kear and Rossman, *Kay Francis*.
10. "Movie Star Visits N.O.," 1.
11. "Film Star Here for Visit Wins Heart of Crowd," *The Times-Picayune*, 23 March 1930, 15.
12. "Film Star Here for Visit Wins Heart of Crowd," *The Times-Picayune*, 23 March 1930, 15.
13. "Movie Star Visits N.O," 2.
14. Kear and Rossman, *Kay Francis*.
15. "Kay Francis Aided by N.O. Girl in Foot Excursion," *New Orleans Item*, 8 April 1936, 21.
16. Francis Diary, 22 March 1930, RCA [Reid Cinema Archives].
17. Kear and Rossman, *Kay Francis*.
18. "Polly Pursue's Society Gossip," *New Orleans States*, 30 March 1930, 16.
19. "Society's Eyes on Junior League Revue," *New Orleans Item*, 30 March 1930, 55.
20. Kear and Rossman, *Kay Francis*.
21. Francis Diary, 25 March 1930, RCA [Reid Cinema Archives].
22. John Shelton Reed, *Dixie Bohemia: A French Quarter Circle in the 1920s* (Baton Rouge: Louisiana State University Press, 2012), 19.
23. Reed, *Dixie Bohemia*, 18–19.
24. Francis Diary, RCA [Reid Cinema Archives].
25. Oscar Wilde, Quotable Quote, https://www.goodreads.com/quotes/3355 53-after-the-first-glass-of-absinthe-you-see-things-as, retrieved 16 April 2020.
26. Reed, *Dixie Bohemia*, 21.
27. Reed, *Dixie Bohemia*, 21.
28. Francis Diary, RCA [Reid Cinema Archives].
29. Kear and Rossman, *Kay Francis*.
30. "Society Folk Go Gypsy," *New Orleans Item*, 6 April 1930, 32.
31. Reed, *Dixie Bohemia*, 8.
32. Will Fellows, *A Passion to Preserve: Gay Men as Keepers of Culture* (Madison: University of Wisconsin Press, 2005), 233.
33. Reed, *Dixie Bohemia*, 234.
34. Kear and Rossman, *Kay Francis*.
35. Francis Diary, 6 April 1930, RCA [Reid Cinema Archives].
36. William G. Wiegand, "Knock 'Em Dead Vamp Now in N.O. Rebel," *New Orleans Item*, 6 April 1930, 40.
37. Francis Diary, 7 April 1930, RCA [Reid Cinema Archives].
38. Kear and Rossman, *Kay Francis*.
39. Francis Diary, 10 April 1930, RCA [Reid Cinema Archives].

Chapter 1

1. Martha Ann Brett Samuel and Joseph Raymond Samuel, *The Great Days of the Garden District*, The Project Gutenberg EBook.

2. Laurance Eustis, *One Lucky Fellow* (privately published, 1999), 1.
3. Eustis, *One Lucky Fellow*, xviii. Eustis, born in 1913, was once married to Alice Walton, an heir to the Walmart estate.
4. Jeff Dwyer, *Ghost Hunter's Guide to New Orleans*, revised edition (Gretna, LA: Pelican, 2016), Ebook.
5. Eustis, *One Lucky Fellow*, 1.
6. Jim Fraiser, *The Garden District Of New Orleans* (Jackson: University of Mississippi Press, 2012), 71.
7. B. Brian Foster, "What About the Houses?" *Veranda*, July–August 2021, 88.
8. Eustis, *One Lucky Fellow*, xi.
9. The Issaquena Genealogy & History Project, https://sites.rootsweb.com/~msissaq2/eustis.html, retrieved July 20, 2020.
10. "Mimi Carte Blanche Writes Peggy Passe Partout," *New Orleans States*, 24 January 1925, 40.
11. Anthony J. Huebner, "Natalie Scott and the Great War Love Story," 21 March 2018, https://werehistory.org/natalie-scott-and-the-great-war-love-story/, retrieved June 13, 2020.

Chapter 2

1. "The Knights of Momus," *Times-Picayune*, 18 February 1898, 1.
2. Maunsel White, email communication, July 24, 2021.
3. "Andrew Stewart Dead," *New Orleans Item*, 7 February 1903, 3.
4. "Andrew Stewart, Former President of the Cotton Exchange, Dies Suddenly," *Times-Picayune*, February 7, 1903, 3.
5. "Society," *The Daily Item*, April 20, 1902, 12.
6. Eustis, *One Lucky Fellow*, 2.
7. Eustis, *One Lucky Fellow*, 1.
8. Reed, *Dixie Bohemia*, 33.
9. "Society," *Times-Picayune*, 17 December 1911, 20.
10. "Society," *Times-Picayune*, 14 April 1912, 18.
11. "Society," *New Orleans Item*, 11 April 1912, 11.
12. Eustis, *One Lucky Fellow*, 2.

Chapter 3

1. Bell Lawrason, "Canaries," http://www.poetryexplorer.net/poem.php?Id=10080096, retrieved May 6, 2020.
2. John Wyeth Scott II, "Natalie Vivian Scott: The Origins, People and Times of the French Quarter Renaissance (1920–1930)."
3. "'Fortnightlies' to Give Second of Three Dances Monday Night in Grunewald," *New Orleans Item*, 30 November 1913, 3.
4. Maunsel White, email correspondence, 24 July 2021.
5. Maunsel White, email communication, 24 July 2021.
6. Maunsel White, email communication, 22 July 2021.
7. Maunsel White, email communication, 22 July 2021.
8. Maunsel White, email communication, 25 July 2021.
9. "Lady Gwendolyn's Society Chat," *New Orleans Item*, 22 April 1906, 12.
10. "Society," *Times-Picayune*, 2 March 1913, 49.
11. "Social Events," *Times-Picayune*, 6 May 1916, 6.
12. "Society," *Times-Picayune*, 23 July 1916, 5.
13. "Society," *Times-Picayune*, 31 December 1916, 33.
14. Harry B. Loeb, "Gambol of the Gods Is Success in Every Way," *New Orleans Item*, 12 January 1917, 10.
15. *The New Orleans States*, 1 May 1917, 8.
16. Maunsel White, email communication, 25 July 2021.
17. "School Set Give Dance at S. Yacht Club," *New Orleans Item*, 2 April 1918, 8.
18. "Social Events," *Times-Picayune*, 19 April 1918, 6.
19. "Entertaining Paulist Choristers, N.O.'s Society's Latest, Says Louisianne," *New Orleans Item*, 21 April 1918, 20.
20. "Social Events," *Times-Picayune*, 7 June 1918, 6.
21. Lucile Rutland, "Who's Who Among the Debutantes," *New Orleans Item*, 31 December 1922, 38.
22. "Society News-Notes," *New Orleans Item*, 21 August 1918, 7.
23. "Social Events," *Times-Picayune*, 18 September 1918, 8.
24. Wiegand, "Knock 'Em Dead Vamp Now In N.O. Rebels," 40.
25. Kear and Rossman, *Kay Francis*, 107.
26. "Social Events," *Times-Picayune*, 13 December 1918, 6.

27. "Smart Event for School Set," *New Orleans Item*, 29 December 1918, 18.
28. "Society," *New Orleans States*, 30 December 1918, 7.
29. "Society," *New Orleans States*, 27 June 1919, 14.
30. "Society," *Times-Picayune*, 3 August 1919, 5.

Chapter 4

1. "Eustis Suicide Laid to Effect of 'Flu' Attack," *New Orleans Item*, 28 October 1919, 7.
2. "Body of Richard Eustis Is Buried on Tuesday," *New Orleans Item*, 29 October 1919, 20.
3. "Members of 'Tau Sigma' Club Give Annual Dance," *New Orleans Item*, 21 December 1919, 46.
4. "Society," *New Orleans States*, 22 March 1918, 10.
5. "Thoughts of Causerie Du Lundi Bring Delight to Reminiscent Louisianne," *New Orleans Item*, 8 December 1918, 17.
6. "Cynthia St. Charles' Letter," *New Orleans States*, 8 February 1920, 35.
7. Reed, *Dixie Bohemia*, 35.
8. "The Diary of Diana," *New Orleans Item*, 12 December 1920, 30.
9. Reed, *Dixie Bohemia*, 185.
10. Lucile M. Lombard, "Society," *New Orleans States*, 22 December 1920, 11.

Chapter 5

1. "Society," *Times-Picayune*, 25 September 1932, 25.
2. John Wyeth Scott II, "Natalie Vivian Scott: The Origins, People and Times of the French Quarter Renaissance (1920–1930)," 1999, LSU Historical Dissertations and Theses, 6924, https://digitalcommons.lsu.edu/gradschool_disstheses/6924, retrieved June 13, 2020.
3. "Peggy Passe Partout's Letter," *New Orleans States*, 26 December 1920, 19.
4. Reed, *Dixie Bohemia*, 34.
5. "Peggy Passe Partout's Letter," *New Orleans States*, 2 January 1921, 33.
6. "Peggy Passe Partout's Letter," *New Orleans States*, 3 April 1921, 3.
7. John Wyeth Scott II, "Natalie Vivian Scott: The Origins, People and Times of the French Quarter Renaissance (1920–1930)."
8. Anna B. Ellis, "Country Clubs, Golf Courses, Tennis Courts, Very Popular," *Times-Picayune*, 27 February 1921, 31.
9. Reed, *Dixie Bohemia*, 53.
10. "Kay Francis Aided by N.O. Girl in Footlight Excursion," 21.
11. "Peggy Passe Partout's Letter," *New Orleans States*, 16 October 1921, 38.
12. "The Diary of Diana," *New Orleans Item*, 23 October 1921, 44.
13. "Peggy Passe Partout's Letter," *New Orleans States*, 16 October 1921, 38.
14. "The Diary of Diana," *New Orleans Item*, 23 October 1921, 44.
15. "Diary of Diana," *New Orleans Item*, 31 July 1921, 33.
16. "Latest Social Events," *Times-Picayune*, 11 October 1921, 10.
17. *Times-Picayune*, 13 November 1921, 34.
18. "Peggy Passe Partout's Letter," *New Orleans State*, 13 November 1921, 52.
19. "Peggy Passe Partout's Letter," *New Orleans States*, 18 December 1921, 39.
20. "Dr. and Mrs. Souchon Entertain at Louisiane for Debutante Daughter," *New Orleans Item*, 25 December 1921, 24.

Chapter 6

1. "Caswell P. Ellis Widely Mourned," *New Orleans States*, 30 June 1924, 5.
2. *St. Nicholas*, Volume 30, part 1 (17 December 1897): 96.
3. "Contributions Received," *Times-Democrat*, 17 December 1897, 3.
4. "Erl Mallam Ellis: Death Robs Tulane of One of Its Brightest Students," *Times-Picayune*, 8 October 1901, 3.
5. "Erl Mallam Ellis," *New Orleans Item*, 7 October 1901, 10.
6. "Dixon Academy," *Times-Picayune*, 17 June 1907, 3.
7. Donald Marsden, *The Long Kickline: A History of the Princeton Triangle Club* (Princeton: Princeton University Press, 1968), 74.
8. Marsden, *The Long Kickline*, 76.
9. Marsden, *The Long Kickline*, 76.
10. "Society," *Times-Picayune*, 14 June 1913, 13.
11. "Society," *Times-Picayune*, 2 July 1913, 14.

12. "Society," *Times-Picayune*, 6 July 1913, 17.
13. Marsden, *The Long Kickline*, 83.
14. Marsden, *The Long Kickline*, 84–85.
15. Marsden, *The Long Kickline*, 83.
16. Marsden, *The Long Kickline*, 83–84.
17. Marsden, *The Long Kickline*, 84.
18. Marsden, *The Long Kickline*, 85.
19. "Society," *Times-Picayune*, 20 September 1914, 16.
20. Matthew J. Bruccoli and George Parker Anderson, eds., *Dictionary of Literary Biography: F. Scott Fitzgerald's Tender Is the Night: A Documentary Volume*, 273 (Farmington Hills, MI: Gale, 2003), 16.
21. Bruccoli and Anderson, *F. Scott Fitzgerald's Tender Is the Night*, 16.
22. F. Scott Fitzgerald, *Delphi Complete Works of F. Scott Fitzgerald*, 3rd edition (East Sussex, UK: Delphi Classics, 2011).
23. James L.W. West, *The Perfect Hour: The Romance of F. Scott Fitzgerald and Ginevra King, His First Love* (New York: Random House, 2006), 18.
24. Jerome Karabel, *The Chosen: The Hidden History of Admission and Exclusion at Harvard, Yale, and Princeton* (New York: Houghton Mifflin Harcourt, 2005), 73.
25. F. Scott Fitzgerald, *This Side of Paradise*, Project Gutenberg eBook #805, 2008.
26. Matthew Joseph Bruccoli, *Some Sort of Grandeur: The Life of F. Scott Fitzgerald* (New York: Harcourt, 1981), 52–53.
27. Karabel, *The Chosen*, 73.
28. Bruccoli, *Some Sort of Grandeur*, 53.
29. Bruccoli and Anderson, *F. Scott Fitzgerald's* Tender Is the Night, 13.
30. Marsden, *The Long Kickline*, 90.
31. Marsden, *The Long Kickline*, 90–91.
32. Matthew J. Bruccoli and Richard Layman, eds., *Fitzgerald-Hemingway Annual 1978* (Farmington Hills, MI: Cengage Gale, 1979).
33. Marsden, *The Long Kickline*, 94.
34. Bruccoli, *Some Sort of Grandeur*, 53.
35. Marsden, *The Long Kickline*, 95.
36. Marsden, *The Long Kickline*, 98.
37. "Affairs of the Week in the Playhouses," *New York Daily Tribune*, 6 December 1914, 23.
38. "Affairs of the Week in the Playhouses," *New York Daily Tribune*, 6 December 1914, 23.
39. "Social Events," *Times-Picayune*, 27 April 1915, 6.
40. "Cynthia St. Charles' Letter," *New Orleans Item*, 20 June 1915, 53.
41. "Society," *New Orleans Item*, 3 July 1917, 4.
42. Caroline Ticknor, *New England Aviators 1914–1918: Their Portraits and Their Records*, Volume 1 (Boston: Houghton Mifflin, 1919), 354.
43. Jonathan H. Ebel, *Faith in the Fight: Religion and the American Soldier in the Great War* (Princeton: Princeton University Press, 2010).
44. Liza Klaussmann, *Villa America* (New York: Little, Brown, 2015).
45. Klaussmann, *Villa America*.
46. "Cynthia St. Charles' Letter," *New Orleans States*, 25 August 1918, 16.
47. "Cynthia St. Charles' Letter," *New Orleans States*, 25 August 1918, 16.
48. "Social Events," *Times-Picayune*, 12 December 1918, 10.
49. "Society News and Notes," *New Orleans Item*, 28 December 1918, 6.
50. "Swimming Party, Smart Feature of This Week," *New Orleans Item*, 26 June 1919, 8.
51. "Due: On Dit," *New Orleans Item*, 29 June 1919, 26.
52. "Society News Notes," *New Orleans Item*, 31 October 1919, 15.
53. "Society News Notes," *New Orleans Item*, 4 November 1919, 13.
54. Raymond N. O'Neil, "Many-Ringed Virtuous Hates Popularity and Fat; Boston Provincial," *Cleveland Leader*, 16 January 1913, 12.
55. *Times-Picayune*, 12 December 1919, 12.
56. "The Diary of Diana," *New Orleans Item*, 12 December 1920, 30.

Chapter 7

1. John P. Coleman, "Fine Old New Orleans Mansions: The Jackson Avenue Stauffer Residence," *New Orleans States*, 30 December 1923, 46.
2. Coleman, "Fine Old New Orleans Mansions," 46.
3. Coleman, "Fine Old New Orleans Mansions," 46.

4. "Walter Stauffer, Head of Hospital, Claimed by Death," *Times-Picayune*, 31 July 1932, 1.
5. Coleman, "Fine Old New Orleans Mansions," 46.
6. "Society," *Times-Picayune*, 22 December 1912, 19.
7. "Orleanians Appointed to Security League," *New Orleans Item*, 6 November 1915, 7.
8. "Society," *Time-Picayune*, 30 January 1916, 21.
9. "N.O. Warriors Leave Big Salaries Behind," *New Orleans Item*, 20 June 1916, 8.
10. "Cynthia St. Charles Letter," *New Orleans Item*, 2 July 1916, 15.
11. Meigs O. Frost, "Artillerymen 'Find' Selves On Border: Girths Subside Under Grind of Drills," *New Orleans Item*, 21 July 1916, 2.
12. Meigs O. Frost, "'And the Caissons Keep Rollin' Along,'" *Times-Picayune*, 21 February 1937, 74.
13. "Women Help Gives Troops Welcome," *New Orleans States*, 31 January 1917, 2.
14. "Orleans Soldiers to Be Mustered on February 20," *Times-Picayune*, 31 January 1917, 5.
15. Maunsel White, email communication, 29 July 2021.
16. "The Wanderings of a War Widow," *New Orleans Item*, 20 May 1917, 18.
17. "Walter Stauffer to Wed Chicago Girl," *New Orleans States*, 21 November 1916.
18. "Society," *New Orleans Item*, 23 November 1916, 10.
19. "Stauffer's Fiancée Will Remain in the U.S.," *New Orleans Item*, 8 February 1917, 3.
20. "Chicago Girl Will Be Bride of Orleans Man," *New Orleans States*, 9 June 1917, 5.
21. "Venus Bests Mars," *Richmond Palladium and Sun-Telegram*, 14 June 1917, 11.
22. "Would-Be War Nurse Bride of Orleanian," *New Orleans Item*, 15 June 1917, 1.
23. "Real War Romance Has Louisiana Hero," *Times-Picayune*, 15 June 1917, 13.
24. "Walter J. Stauffer Weds Chicago Girl," *New Orleans States*, 15 June 1917, 14.
25. "Chicago Society Girl Weds Mr. W. Stauffer," *New Orleans States*, 16 June 1917, 5.
26. "Wanderings of a War Widow," *New Orleans Item*, 12 August 1917, 3.
27. "Wanderings of a War Widow," *New Orleans Item*, 30 September 1917, 16.
28. "Third Death in Month For Stauffer Family," *New Orleans States*, 24 January 1918, 5.
29. "Dies in War Work," *Rockford Republic*, 28 January 1918, 6.
30. "Death of Lovely Woman," *Times-Picayune*, 24 January 1918, 5.
31. "Relatives Are Left Handsome Legacies," *Times-Picayune*, 15 June 1918, 7.
32. "Cooke and Dickason Wills Are Probated," *New Orleans States*, 14 June 1918, 13.
33. "Diary of Diana," *New Orleans Item*, 11 January 1925, 40.
34. Frost, "'And the Caissons Keep Rollin' Along,'" *Times-Picayune*, 74.

Chapter 8

1. Reed, *Dixie Bohemia*, 69.
2. John Wyeth Scott II, "Natalie Vivian Scott: The Origins, People and Times of the French Quarter Renaissance (1920–1930)."
3. Historic American Buildings Survey, National Park Service, HABS No. LA-33. http://lcweb2.loc.gov/master/pnp/habshaer/la/la0000/la0021/data/la021data.pdf. Retrieved April 12, 2020.
4. Lyle Saxon, "Vieux Awakening; Is Coming Into Own Again," *Times-Picayune*, 6 June 1920, 64.
5. John W. Scott, *Natalie Scott: A Magnificent Life* (Gretna, LA: Pelican, 2008), 231–232.
6. "Ellis Named Commander of Soniat Legion Post," *Times-Picayune*, 23 June 1920, 9.
7. "Soniat Legion Post Charter Is Revoked," *New Orleans Item*, 8 August 1920, 52.
8. "Soniat Post Opposed to Cash Bonus Plan," *New Orleans Item*, 1 July 1920, 17.
9. "Leon Soniat Legion Post Charter Is Revoked," *New Orleans Item*, 9 August 1920, 1.
10. "Says Bonus Not Call for Action," *New Orleans States*, 11 August 1920, 8.

11. "Leon Soniat Legion Post Charter Is Revoked," 13.
12. "Soniat Post to Be a Private Club," *New Orleans Item*, 10 August 1920, 7.
13. *Times-Picayune*, 11 August 1920, 3.
14. "Leon Soniat Post No More Member of Legion Group," *Times-Picayune*, 27 September 1920, 1.
15. "Cancel Soniat Charter," *New Orleans States*, 27 September 1920, 3.
16. "Peggy Passe Partout's Letter," *New Orleans States*, 20 June 1920, 33.
17. Scott, *Natalie Scott*, 234.
18. "Due: On Dit," *New Orleans Item*, 27 June 1920, 41.
19. Reed, *Dixie Bohemia*, 17.
20. "Due: On Dit," *New Orleans Item*, 10 October 1920, 37.
21. "Peggy Passe Partout's Letter," *New Orleans States*, 5 December 1920, 39.
22. Maybe not. An extensive history of the property, including the land and the house construction, is detailed in the Historic American Buildings Survey: Historic American Buildings Survey, National Park Service. HABS No. LA-33. http://lcweb2.loc.gov/master/pnp/habshaer/la/la0000/la0021/data/la0021data.pdf.
23. "Peggy Passe Partout's Letter," *New Orleans States*, 5 December 1920, 39.
24. "New Orleans Society Events," *New Orleans Item*, 28 December 1920, 12.
25. "Diary of Diana," *New Orleans Item*, 2 January 1921, 35.
26. Reed, *Dixie Bohemia*, 68.
27. Maunsel White, email communication, 22 July 2021.
28. "Featuring Orleans Society," *New Orleans Item*, 13 March 1921, 40.
29. "Featuring Orleans Society," *New Orleans Item*, 20 March 1921, 30.
30. "Peggy Passe Partout's Letter," *New Orleans States*, 2 October 1921, 35.
31. "Featuring Orleans Society," *New Orleans Item*, 27 March 1921, 39.
32. "Peggy Passe Partout's Letter," *New Orleans States*, 17 July 1921, 33.
33. "Society," *New Orleans States*, 28 July 1921, 11.
34. "Diary of Diana," *New Orleans Item*, 31 July 1921, 33.
35. "Peggy Passe Partout's Letter," *New Orleans States*, 25 September 1921, 34.
36. "Featuring Orleans Society," *New Orleans Item*, 16 October 1921, 46.

Chapter 9

1. "Exodus to Mountains and Seashore Will Be on Soon Now," *Times-Picayune*, 4 June 1922, 1.
2. "Society," *New Orleans States*, 6 January 1922, 15.
3. Anna B. Ellis, "Parties Given in Vieux Carre Proving Notable Features in Social Life of New Orleans," *Times-Picayune*, 8 January 1922, 1.
4. "This Year's Carnival to Be Like Its Old Time Glory," *Times-Picayune*, 22 January 1922, 27.
5. "Peggy Passe Partout's Letter," *New Orleans States*, 8 January 1922, 40.
6. "Peggy Passe Partout's Letter," *New Orleans States*, 22 January 1922, 26.
7. "Good Horsewomen Are Members of the New Orleans Bridle Club," *New Orleans States*, 1 February 1922, 19.
8. "New Orleans Society," *New Orleans Item*, 4 February 1922, 7.
9. "Rulers of French Opera Ball," *New Orleans States*, 26 February 1922, 13.
10. "Society," *Times-Picayune*, 26 February 1922, 52.
11. "The Marriage Market," *New Orleans States*, 1 February 1922, 17.
12. "Wherein Brownie Makes Date with His Master-to-Be," *Times-Picayune*, 3 February 1922, 3.
13. "Brownie to Pick Future Master in Square Today," *Times-Picayune*, 4 February 1922, 2.
14. "Oldest Servant Dead," *Times-Picayune*, 17 February 1922, 2.
15. "Air Thrills for Legion Meeting," *New Orleans States*, 12 March 1922, 35.
16. "Society," *New Orleans States*, 11 March 1922, 7.
17. "New Orleans Society," *New Orleans Item*, 12 March 1922, 36.
18. William Wiegand, "Down the Spillway," *New Orleans Item*, 30 March 1932, 1.
19. Lyle Saxon, "New Orleans' Vieux Carre Now Coming Into Its Own," *Times-Picayune*, 16 April 1922, 77.
20. Historic American Buildings Survey, National Park Service, HABS No. LA-33.
21. "The Diary of Diana," *New Orleans Item*, 30 April 1922, 29.
22. "Society," *Times-Picayune*, 21 May 1922, 33.
23. "Sir Knights and Visiting Ladies

Made Last Week Notable," *Times-Picayune*, 30 April 1922, 1.
24. Scott, *Natalie Scott*, 245.
25. "Latest Social Events," *Times-Picayune*, 31 May 1922, 10.
26. Reed, *Dixie Bohemia*, 9.
27. Reed, *Dixie Bohemia*, 128.
28. Scott, "Natalie Vivian Scott: The Origins, People and Times of the French Quarter Renaissance (1920–1930)."
29. "New Orleans Society," *New Orleans Item*, 21 July 1922, 9.
30. "Many Orleanians See Grand Prix Classic Hold Society Reunion," *New Orleans States*, 23 July 1922, 23.
31. "Mardi Gras Staged by N.O. Girls on Liner," *New Orleans States*, 9 July 1922, 1.
32. "Peggy Passe Partout's Letter," *New Orleans States*, 30 July 1922, 24.
33. "Peggy Passe Partout's Letter," *New Orleans States*, 30 July 1922, 24.
34. Scott, "Natalie Vivian Scott: The Origins, People and Times of the French Quarter Renaissance (1920–1930)."
35. "Peggy Passe Partout's Letter," *New Orleans States*, 30 July 1922, 24.
36. "Peggy Passe Partout's Letter," *New Orleans States*, 6 August 1922, 28–29.
37. "All of New Orleans Society Busy Making Plans for Summer...," *Times-Picayune*, 11 August 1922, 1.
38. Eustis, *One Lucky Fellow*, 2.
39. "Real Estate for Sale," *Times-Picayune*, 28 May 1922, 5.
40. "Peggy Passe Partout's Letter," *New Orleans States*, 3 September 1922, 31.
41. "Ten Girls Slip by Gougers in Europe," *New Orleans States*, 12 September 1922, 13.

Chapter 10

1. "Debutante," Wikipedia, https://en.wikipedia.org/wiki/Debutante. Retrieved July 8, 2020.
2. "Peggy Passe Partout's Letter," *New Orleans States*, 24 September 1922, 41.
3. "Orleans Society," *Times-Picayune*, 15 October 1922, 2.
4. Pauline Breustedt, interview by Janelle Easley, February 23, 1977, in Waco, Texas, transcript, Baylor University Institute for Oral History, Waco, TX, available online at https://digitalcollections-baylor. quartexcollections.com/Documents/Detail/oral-memoirs-of-pauline-breustedt-transcript/1559348?item=1559349. Retrieved August 13, 2021.
5. "Peggy Passe Partout's Letter," *New Orleans States*, 24 September 1922, 40.
6. "Peggy Passe Partout's Letter," *New Orleans States*, 8 October 1922, 26.
7. Elbert Deets, ed., *The Cyclopedia of Temperance, Prohibition, and Public Morals* (Methodist Book Concern, 1917), 398.
8. Alice Dameron, "Summer Tourists, En Route Home, Linger in Metropolis," *Times-Picayune*, 8 October 1922, 35.
9. "Peggy Passe Partout's Letter," *New Orleans States*, 5 November 1922, 48.
10. "Orleans Society," *Times-Picayune*, 22 October 1922, 33.
11. "Society," *New Orleans States*, 21 October 1922, 5.
12. "Engagements in Social Circles Claiming Interest," *New Orleans Item*, 22 October 1922, 9.
13. "Notes of Crescent City," *New Orleans Item*, 22 October 1922, 12.
14. "Latest Social Events," *Times-Picayune*, 8 November 1922, 13.
15. "Latest Social Events," *Times-Picayune*, 21 November 1922, 10.
16. "Latest Social Events," *Times-Picayune*, 22 November 1922, 12.
17. "News of Social Incident and of Women's Varying Activities," *New Orleans Item*, 24 November 1922, 16.
18. "Latest Social Events," *Times-Picayune*, 6 December 1922, 12.
19. "News of Social Incident and of Women's Varying Activities," *New Orleans Item*, 6 December 1922, 13.
20. "News of Social Incident and Women's Varying Activities," *New Orleans Item*, 7 December 1922, 22.
21. "The Diary of Diana," *New Orleans Item*, 10 December 1922, 84.
22. "News of Social Interest and of Women's Varying Activities," *New Orleans Item*, 11 December 1922, 12.
23. "Latest Social Events," *Times-Picayune*, 12 December 1922, 12.
24. "Peggy Passe Partout's Letter," *New Orleans States*, 10 December 1922, 47.
25. "The Diary of Diana," *New Orleans Item*, 3 December 1922, 34.
26. "Peggy Passe Partout's Letter," *New Orleans States*, 10 December 1922, 47.

27. "Peggy Passe Partout's Letter," *New Orleans States* 17 December 1922, 30.
28. "Latest Social Events," *Times-Picayune*, 19 December 1922, 19.
29. "News of Social Interest and of Women's Varying Activities," *New Orleans Item*, 19 December 1922, 18.
30. "Peggy Passe Partout's Letter," *New Orleans States*, 24 December 1922, 31.
31. "The Diary of Diana," *New Orleans Item*, 24 December 1922, 34.
32. "News of Social Incident and of Women's Varying Activities," *New Orleans Item*, 18 December 1922, 13.
33. "News of Social Interest and of Women's Varying Activities," *New Orleans Item*, 22 December 1922, 12.
34. "Receptions and Dejeuners for Debutante Set Open Christmas Eve Festivities," *New Orleans Item*, 24 December 1922, 33.
35. "Receptions and Dejeuners Set Open Christmas Eve Festivities," 33.
36. "Peggy Passe Partout's Letter," *New Orleans States*, 24 December 1922, 32.
37. Lucile Rutland, "Who's Who Among the Debutantes," *New Orleans Item*, 31 December 1922, 31.
38. Rutland, "Who's Who Among the Debutantes," 31.
39. Rutland, "Who's Who Among the Debutantes," 38.
40. Maunsel White, email correspondence, 22 July 2021.
41. "News of Social Incident and of Women's Varying Activities," *New Orleans Item*, 21 November 1922, 16.
42. David Rankin Barbee, "Le Petit Theatre Has Splendid Inaugural," *New Orleans States*, 21 November 1922, 11.
43. "Featuring Orleans Society," *New Orleans Item*, 26 November 1922, 47.
44. "Peggy Passe Partout's Letter," *New Orleans States*, 26 November 1922, 31.
45. Cay Saunders, "Brilliant Plays at Little Theater Society Feature of the Week," *New Orleans States*, 26 November 1922, 27.
46. "Orleans Society," *Times-Picayune*, 14 January 1923, 41.
47. "Latest Social Events," *Times-Picayune*, 17 January 1923, 12.
48. "Peggy Passe Partout's Letter," *New Orleans States*, 14 January 1923, 40.
49. "Peggy Passe Partout's Letter," *New Orleans States*, 14 January 1923, 40.
50. "Peggy Passe Partout's Letter," *New Orleans States*, 14 January 1923, 40.
51. Bruccoli and Anderson, *F. Scott Fitzgerald's Tender Is the Night*, 13.
52. "Latest Social Events," *Times-Picayune* 19 January 1923, 10.
53. "Peggy Passe Partout's Letter," *New Orleans States*, 11 February 1923, 40.
54. "News of Social Incident and of Women's Varying Activities," *New Orleans Item*, 12 March 1923, 16.
55. "Peggy Passe Partout's Letter," *New Orleans States*, 25 February 1923, 38.
56. Fred Digby, "Poloists Will Form Club Here," *New Orleans Item*, 14 March 1923, 10.
57. "New Orleans Society," *Times-Picayune*, 8 April 1923, 35.
58. "Out-of-Door Recreations," *New Orleans States*, 1 April 1923, 38.
59. "Peggy Passe Partout's Letter," *New Orleans States*, 15 April 1923, 41.
60. "Peggy Passe Partout's Letter," *New Orleans States*, 1 April 1923, 41.
61. "Peggy Passe Partout's Letter," *New Orleans States*, 29 April 1923, 40.
62. "Peggy Passe Partout's Letter," *New Orleans States*, 24 June 1923, 38.
63. "Peggy Passe Partout's Letter," *New Orleans States*, 12 August 1923, 37.
64. "Gulf Coast Is Social Center for Orleanians," *New Orleans States*, 2 August 1923, 12.
65. "Society Plans Many Parties for Debutantes," *Times-Picayune*, 14 October 1923, 42.
66. "Le Blanc-Gilbert [sic] Nuptial Notable Autumn Event," *Times-Picayune*, 6 November 1923, 10.
67. "The Gay World Versus Mrs. Grundy," *Times-Picayune*, 11 November 1923, 43.
68. "The Gay World Versus Mrs. Grundy," *Times-Picayune*, 18 November 1923, 45.
69. "States Social Side," *New Orleans States*, 25 December 1923, 10.
70. "States Social Side," *New Orleans States*, 7 December 1923, 16.
71. "Diary of Diana," *New Orleans Item*, 16 December 1923, 34.
72. "Peggy Passe Partout's Letter," *New Orleans States*, 24 February 1924, 40.

Chapter 11

1. "Peggy Pass Partout's Letter," *New Orleans States*, 10 February 1924, 40.
2. "Balmy Sunshine Entices Society Into Open Spaces," *Times-Picayune*, 27 March 1924, 12.
3. "Week of Social Calm Follows Post-Easter Wedding Storm," *Times-Picayune*, 30 April 1924, 12.
4. "Peggy Passe Partout's Letter," *New Orleans States*, 27 April 1924, 41.
5. "Mail Addresses of Some New Orleanians Who Are Now Touring the Continent," *New Orleans States*, 8 June 1924, 25.
6. "Summer Departures Thin Ranks of Society's Stay-at-Homes," *Times-Picayune*, 27 June 1924, 12.
7. "'Message of Hope' Will Be Shown at K. of C. Home," *New Orleans States*, 4 June 1924, 14. The film appears to be lost.
8. "Caswell P. Ellis Widely Mourned," *New Orleans States*, 30 June 1924, 5.
9. "Ellis Will Probated," *Times-Picayune*, 3 June 1924, 7.
10. "Peggy Passe Partout's Letter," *New Orleans States*, 13 July 1924, 41.
11. "News of Social Incident and of Women's Varying Activities," *New Orleans Item*, 17 July 1924, 14.
12. Maunsel White, email communication, 7 November 2021.
13. "Peggy Passe Partout's Letter," *New Orleans States*, 3 August 1924, 38.
14. "Peggy Passe Partout's Letter," *New Orleans States*, 14 September 1924, 49.
15. Colin W. Sargent, "So Much More Than Waldo's Wives," *Portland Monthly*, September 2018. https://www.portlandmonthly.com/portmag/2018/08/so-much-more-than-waldos-wives/. Retrieved August 10, 2021.
16. Maunsel White, email communication, 28 July 2021.
17. William Gallagher, "Waldo Peirce: Brief Life of a Vibrant Artist: 1884–1970," *Harvard Magazine*, January–February 2002. https://www.harvardmagazine.com/2002/01/waldo-peirce.html. Retrieved August 8, 2021.
18. Sargent, "So Much More Than Waldo's Wives."
19. Sargent, "So Much More Than Waldo's Wives."
20. Maunsel White, email communication, 27 July 2021.
21. Gallagher, "Waldo Peirce."
22. Elizabeth (Moosie) White, undated letter, property of Maunsel White.
23. "States Social Side," *New Orleans States*, 8 October 1924, 14.
24. "Peggy Passe Partout's Letter," *New Orleans States*, 5 October 1924, 32.
25. *Times-Picayune*, 19 October 1924, 62.
26. "Entre Nous," *Times-Picayune*, 21 December 1924, 43.

Chapter 12

1. "Mrs. Eustis Leaves $209,000 Estate," *Times-Picayune*, 28 November 1924, 4.
2. Alice Elizabeth Eustis was born in 1913. She was six when her father committed suicide and eleven when she received her inheritance. She was a writer and actor who moved to New York. Never married, she died in 1989. She left behind a scandalous diary describing much drinking and many affairs.
3. "Peggy Passe Partout's Letter," *New Orleans States*, 28 August 1921, 44.
4. "Reduced Port Charges Urged as Big N.O. Need," *New Orleans Item*, 11 November 1921, 27.
5. "Latest Social Events," *Times-Picayune*, 31 October 1922, 10.
6. "Latest Social Events," *Times-Picayune*, 30 January 1923, 12.
7. "Roof Garden Dinner Dance Attracts Society Folks," *Times-Picayune*, 16 May 1923, 12.
8. Moosie White, undated letter, property of Maunsel White.
9. "Miss Hopkins Introduced to N.O. Society," *New Orleans States*, 2 December 1924, 16. Coincidentally, the same paper reported Miriam Hopkins' debut.
10. "Opening of Month Gives Impetus to Local Society," *Times-Picayune*, 2 December 1924, 20.
11. Francis Diary, 17 Dec 1924, RCA [Reid Cinema Archives].
12. Francis Diary, 31 Dec 1924, RCA [Reid Cinema Archives].
13. "Mimi Carte-Blanche Writes Peggy Passe Partout," *New Orleans States*, 4 January 1925, 40.
14. "Mimi Carte Blanche Writes Peggy Passe Partout," *New Orleans States*, 4 January 1925, 40.

15. "Peggy Passe Partout's Letter," *New Orleans States*, 22 March 1925, 42.
16. "Notable Dance Given in Honor of Miss Butler," *New Orleans States*, 6 February 1925, 6.
17. "Entre Nous," *Times-Picayune*, 15 March 1925, 52.
18. "Society," *Times-Picayune*, 12 March 1925, 17.
19. "Daily Magazine," *New Orleans States*, 14 March 1925, 7.
20. "Peggy Passe Partout's Letter," *New Orleans States*, 22 March 1925, 41.
21. "Society," *Times-Picayune*, 29 March 1925, 45.
22. Reed, *Dixie Bohemia*, 84, 85.
23. "States Social Side," *New Orleans States*, 6 April 1925, 8.
24. Maunsel White, email communication, 7 November 2021.
25. "Daughters in Session," *New Orleans States*, 8 April 1925, 8.
26. "Peggy Passe Partout's Letter," *New Orleans States*, 26 April 1925, 38.
27. "Peggy Passe Partout's Letter," *New Orleans States*, 17 May 1925, 29.
28. John Wyeth Scott II, "Natalie Vivian Scott: The Origins, People and Times of the French Quarter Renaissance (1920–1930)."

Chapter 13

1. "Society," *Times-Picayune*, 15 June 1925, 15.
2. "Peggy Passe Partout's Letter," *New Orleans States*, 21 June 1925, 40.
3. "Entre Nous," *Times-Picayune*, 21 June 1925, 46.
4. "More Society Folk to Sail for Europe," *New Orleans States*, 27 June 1925, 6.
5. Tony Allen, *Americans in Paris* (Chicago: Contemporary Books, 1977), 131.
6. "Peggy Passe Partout's Letter," *New Orleans States*, 19 July 1925, 38.
7. "Peggy Passe Partout's Letter, *New Orleans States*, 9 August 1925, 27.

Chapter 14

1. "Peggy Passe Partout's Letter," *New Orleans States*, 1 November 1925, 42.
2. "Society," *Times-Picayune*, 7 November 1925, 17.
3. "Peggy Passe Partout's Letter," *New Orleans States*, 13 December 1925, 57.
4. "Peggy Passe Partout's Letter," *New Orleans States*, 13 December 1925, 57.
5. "Peggy Passe Partout's Letter," *New Orleans States*, 20 November 1925, 38.
6. "Society," *New Orleans Item*, 30 January 1926, 5.
7. "Arts, Crafts Club Elects Westfeldt Next President," *Times-Picayune*,17 April 1926, 18.
8. Reed, *Dixie Bohemia*, 281.
9. Reed, *Dixie Bohemia*, 45–46.
10. Reed, *Dixie Bohemia*, 59–60.
11. Reed, *Dixie Bohemia*, 72.
12. "Entres Nous," *Times-Picayune*, 14 February 1926, 45.
13. "Little Theater in Biggest Triumph," *New Orleans States*, 23 February 1926, 7.
14. "Little Theater Audience Gives 'Mardi Gras' Ballet Loud Acclaim at Opening," *Times-Picayune*, 23 February 1926, 2.
15. "Peggy Passe Partout's Letter," *New Orleans States*, 28 February 1926, 48.
16. "Italy-American Society Branch Formed Here," *Times-Picayune*, 30 April 1926, 16.
17. "Society," *Times-Picayune*, 21 April 1926, 19.
18. "Peggy Passe Partout's Letter," *New Orleans States*, 14 March 1926, 42.
19. Ann Gilbert, *Covington: 200 Years*, Expanded Ebook, 9 May 2013. Reprinted from *Inside Northside*, February–March 2002, 79–80.
20. "Peggy Passe Partout's Letter," *New Orleans States*, 14 March 1926, 42.
21. Norman Bel Geddes, *Miracle in the Evening* (Chicago: Papamoa Press, 2018).
22. Ernest Albrecht, *From Barnum & Bailey to Feld* (Jefferson, NC: McFarland, 2014), 154.
23. Arthur Laurents, *Original Story By: A Memoir of Broadway and Hollywood* (New York: Applause, 2001), 38.
24. Esther Newton, *Cherry Grove, Fire Island: Sixty Years in America's First Gay and Lesbian Town* (Durham: Duke University Press Books, 2015). Ebook.
25. "Entre Nous," *Times-Picayune*, 28 March 1926, 48.
26. "Peggy Passe Partout's Letter," *New Orleans States*, 10 May 1926, 55.
27. "Peggy Passe Partout's Letter," *New Orleans States*, 28 March 1926, 38.

Chapter 15

1. Linda Patterson Miller, ed., *Letters from the Lost Generation: Gerald and Sara Murphy and Friends* (Gainesville: University of Florida Press, 2002), xvii.
2. Miller, *Letters from the Lost Generation*, xxvi.
3. Miller, *Letters from the Lost Generation*, xxv.
4. Margalit Fox, "Honoria Murphy Donnelly, of Artistic Milieu, Dies at 81," *New York Times*, 28 December 1998. https://www.nytimes.com/1998/12/28/arts/honoria-murphy-donnelly-of-artistic-milieu-dies-at-81.html. Retrieved June 11, 2020.
5. Allen, *Americans in Paris*, 85.
6. Miller, *Letters from the Lost Generation*, xix.
7. Fox, "Honoria Murphy Donnelly, of Artistic Milieu, Dies at 81."
8. Amanda Vaill, *Everybody Was So Young: Gerald and Sara Murphy, a Lost Generation Love Story* (New York: Houghton Mifflin, 1998), 158.
9. "Peggy Passe Partout's Letter," *New Orleans States*, 10 May 1926, 55.
10. "Peggy Passe Partout's Letter," *New Orleans States*, 2 May 1926, 38.
11. "Peggy Passe Partout's Letter," *New Orleans States*, 16 May 1926, 48.
12. Allen, *Americans in Paris*, 14.
13. "Entre Nous," *Times-Picayune*, 16 May 1926, 51.
14. "Suburban Clubs Gay with Evening Affairs for Folk Passing Summer at Home," *New Orleans States*, 25 July 1926, 35.
15. Count de Witte was an eccentric New Orleans celebrity who Natalie Scott often wrote about in her society columns.
16. "Peggy Passe Partout's Letter," *New Orleans States*, 1 August 1926, 46.
17. "Society," *Times-Picayune*, 1 September 1926, 17.
18. "Society," *Times-Picayune*, 29 September 1926, 17.
19. "Peggy Passe Partout's Letter," *New Orleans States*, 24 October 1926, 45.
20. "Peggy Passe Partout's Letter," *New Orleans States*, 24 October 1926, 45.
21. "Society Turns to Sewanee, Tulane Game," *New Orleans States*, 13 November 1926, 9.
22. "Stratford Club Will Give First of Dinner-Dances," *Times-Picayune*, 19 November 1926, 27.
23. "Peggy Passe Partout's Letter," *New Orleans States*, 21 November 1926, 45.
24. Francis Diary, 28 Dec 1926, RCA [Reid Cinema Archives].
25. "Entre Nous," *Times-Picayune*, 26 December 1926, 33.
26. Reed, *Dixie Bohemia*, 3.
27. Reed, *Dixie Bohemia*, 152.
28. Frank Perez, "The Gay Lens: Frances Benjamin Johnston and Pops Whitesell," *French Quarter Journal*, 30 August 2020. https://www.frenchquarterjournal.com/archives/the-gay-lens-frances-benjamin-johnston-and-pops-whitesell Retrieved 19 November 2021.
29. Perez, "The Gay Lens." A large collection of Joseph Woodson "Pops" Whitesell's photographs can be viewed on the Tulane University Digital Library site: https://digitallibrary.tulane.edu/islandora/object/tulane%3Awhitesell.

Chapter 16

1. "Society," *Times-Picayune*, 11 January 1927, 17.
2. "Entre Nous," *Times-Picayune*, 6 February 1927, 43.
3. "Affairs Honoring Visitors to Hold Society's Attention During Week," *Times-Picayune*, 17 March 1927, 19.
4. "Society News of the Week, " *New Orleans States*, 20 March 1927, 37.
5. "Many Informal Parties Given," *New Orleans Item*, 27 March 1927, 39.
6. "Society Followers Continue Exodus from City on Summer Journeys," *Times-Picayune*, 22 June 1927, 17.
7. Maunsel White, email communication, 25 July 2021.
8. "Entre Nous," *Times-Picayune*, 24 July 1927, 34.
9. Allen, *Americans in Paris*, 11.
10. Kear and Rossman, *Kay Francis*, 26.
11. Miller, *Letters from the Lost Generation*, 29.
12. Miller, *Letters from the Lost Generation*, 30.
13. "Touch of Autumn in Air Gives Impetus to Plans of Fashionables," *Times-Picayune*, 23 August 1927, 15.
14. "Peggy Passe Partout's Letter," *New Orleans States*, 23 October 1927, 33.

15. "Entre Nous," *Times-Picayune*, 30 October 1927, 31.
16. "As Diana Sees Society," *New Orleans Item*, 6 November 1927, 43.
17. "Entre Nous," *Times-Picayune*, 20 November 1927, 44.
18. "New Orleans Girls Save Parisian from Suicide," *New Orleans States*, 27 November 1927, 1.
19. "$67,628 Is Sought in Damage Suit," *Times-Picayune*, 27 September 1927, 13.
20. "Entre Nous," *Times-Picayune*, 27 November 1927, 45.
21. "Entre Nous," *Times-Picayune*, 25 December 1927, 19.
22. "Entre Nous," *Times-Picayune*, 8 January 1928, 37.

Chapter 17

1. "Entre Nous," *Times-Picayune*, 29 January 1928, 35.
2. "Society," *Times-Picayune*, 19 March 1928, 17.
3. "Polly Pursue's Society Gossip," *New Orleans States*, 13 May 1928, 41.
4. Bruccoli and Anderson, *F. Scott Fitzgerald's* Tender Is the Night, 16.
5. Karabel, *The Chosen*.
6. Arthur Mizener, *The Far Side of Paradise: A Biography of F. Scott Fitzgerald* (London: Lume Books, 2020). Ebook.
7. Matthew J. Bruccoli, *The Composition of* Tender Is the Night (Pittsburgh: University of Pittsburgh Press, 1963), 21–22.
8. West, *The Perfect Hour*, 95.
9. "Society," *Times-Picayune*, 31 August 1928, 23.
10. Francis Diary, 11 Dec 1928, RCA [Reid Cinema Archives].
11. "Society," *Times-Picayune*, 6 March 1929, 23.
12. "Society," *Times-Picayune*, 11 June 1929, 20.
13. "Death of Brazil Consul Reported," *Times-Picayune*, 24 January 1955, 4.

Chapter 18

1. Francis Diary, 12 April 1929, RCA [Reid Cinema Archives].
2. Francis Diary, 15 April 1929, RCA [Reid Cinema Archives].
3. Francis Diary, 21 April 1929, RCA [Reid Cinema Archives].
4. Francis Diary, 23 May 1929, RCA [Reid Cinema Archives].
5. Francis Diary, 27 May 1929, RCA [Reid Cinema Archives].
6. Francis Diary, 1 June 1929, RCA [Reid Cinema Archives].
7. Francis Diary, 2 June 1929 RCA [Reid Cinema Archives].
8. Anna B. Ellis, "More Activities Are Promised This Week Than in One Just Past," *Times-Picayune*, 39.
9. Anna B. Ellis, "Outdoor Diversions of Clubs Take Stage for Rest of Summer," *Times-Picayune*, 5 May 1929, 45.
10. "Society and Its Interests," *New Orleans States*, 5 May 1929, 32.
11. "Polly Pursue's Society Gossip," *New Orleans States*, 15 May 1929, 35.
12. "Society," *Times-Picayune*, 5 May 1929, 49.
13. "Impressive Events for Notables Are Week's Brightest Features," *Times-Picayune*, 2 June 1929, 37.
14. "Polly Pursue's Society Gossip," *New Orleans States*, 16 June 1929, 35.
15. "Down the Spillway with Wiegand," *New Orleans Item*, 16 October 1939, 16.
16. "Society," *Times-Picayune*, 16 June 1929, 56.
17. "Coleman E. Adler [advertisement]," *Times-Picayune*, 14 June 1929, 26.
18. "Coleman E. Adler [advertisement]," *Times-Picayune*, 18 June 1929, 18.
19. Maunsel White, email communication, 25 July 2021.

Chapter 19

1. "College Circle Parties Now Claim Chief Interest," *Times-Picayune*, 11 June 1929, 20.
2. "Football, Yachting and Engagements Interest New Orleans Society," *New Orleans Item*, 29 September 1929, 30.
3. "Social Whirl Well Under Way with Large Affairs Frequent," *Times-Picayune*, 17 November 1929, 35.
4. "Le Petit Theatre Presents Shavian Drama This Week," *Times-Picayune*, 24 November 1929, 69.
5. "Society," *Times-Picayune*, 28 December 1929, 15.
6. Carrie Walmsley, "Society in New

Orleans," *New Orleans Item*, 7 November 1929, 21.
7. "Society," *Times-Picayune*, 25 September 1932, 25.
8. "Deb Dance for Miss Cordill Set Thursday," *New Orleans Item*, 5 January 1930, 29.
9. U.S. Census Bureau, Annual Social and Economic Supplement: 2003 Current Population Survey, Current Population Reports, Series P20–553, "America's Families and Living Arrangements: 2003" and earlier reports
10. "Last of Lyceum Lectures Will Be Given Tonight," *Times-Picayune*, 10 March 1930, 21.
11. "Polly Pursue's Society Gossip," *New Orleans States*, 23 March 1930, 30.
12. Francis Diary, 25 January 1930, RCA [Reid Cinema Archives].
13. Fox, "Honoria Murphy Donnelly, of Artistic Milieu, Dies at 81," https://www.nytimes.com/1998/12/28/arts/honoria-murphy-donnelly-of-artistic-milieu-dies-at-81.html. Retrieved June 11, 2020.
14. Carrie Walmsley, "Society in New Orleans," *New Orleans Item*, 29 April 1930, 15.
15. Carrie Walmsley, "Society in New Orleans," 15.
16. Reed, *Dixie Bohemia*, 29.
17. "Polly Pursue's Hollywood Gossip," *New Orleans States*, 8 June 1930, 23.
18. "Polly Pursue's Society Gossip," *New Orleans States*, 12 June 1930, 37.

Chapter 20

1. Carrie Walmsley, "Society in New Orleans," *New Orleans Item*, 23 May 1930, 15.
2. "Departures Shrink N.O. Society Colony," *New Orleans Item*, 10 August 1930, 45.
3. "Society," *New Orleans States*, 5 September 1930, 11.
4. Carrie Walmsley, "Society in New Orleans," *New Orleans Item*, 7 October 1930, 37.
5. "Out-of-Town Weddings to Hold Interest in Social Circles Here," *Times-Picayune*, 7 October 1930, 17.
6. "Society," *New Orleans States*, 7 October 1930, 15.
7. "Prominent Weddings Set for This Month," *New Orleans Item*, 12 October 1930, 44.
8. "Society," *Times-Picayune*, 15 October 1930, 21.
9. "Runs Big Firm by Telegraph," *New Orleans Item*, 7 October 1930, 1, 3.
10. "Football Sharing Interest in Social Circles of City," *Times-Picayune* 7 November 1930, 26.
11. "Society in New Orleans," *New Orleans States*, 4 November 1930, 16.
12. "Buffet Supper Planned Tonight for Bridal Pair," *Times-Picayune*, 10 November 1930, 20.
13. Anthony Slide, *It's the Pictures That Got Small* (New York: Columbia University Press), 30.
14. Newton, *Cherry Grove*.
15. Reed, *Dixie Bohemia*, 69.
16. "Society," *Times-Picayune*, 12 March 1931, 19.
17. "Tells How Richard Ellis Lost His Life," *New Orleans Item*, 27 May 1931, 1.
18. "June Weddings to Intrigue Society Here," *New Orleans Item*, 31 May 1931, 41.
19. "Through the Lorgnette," *Times-Picayune*, 1 November 1931, 29.

Chapter 21

1. "Society," *Times-Picayune*, 15 December 1931, 19.
2. Elizabeth Kell, "Living in the Sea," *Times-Picayune*, 17 December 1931, 15.
3. "Chic Chatter of N.O.," *New Orleans Item*, 20 December 1931, 49.
4. Moosie White, undated letter, property of Maunsel White.
5. William Wiegand, "Down the Spillway," *New Orleans Item*, 7 January 1932, 1.
6. Elizabeth Kell, "Society Chat," *New Orleans Item*, 16 February 1932, 21.
7. "'On Approval' at Little Theatre," *New Orleans States*, 21 February 1932, 32.
8. Daily Weinberg, "'On Approval' Wins Praise," *New Orleans Item*, 1 March 1932, 6.
9. Selby Noel Mayfield, "Farce Presented by Petit Theatre," *Times-Picayune*, 1 March 1932, 6.
10. Carrie G. Walmsley, "Society in New Orleans," *New Orleans Item*, 2 March 1932, 13.
11. "Parties and Events," *Times-Picayune*, 6 March 1932, 30.

12. "Gulf Hills Horse Show Claims Wide Interest Among Elite," *New Orleans Item*, 6 March 1932, 32.
13. "In Society," *New Orleans States*, 2 March 1932, 10.
14. "In Society," *New Orleans States*, 4 March 1932, 8.
15. Carrie G. Walmsley, "Society in New Orleans," *New Orleans Item*, 1 April 1932, 16.
16. Elizabeth Kell, "Society Chat," *New Orleans Item*, 6 April 1932, 15.
17. Elizabeth Kell, "Society Chat," *New Orleans Item*, 8 April 1932, 15.
18. "Walter Stauffer, Head of Hospital, Claimed by Death," *Times-Picayune*, 31 July 1932, 1.
19. "Citizens Invited to Join in Movement for 'Fair Election,'" *Times-Picayune*, 7 August 1932, 1.
20. "Long, Walmsley, Overton Heard," *New Orleans States*, 10 September 1932, 3.

Chapter 22

1. "F. Edw. Hebert House Boating," *New Orleans States*, 2 August 1932, 3.
2. Reed, *Dixie Bohemia*, 60–61.
3. The Black Bridge, now gone, was used by the railroad and located near Metairie Cemetery. Built in the 19th century, its construction resulted in the deaths of thousands of immigrants.
4. "Through the Lorgnette," *Times-Picayune*, 7 August 1932, 14.
5. Carrie G. Walmsley, "Society in New Orleans," *New Orleans Item*, 14 September 1932, 15.
6. Austin Boyle, "Russian Play Big Success," *New Orleans Item*, 29 November 1932, 10.
7. Charles P. Jones, "'Cherry Orchard' Ably Performed," *Times-Picayune*, 29 November 1932, 17.
8. William Wiegand, "Down the Spillway," *New Orleans Item*, 27 February 1933, 1.
9. William Wiegand, "Down the Spillway," *New Orleans Item*, 14 February 1933, 1.
10. "Society," *Times-Picayune*, 16 July 1933, 45.
11. Maunsel White, email communication, 2 October 2021.
12. Reed, *Dixie Bohemia*, 228.
13. Reed, *Dixie Bohemia*, 229.
14. Reed, *Dixie Bohemia*, 53.
15. Elizabeth Kell, "In Society," *New Orleans States*, 1 September 1933, 6.
16. "Social Sets Plan Jaunts Over the Week-End," *Times-Picayune*, 1 September 1933, 21.
17. Elizabeth Kell, "In Society," *New Orleans States*, 3 October 1933, 8.
18. "Elite While Away Summer Days with Tournaments, Regattas," *New Orleans Item*, 3 September 1933, 47.
19. Elizabeth Kell, "In Society," *New Orleans States*, 6 November 1933, 6.
20. "Walker M. Ellis Injures His Hand," *New Orleans Item*, 1 November 1933, 2.
21. "Attention Is Claimed by Events," *Times-Picayune*, 15 November 1933, 21.
22. "Many Hostesses Give Parties for Buds of Societies," *Times-Picayune*, 22 November 1933, 18.
23. Elizabeth Kell, "In Society," *New Orleans States*, 17 November 1933, 10.
24. Elizabeth Kell, "In Society," *New Orleans States*, 28 November 1933, 8.
25. "Harlequin's Ball to Be Attraction for Society Folk," *Times-Picayune*, 29 December 1933, 19.

Chapter 23

1. William Wiegand, "Down the Spillway," *New Orleans Item*, 17 January 1934, 6.
2. "John Chapin Mosher," Wikipedia, https://en.wikipedia.org/wiki/John_Mosher_(writer). Retrieved 15 October 2021.
3. "Chic Chatter of New Orleans," *New Orleans Item*, 18 February 1934, 32.
4. Val Flanagan, "S.Y.C. Schedule for First Half of 1934 Season Includes 66 Races," *Times-Picayune*, 25 March 1934, 48.
5. Elizabeth Kell, "In Society," *New Orleans States*, 26 March 1934, 11.
6. Maunsel White, email communication, 20 July 2021.
7. Sue Bryan, "Chat," *New Orleans Item*, 2 April 1934, 10.
8. Elizabeth Kell, "In Society," *New Orleans States*, 30 March 1934, 13.
9. Sue Bryan, "Chat," *New Orleans Item*, 18 April 1934, 12.
10. "Through the Lorgnette," *Times-Picayune*, 20 May 1934, 40.

11. "Records of the Day," *Times-Picayune*, 26 April 1934, 22.
12. *Southern Reporter*, Volume 159, West Publishing Company, 1935, 325–326.
13. Elizabeth Kell, "In Society," *New Orleans States*, 8 June 1934, 17.
14. "Artists Will Spend Week at Grand Isle," *New Orleans Item*, 10 June 1934, 16.
15. Irene Cooper, "Pen, Chisel and Brush," *Times-Picayune*, 17 June 1934, 24.
16. Elizabeth Kell, "In Society," *New Orleans States*, 24 July 1934, 15.
17. Burdette Waldo Huggins, "Dance and Party Are Arranged," *New Orleans Item*, 22 November 1934, 16.
18. "A.S. White Passes," *New Orleans Item*, 26 December 1934, 3.
19. Maunsel White, email communication, 22 July 2021, 25 July 2021.
20. Burdette W. Huggins, "Prominent Winter Nuptial," *New Orleans States*, 12 February 1935, 14.
21. Burdette W. Huggins, "Exodus to Gulf Coast," *New Orleans Item*, 26 July 1935, 13.
22. Elizabeth Kell, "In Society," *New Orleans States*, 6 March 1935, 15.
23. Elizabeth Kell, "In Society," *New Orleans States*, 27 March 1935, 17.
24. Esther Dupuy, "New Prints and Triple Sheers Seen by Chic Chatter," *New Orleans Item*, 24 March 1935, 41.
25. Burdette W. Huggins, "Orleans Club Reception Today," *New Orleans Item*, 28 May 1935, 20.
26. "Banquets to Close Fetes for Envoy," *New Orleans Item*, 3 April 1935, 15.
27. Elizabeth Kell, "In Society," *New Orleans States*, 10 June 1935, 13.
28. Elizabeth Kell, "In Society," *New Orleans States*, 27 June 1935, 17.
29. Sue Bryan, "Society Chats About Variety of Bathing Spots Along Seawall," *New Orleans Item* 4 August 1935, 32.
30. Burdette W. Huggins, "Informal Fetes Break Monotony," *New Orleans Item*, 20 August 1935, 13.
31. Burdette W. Huggins, "Gay Week-End for Fashionables," *New Orleans Item*, 18 October 1935, 17.
32. Allen, *Americans in Paris*, 152–153.
33. Elizabeth Kell, "In Society," *New Orleans States*, 17 November 1935, 11.
34. "Bullet Fired Into White Residence; None Is Injured," *Times-Picayune*, 9 November 1935, 1.
35. Maunsel White, email communication, 24 July 2021.
36. Sue Bryan, "Beaming," *New Orleans Item*, 23 February 1936, 28.
37. Sue Bryan, "Prepare for High Flying and Cheer," *New Orleans Item*, 23 February 1936, 28.
38. "Kay Francis Aided by N.O. Girl in Footlight Excursion," *New Orleans Item*, 21.
39. "Prominent Group Stopping in City," *New Orleans Item*, 5 May 1936, 15.
40. Peggy Poor, "Chat.," *New Orleans Item*, 22 May 1936, 18.
41. "Much Activity in Fashionable Circles with a Variety of Affairs Scheduled," *New Orleans Item*, 27 May 1936, 13.
42. Hildegarde Lyons, "Chat," *New Orleans Item*, 10 December 1936, 18.
43. Mel Washburn, "Kay Francis Builds Fire Under Herself: Washburn Tells How Cigarette Started Her Talking, Star Known as Reticent Woman," *New Orleans Item*, 14 April 1937, 7.
44. Hildegarde Lyons, "Cosmopolites," *New Orleans Item*, 6 June 1937, 35,
45. Julia Harden, "A Competitor," *New Orleans States*, 18 June 1937, 19.
46. Hildegarde Lyons, "Ramblings," *New Orleans Item* 25 July 1937, 34.
47. "Weigand's Down the Spillway," *New Orleans Item*, 7 August 1937, 8.
48. Hildegarde Lyons, "Society Chats About Modern Proposals and Who Does 'Em," *New Orleans Item*, 22 August 1937, 35.
49. Burdette W. Huggins, "Prominent N.O. Couple Wed Tonight," *New Orleans Item*, 10 September 1937, 13.
50. Elizabeth Kell, "In Society," *New Orleans States*, 25 September 1937, 5.

Chapter 24

1. "'Arms Plot' Here May Bring on Some International Chuckles," *New Orleans Item*, 20 November 1937, 1–2.
2. "'Munitions' Case Here Cleared Up," *New Orleans Item*, 23 November 1937, 2.
3. "Fifth Defendant Freed on Bond in Gun Export Case," *Times-Picayune*, 3 December 1937, 1.
4. "Four Arrested, Accused of Plot To Export Arms To Honduras," *Times-Picayune*, 20 November 1937, 1.

5. "No True Bill In Arms Plot," *New Orleans Item*, 14 December 1937, 2.
6. Elizabeth Kell, *New Orleans States*, 6 January 1938, 19.
7. Irene Cooper, "Pen, Chisel and Brush," *Times-Picayune*, 16 January 1938, 23.
8. Burdette W. Huggins, "Society," *New Orleans Item*, 24 May 1938, 12.
9. K.T. Knoblock, "Gourmet Is Now Viewing with Alarm," *New Orleans Item*, 23 January 1939, 3.
10. K.T. Knoblock, "Gourmet Is Now Viewing with Alarm," *New Orleans Item*, 23 January 1939, 3, 6.
11. K.T. Knoblock, "Gourmet Is Now Viewing with Alarm," *New Orleans Item*, 23 January 1939, 6.
12. Elizabeth Kell, "Social Activities Run to Lunches and Dinners," *New Orleans States*, 10 November 1939, 23.

Chapter 25

1. "Society," *Times-Picayune*, 1 February 1940, 21.
2. Elizabeth Kell, "Play Reading," *New Orleans States*, 3 April 1940, 15.
3. Elizabeth Kell, "Play Reading," *New Orleans States*, 15 April 1940, 13.
4. "Society," *Times-Picayune*, 19 June 1940, 27.
5. Burdette Huggins, "All the Activities of Society," *New Orleans Item*, 9 June 1941, 13.
6. "Time-Out," *New Orleans Item*, 5 September 1941, 20.
7. Ken Gormin, "The Spotlight," *New Orleans Item*, 8 July 1941, 18.
8. "Little Theater 1941-42 Season to Open October 15," *Times-Picayune*, 24 September 1941, 3.
9. "Stage Season to Open Here Wednesday," *Times-Picayune*, 12 October 1941, 55.
10. Cleveland Sessums, "Little Theater Patrons Applaud Season's Opener," *Times-Picayune*, 16 October 1941, 10.
11. "Parties and Events," *Times-Picayune*, 22 March 1942, 43.
12. "Play Leads at Little Theater," *Times-Picayune*, 25 March 1942, 10.
13. Cleveland Sessums, "Drama of 1840s Offered Here By Little Theater," *Times-Picayune*, 26 March 1942, 38.

14. "Little Theater Comedy Makes Hit at Opening," *Times-Picayune*, 26 April 1942, 25.
15. Burdette Huggins, "Society," *New Orleans Item*, 5 January 1943, 9.
16. "Sunday Radio Programs [advertisement]," *Times-Picayune*, 31 January 1943, 35.
17. "Coast-to-Coast," *Radio Daily*, 3 September 1943, 8.
18. "Drama," *Times-Picayune*, 9 September 1944, 21.
19. "Stauffer New Hospital V.P.," *New Orleans Item*, 21 July 1944, 22.
20. "Officers Installed by Legion Post," *New Orleans States*, 16 August 1944, 6.
21. "Drama," *Times-Picayune*, 13 January 1945, 21.
22. "Mrs. C.P. Ellis, Sr. Taken by Death," *Times-Picayune*, 19 July 1945, 2.
23. Burdette Huggins, "Society," *New Orleans Item*, 29 March 1946, 20.
24. "It's the Metropolitan's Opening Night in New Orleans," *New Orleans States*, 9 May 1947, 10.
25. Alice Dameron, "Lull in Social Activities Will Follow Brilliant 'Met' Season," *Times-Picayune*, 11 May 1947, 59.

Chapter 26

1. "W.P. Stewart Taken by Death," *Times-Picayune*, 7 March 1948, 1.
2. "Walker M. Ellis Takes Own Life," *Times-Picayune*, 7 December 1948, 1.
3. *Princeton Alumni Weekly*, 4 February 1949, 25-26.
4. Marie Louise Miltenberger, "Fishing Trip," *New Orleans States*, 9 December 1948, 38.
5. *Princeton Alumni Weekly*, 14 October 1969, 19.
6. "Society," *Times-Picayune*, 17 January 1949, 34.
7. "White League's Fight Observed," *Times-Picayune*, 15 September 1953, 3.
8. Cain Burdeau, "New Orleans Council Votes to Remove Monument to White Supremacists," *Christian Science Monitor*, 3 September 2015. https://www.csmonitor.com/USA/Society/2015/0903/New-Orleans-council-votes-to-remove-monument-to-white-supremacists.
9. "Mrs. White's Rites Held," *New Orleans States*, 13 December 1954, 5.

10. "Named by Trustees," *New Orleans States*, 17 April 1958, 16.

Chapter 27

1. Maunsel White, email communication, 26 July 2021.
2. Maunsel White, email communication, 22 July 2021.
3. Maunsel White, email communication, 26 July 2021.
4. Thomas Griffin, "Lagniappe," *New Orleans States-Item*, 25 January 1916, 12.
5. "Society," *Times-Picayune*, 12 June 1961, 44.
6. Maunsel White, email communication, 25 July 2021.
7. Maunsel White, email communication, 25 July 2021.
8. "Society," *Times-Picayune*, 14 September 1962, 40.
9. "Society," *Times-Picayune*, 13 April 1963, 32.
10. Maunsel White, email correspondence, 22 July 2021.
11. Maunsel White, email communication, 24 July 2021.
12. Maunsel White, email communication, 24 July 2021.
13. Maunsel White, email communication, 25 July 2021.
14. Deaths, "Eustis," *Times-Picayune*, 8 July 1969, Section 1, 14.
15. Maunsel White, email correspondence, 22 July 2021.
16. "Real Estate Transfers," *Times-Picayune*, 26 December 1992, 125.

Bibliography

Newspapers include *The Daily Item* (1902), *New Orleans Item* (1901–1936), *New Orleans States* (1917–1930), *New York Daily Tribune* (1914), *Times-Democrat* (1897), *Times-Picayune* (1898–1955).

Albrecht, Ernest. *From Barnum & Bailey to Feld*. Jefferson, NC: McFarland, 2014.
Allen, Tony. *Americans in Paris*. Chicago: Contemporary Books, 1977.
Bel Geddes, Norman. *Miracle in the Evening*. Chicago: Papamoa Press, 2018.
Breustedt, Pauline. Interview by Janelle Easley, February 23, 1977, in Waco, Texas, transcript, Baylor University Institute for Oral History, Waco, Texas, available online at https://digitalcollections-baylor.quartexcollections.com/Documents/Detail/oral-memoirs-of-pauline-breustedt-transcript/1559348?item=1559349. Retrieved August 13, 2021.
Bruccoli, Matthew J. *The Composition of Tender Is the Night*. Pittsburgh: University of Pittsburgh Press, 1963.
Bruccoli, Matthew Joseph. *Some Sort of Grandeur: The Life of F. Scott Fitzgerald*. New York: Harcourt, 1981.
Bruccoli, Matthew J., and Richard Layman, eds. *Fitzgerald-Hemingway Annual 1978*. Farmington Hills, MI: Cengage Gale, 1979.
Bruccoli, Matthew J., and George Parker Anderson, eds. *Dictionary of Literary Biography: F. Scott Fitzgerald's Tender Is the Night: A Documentary Volume*. Farmington Hills, MI: Gale, 2003.
Burdeau, Cain. "New Orleans Council Votes to Remove Monument to White Supremacists." *Christian Science Monitor*, September 3, 2015. https://www.csmonitor.com/USA/Society/2015/0903/New-Orleans-council-votes-to-remove-monument-to-white-supremacists.
"Coast-To-Coast." *Radio Daily*, September 3, 1943.
"Debutante." Wikipedia. https://en.wikipedia.org/wiki/Debutante. Retrieved July 8, 2020.
Deets, Elbert, ed. *The Cyclopedia of Temperance, Prohibition, and Public Morals*. New York: Methodist Book Concern, 1917.
"Dies in War Work." *Rockford Republic*, January 28, 1918.
Dwyer, Jeff. *Ghost Hunter's Guide to New Orleans*, rev. ed. Gretna, LA: Pelican, 2016. Ebook.
Ebel, Jonathan H. *Faith in the Fight: Religion and the American Soldier in the Great War*. Princeton: Princeton University Press, 2010.
Eustis, Laurance. *One Lucky Fellow*. Privately published, 1999.
Fellows, Will. *A Passion to Preserve: Gay Men as Keepers of Culture*. Madison: University of Wisconsin Press, 2005.
Fitzgerald, F. Scott *Delphi Complete Works of F. Scott Fitzgerald*, 3d ed. East Sussex, UK: Delphi Classics, 2011.
Fitzgerald, F. Scott. *This Side of Paradise*. Project Gutenberg ebook #805, 2008.
Foster, B. Brian. "What About the Houses?" *Veranda*, July–August 2021.
Fox, Margalit. "Honoria Murphy Donnelly, of Artistic Milieu, Dies at 81." *New York Times*, December 28, 1998.

Bibliography

Francis, Kay. Diary. Kay Francis Collection, Ogden and Mary Louise Reed Cinema Archives, Wesleyan University, Middleton, CT.

Fraiser, Jim. *The Garden District of New Orleans*. Jackson: University of Mississippi Press, 2012.

Gallagher, William. "Waldo Peirce: Brief Life of a Vibrant Artist: 1884–1970." *Harvard Magazine*, January–February 2002. https://www.harvardmagazine.com/2002/01/waldo-peirce.html. Retrieved August 8, 2021.

Gilbert, Ann. *Covington: 200 Years*. Expanded ebook. May 9, 2013. Reprinted From *Inside Northside*, February–March 2002.

Historic American Buildings Survey. National Park Service. HABS No. LA-33. http://lcweb2.loc.gov/master/pnp/habshaer/la/la0000/la0021/data/la0021data.pdf. Retrieved April 12, 2020.

Huebner, Anthony J. "Natalie Scott and the Great War Love Story." March 21, 2018, https://werehistory.org/natalie-scott-and-the-great-war-love-story/. Retrieved June 13, 2020.

The Issaquena Genealogy & History Project. https://sites.rootsweb.com/~msissaq2/eustis.html. Retrieved July 20, 2020.

Karabel, Jerome. *The Chosen: The Hidden History of Admission and Exclusion at Harvard, Yale, and Princeton*. New York: Houghton Mifflin Harcourt, 2005.

Kear, Lynn, and John Rossman. *Kay Francis: A Passionate Life and Career*. Jefferson, NC: McFarland, 2006.

Klaussmann, Liza. *Villa America*. New York: Little, Brown, 2015.

Laurents, Arthur. *Original Story By: A Memoir of Broadway and Hollywood*. New York: Applause, 2001.

Lawrason, Bell. "Canaries." http://www.poetryexplorer.net/poem.php?Id=10080096. Retrieved May 6, 2020.

Marsden, Donald. *The Long Kickline: A History of the Princeton Triangle Club*. Princeton: Princeton University Press, 1968.

Miller, Linda Patterson, ed. *Letters from the Lost Generation: Gerald and Sara Murphy and Friends*. Gainesville: University of Florida Press, 2002.

Mizener, Arthur. *The Far Side of Paradise: A Biography of F. Scott Fitzgerald*. London: Lume Books, 2020. Ebook.

"Mosher, John Chapin." Wikipedia. https://en.wikipedia.org/wiki/John_Mosher_(writer). Retrieved October 15, 2021.

Newton, Esther. *Cherry Grove, Fire Island: Sixty Years in America's First Gay and Lesbian Town*. Durham: Duke University Press, 2015. Ebook.

Perez, Frank. "The Gay Lens: Frances Benjamin Johnston and Pops Whitesell. *French Quarter Journal*, August 30, 2020. https://www.frenchquarterjournal.com/archives/the-gay-lens-frances-benjamin-johnston-and-pops-whitesell. Retrieved November 19, 2021.

Princeton Alumni Weekly. February 4, 1949, 25–26.

Princeton Alumni Weekly. October 14, 1969, 19.

Reed, John Shelton. *Dixie Bohemia: A French Quarter Circle in the 1920s*. Baton Rouge: Louisiana State University Press, 2012.

St. Nicholas. Volume 30, part 1. December 17, 1897.

Samuel, Martha Ann Brett, and Joseph Raymond Samuel. *The Great Days of the Garden District*. Project Gutenberg ebook.

Sargent, Colin W. "So Much More Than Waldo's Wives," *Portland Monthly*, September 2018. https://www.portlandmonthly.com/portmag/2018/08/so-much-more-than-waldos-wives/ Retrieved August 10, 2021.

Scott, John W. *Natalie Scott: A Magnificent Life*. Gretna, LA: Pelican, 2008.

Scott, John Wyeth II. "Natalie Vivian Scott: The Origins, People and Times of the French Quarter Renaissance (1920–1930)." 1999. LSU Historical Dissertations and Theses, 6924, https://digitalcommons.lsu.edu/gradschool_disstheses/6924. Retrieved June 13, 2020.

Slide, Anthony. *It's the Pictures That Got Small*. New York: Columbia University Press, 2015.

Ticknor, Caroline. *New England Aviators 1914–1918: Their Portraits and Their Records*, Volume 1. Boston: Houghton Mifflin, 1919.

Vaill, Amanda. *Everybody Was So Young: Gerald and Sara Murphy, a Lost Generation Love Story*. New York: Houghton Mifflin, 1998.
"Venus Bests Mars." *Richmond Palladium and Sun-Telegram*, June 14, 1917.
West, James L.W. *The Perfect Hour: The Romance of F. Scott Fitzgerald and Ginevra King, His First Love*. New York: Random House, 2006.
White, Elizabeth (Moosie). Undated letter.
White, Maunsel. Email communication.
Wilde, Oscar. Quotable Quote. https://www.goodreads.com/quotes/335553-after-the-first-glass-of-absinthe-you-see-things-as. Retrieved April 16, 2020.

Index

Abbott, Berenice 106
Abbott, Cornelius 191
Abbott, Paul 110
Absinthe 7–8
Allen, Peaceful 122
Allen, Tony 170–171
Allen Thomas Post 68
L'Alliance Française 34
American Horror Story 11
American Legion 67, 68, 69, 183
Amor, Juan Vasquez 109
Anderson, Elizabeth 7
Anderson, John Murray 122
Anderson, Sherwood 7, 128
Andrey, Octavia 26
Anna Karenina 190
Antoine's 177, 186, 188
Archibald, Mrs. Ben 167
Architects' Club 64
La Argentina 152
Arlen, Richard 139, 140
Arnaud's 7, 37, 177
Arts and Crafts Club 118–119, 146, 149
Astor, Mary 148
L'Atalante 152
Atlanteans Ball 179
Audley, Jack 98
Averardi, Franco Bruno 7

Baldwin, John 39
Baldwin, Mildred 39
Bangs, John Kendrick 100
Barbee, Richard 101
Barbier, George 101
Barclay, Minnie 92
Barney, Natalie 132
Barnum & Bailey Circus 122
Baroness Pontalba 133
Barry, Ellen 132
Barry, Philip 107, 125, 132
Barthel, Harold 131, 133, 134
Battle of New Orleans 24, 167, 172
Beach, Sylvia 106
Beatty, Warren 105
Beauty and the Beast 149

Beck, James M. 44
The Beggar on Horseback 101, 106, 186
Behind the Make-Up 139
Behrman, Martin 55
Bein, Charles 69, 75, 82, 128
Bel Geddes, Norman 122
Belliofsky, Sergie 172
Benchley, Robert 125
Bennett, Joan 139
Bernard, Althee 104
Beyonce 120
Big Kate 34, 119
Black, Bryan 56
Black, Kingsley 31, 56, 113, 171, 172, 191
Black Sun Press 132, 171
Bobb, Mr. and Mrs. Carroll 164
Bow, Clara 3, 139, 140
Brackett, Charles 132
Bradford, Amanda Davis 141, 167
Bradford, Elizabeth Porter 167
Breustedt, Pauline 87–88, 89
Bridle Club 39, 77, 78, 98, 104
Bright, Edgar 67, 100, 111
Bringier, Louise Marie 52
Bringier, Michel 52
Broussard, Blanche 80, 84
Bruccoli, Matthew 97–98
Buckner, Catherine Allen 14
Buckner, Henry Sullivan 11–12, 13–14
Buckner House 11–12, 17, 18, 84–86
Burbank family 78
Burke, Billie 98
Burke-Roche, Denis 157
Burnett, Celeste Stauffer 54, 58, 61, 64
Burnett, Harry 58, 64
Burnett, Peter 61, 64
Burns, Elizabeth 54
Butler, Audrey 111
Byington, Spring 101

Café Lafitte 129
Calliopean Society 55
Camors, Elise 94
Camp, Virginia 183
Camp Quinibeck 28

217

Campbell, Lawton 46
Carmer, Carl 70
Carriere, Marie Olive 26
Carroll, Nancy 139
Case, Pa 122
Catlett, Walter 139
Celeste's 70
Chandler, Roy 101
Chanley, Theodore 136
Chapman, Eleanore 62
Chatterton, Ruth 139
Cherkassky, Shura 127
Cherry Grove 122, 153, 173
The Cherry Orchard 161, 163
Chevalier, Maurice 6, 140
Children of Strangers 174
Christodora, A. J. 95
Claiborne, Clarisse 118
Claiborne, Virginia 100, 119, 122, 126, 131, 134, 135
Claire, Ina 148
Clarence 72
Clark, Ken 45
Clark, Mrs. Sam 135
Clarke, George 57
Clay, Dorothy 31, 35, 104
Clinton, Katherine 4, 29–30
Cole, C. Grenes 185
Coleman E. Adler 145
Colman, Ronald 4, 148
Columbia University 100, 101, 102, 179
Confession 173
Connelly, Marc 101
Coolidge, Hamilton 49
Cooper, Gary 140
Copeland, George 51
Crabbe, Captain and Mrs. 164
Crane, Hart 132, 171
Cromwell, John 139
Crosby, Caresse 132, 170–171
Crosby, Harry 132, 170–171
Crothers, Rachel 140
Crusel, Marion 34

Da Cunha, Victor 38, 108–110, 111, 126, 134, 135, 136, 137
D'Ambricourt, Madame 120
Dameron, Alice 88
The Dance of Life 139
Dangerous Curves 139
Davis, Jefferson 89, 141, 167
Davis, Lucinda Farrar 89
Dearborn, Ellen 108
Dearborn, Nellie Eustis 20
Dearborn, William 20
Deer Range Plantation 24, 167, 171
Déjà vu 120
De la Vasselais, Roger 98
De Mille, William C. 139
Democratic National Convention 67

Denegre, Blaine 44
Deutsch, Rhea Loeb Goldberg *see* Goldberg, Rhea Loeb
The Devil's Disciple 146, 147
De Witte, Count 127, 205
De Wolfe, Elsie 72
Dickason, Ada 58
Dickason, Livingston (Dorothy Stauffer's brother) 58, 62, 63, 98, 99
Dickason, Livingston (Dorothy Stauffer's father) 58, 62
Dickason, Sybil Tinkham 58
Di Robilant, Contessa 120
Dix, Dorothy (Elizabeth Gilmer) 35, 146, 163, 164
Dixon Academy 41, 42
Dos Passos, John 106, 125
Douglas, Norman 163
Downman, Virginia 50, 90, 94
Draper, Marion 128
Drawing Room Players 34
Duchamp, Marcel 122
Dufour, H. Generes 50
Dufour, Helen 28, 29
Dumont, Yvonne 100
Duncan, Isadora 51
DuPont family 74
Dupuy, Esther 113
Dupuy, Marie Elise 113
Durstine, Roy 45

Eagels, Jeanne 139
Ebel, Jonathan H. 49
Egues, Julia 54
Eisner, Michael 54
Ellis, Caswell P. 41, 42, 48, 51, 69, 99, 103, 183
Ellis, Caswell P., Jr. 42, 103, 181, 186
Ellis, Erl Mallam 42
Ellis, Helen (Walker's niece) 51
Ellis, Helen (Walker's sister-in-law) 51
Ellis, Nellie (Walker's mother) 40, 41–42, 48, 51, 69, 103, 104, 118, 137, 140, 147, 150, 152, 153, 156, 163, 168, 183
Ellis, Nellie (Walker's sister) 42
Ellis, Peggy 173
Ellis, Richard (Walker's grandfather) 41
Ellis, Richard (Walker's nephew) 51
Ellis, Richard M. (Walker's brother) 42, 51, 103, 153
Ellis, Sidney 153
Engelbach, Dr. 167
Eustacia Plantation 15
Eustis, Adele Britten 20
Eustis, Alice Aldice 14, 20, 108
Eustis, Allan 20, 33, 108
Eustis, Allan, Jr. 184
Eustis, Mrs. Allan 135
Eustis, Binks 20
Eustis, Cartwright 14, 15, 18
Eustis, Cartwright, Jr. 108

Index

Eustis, Elizabeth 108, 203
Eustis, Herbert, Jr. 20, 108
Eustis, Horatio 15
Eustis, Horatio Sprague (Katty's great-grandfather) 15
Eustis, Jimmy 20
Eustis, Laura Buckner (Mumsie) 11, 14, 15, 18, 20, 21, 22, 23, 31, 84, 86, 108, 109
Eustis, Laurance (Katty's cousin) 12, 13, 18, 21, 84
Eustis, Laurance (Katty's uncle) 12, 13, 14, 84, 108
Eustis, Richard (Katty's great uncle) 15
Eustis, Richard (Katty's uncle) 14, 20, 33, 108
Everett, Joshua B. 47
Ewing, James 77

Fair, Florence 72
Farrar, Beatrice Howard 122, 168, 170
Farrar, Edgar 50, 51, 89
Farrar, Lucinda Stamps 89
Farrar, Maude Ellen (Moosie's niece) 142, 149
Farrar, Maude Tobin White (Maudie) 24, 25, 26, 27, 28, 29, 32, 51, 76, 89, 118, 141, 142, 145, 149, 161, 168, 176, 188, 191, 192
Farrar, Stamps 51, 89, 141, 145, 161, 168, 175, 176
Farrar, Tommy 51, 69, 82, 121, 122, 136, 168, 170, 171, 173
Farrar family 75, 141
Farwell, Charles 112
Farwell, Edwa Stewart (Mrs. Charles Farwell) 26, 27, 28, 80, 93, 112, 183
Fashion 181
Faulkner, William 128
Fellows, Will 8
Ferber, Edna 160
Ferry, James F. 175
Fidelia 122
Fie! Fie! Fi-Fi! 46-47, 48, 95
Field, Sidney 176
Fire Island 122
Fitzgerald, F. Scott 2, 41, 45, 46-47, 95, 97, 106, 124, 125, 135-136, 148-149, 193
Fitzgerald, Zelda 106, 124, 132, 149
Forbes, Malcolm 54
Fox, Ethel 88, 90, 92-93
Fox, Maude 28, 29, 88, 94
France Forever 180
Francis, Dwight 110, 114
Francis, Kay 1, 3-10, 29-31, 37-38, 83, 88, 89, 97, 98, 101, 110, 111, 114-115, 117, 124, 126, 127-128, 130, 136, 138-140, 146, 147, 148, 149, 172, 173, 191, 193
Franks, Edward Gay 30
Franks, Edwin 30
Franks, Henrietta 30
Franks, Isabella Clinton 30
Franks, Moses Benjamin 30

French Opera House 27
French Opera Society Trade Ball 77
French Quarter 5, 6, 7, 8, 37, 64, 65-66, 69, 70, 71, 72, 74, 75, 76, 79, 93, 119, 129, 149, 153, 154, 158, 163, 178, 188
Freret, Virginia 183
Frost, Meigs 128
Funston, Frederick 57

Galatoire's 7, 177
Gallagher, William 106
Gallup, George 158
A Game of Hearts 36, 37
Garbo, Greta 190
Garden, Mary 51
Gaston, Bill 117
Gazzam, Joseph 87, 88
Gazzam, Nellie 87, 88
Gentlemen of the Press 138, 140
George Washington Slept Here 181
Ghost Hunters 120
Gibbons, William J., Jr. 67, 77
Gibbs, Joseph Sprague 4, 29, 30
Gibert, Josephine Stewart LeBlanc (Jo) 7, 20, 27, 28, 31, 34, 80, 84, 91, 92-93, 99, 100, 112-113, 118, 158, 162, 163, 164, 180, 187, 188, 190, 191
Gibert, Leon (Gus, Moosie's uncle) 39, 87, 92, 105, 131, 133, 192
Gibert, Leon (Gussie, Jo's husband) 20, 92, 100, 100, 111, 112-113
Gibert, Maude White (Moosie's aunt) 39, 87, 92, 105, 131, 133, 192
Gibert, Pierre 142
Gibert, Titine 190
Gibert, William 112-113, 121
Gibert family 163, 164
Gilbert, John 148
Gillespie, Jake 100
Gilmer, Elizabeth (see Dorothy Dix)
Godchaux family 119
Goldberg, Abraham 50
Goldberg, Rhea Loeb 34, 50, 95, 96, 164
Goldsborough, Anna Farrar 172
Goldsmith, Oliver 42
Goldstein, Maurice 91
Goldstein, Mrs. Maurice 38, 91, 109
Goldstein, Moise 158
Goulding, Edmund 139
Green, Abel 176
Green, Grace Fenn 176
Griffin, Thomas 189
Griffith, D.W. 8
Grima, Corinne 164
Griswold, Mr. and Mrs. George 186
Gumbel, Joe 98

Hall, Weeks 8, 128
Hamlet 117
Hangar family 83

220 Index

Hanson, Ada 26
Hardie, Alice Stauffer 54, 64
Hardie, Anne 28, 29
Hardie, Betty 64
Hardie, Lewis 64, 175
Hardie, Walter 64
Harlow, Jean 148
Harris, Erdman 45
Harris, Norvin 119
Hart, Moss 179, 180, 181
Harvard University 41, 48, 49, 89, 105, 186
Hawks, Kenneth 148
Hayne, Emily 31, 88, 92–93, 94, 100
Hecht, Mrs. 168
Hecht, Rudolph 158
Hemingway, Ernest 105, 106, 125, 149, 171
Hemingway, Frank 133
Henderson, Ellen 27
Hermitage Plantation 52
Heubert, Ramonde 156
Hibben, James M. 44
Hill School 41, 42–43
Hitchler, Anthony H. 80, 188
Hobson, Mrs. John B. 179
Holditch, Kenneth 74, 153
Hollander, A.J. 161
Holy Cathedral School of St. Mary 5, 29, 30, 31, 37
Hopkins, Corinne 98
Hopkins, Gladys 98
Hopkins, Mr. and Mrs. Guy 98
Hopkins, Miriam 97, 98
Huebner, Anthony J. 16
Huggins, Allen 134, 171
Huggins, Burdette Waldo 7, 28, 29, 31, 34, 91, 94, 98, 99, 100, 119, 122, 126, 134, 155, 161, 171, 180, 183, 187, 188, 192
Hughes, William ("Son") 170
Hume, W.W. 79
Hunter, Juliette 78
Hush…Hush, Sweet Charlotte 120
Huston, Walter 3, 140
Hymes, Chapman H., Jr. 100

Innocents of Paris 140
Interview with the Vampire 120
Irby, William Radcliffe (W.R.) 70, 119
Israel, Helene 38
Issaquena County 15
Italy-American Society 7, 120
Ivey, Mary Nell 182–183

Jackson, Abby Orme 186
Jackson, Andrew 23, 24, 52, 167, 171
Jackson, J. Norcom 186
Johnson, Bessie 80, 86
Johnson, Kay 4, 101, 139, 140
Johnston, Albert Sidney 141
Johnston, Frances Benjamin 129
Joyce, James 106, 171

Kaufman, George S. 101, 179, 180, 181
Kaufman, Olga 50, 115, 117, 164
Kearney, Buddy 164
Kearney, Nell 92
Keiffer, Walter 130–131
Kell, Elizabeth 164, 167
Kemp, Audrey 184
Kemp, Blanche Cook 184
Kemp, Walter 184
Kent, John 183
Kimbrough, Emily 103
King, Grace 128, 163
Kingsley, Betty 14
Kirkland, Alexander 152
Klaussmann, Liza 49
Knights of Momus 17
Koch, Charles 70
Koch, James (Jimmy) 92
Koch, Richard 8, 70, 121, 128
Kock, Heda 28, 29
Kohn, Therese 178
Kolb's 177
Kreegar, Nick 183

Labrot, Sylvester 27
Labrot, William (Bill) 27, 172
Labrot family 88
La Farge, Oliver 112, 128
Lafitte's Blacksmith Shop 129
Larrimore, Francine 140
Laurents, Arthur 122
Lawrason, Bell 22, 69, 75
Lawrence, Joel 149
Lawrenceville School 54–55
LeBlanc, Alfred 20
LeBlanc, Henry 82, 98, 184
LeBlanc, Jane Stewart 20, 28, 34
Legendre, Hennen 118, 166
Legendre, James H. 44
Legendre, Mr. and Mrs. Sidney 147
Leger, Fernand 125
Leon Soniat Post 67, 68
Let Us Be Gay 140
Let's Not and Say We Did 38, 172
The Letter 139
Levert, Stephanie 88
Levy, Stanford J. 161
Lewis, Huey 54
Liberty Place 187
Little, John 63, 102, 104, 110, 148
Little, Stella Hayward 63, 102, 103, 104, 110, 148
Loker, Myra 164
Long, Huey P. 64, 159
Lonsdale, Frederick 157
Lorch, Adam, Jr. 146
Loughborough, Edith 115
Louisiane 39, 98
Luhan, Mabel Dodge 172
Lyons, Elizabeth 187
Lyons, Hildegarde 173, 174

Index 221

Mabon, Mary Frost 171
MacKenna, Kenneth 4, 8, 10, 148
MacLeish, Archibald 106, 125
Maginnis, Mrs. Donald 179
Mahinder, Dr. 131
Main Street 43
The Man in the Stalls 95, 164
The Man Who Came to Dinner 179, 180
Mann, Ray 173
Marbury, Elizabeth 72
March, Fredric 190
Mardi Gras 17, 25–26, 36, 77, 119, 129, 131, 141, 168
Marie Jeanne 156
Marsden, Donald 43, 44, 46–47
Marshall, Herbert 97
Martin, George M. 48
Maugham, Somerset 180
Maunsel White's 1812 Sauce 23–24, 171–172, 177
May, Amelie 31, 80, 92, 94, 100
McCarthy, J.R. 100
McIlhenny, Anita Stauffer 54, 141
McIlhenny, Edmund 141
McIlhenny, John 141
McIlhenny family 23, 141
Mcrand, Paul 156
Meehan, John 6
Mehle, Allen 98
Meller, Raquel 117
The Message of Hope 103
Millay, Edna St. Vincent 94, 167
Miller, Betty 183
Miller, Henry 8
Miller, T.D. 78
Minneapolis Symphony Orchestra 130
Miss Josephine 12
Miss Masters' School 29
Miss Miller's School 28
Mitchell, George 101
Moffatt, Anna Cora 181
Moloney, Guy 56, 176
Monrose, Chick 121
Monrose, Laura 121
Moore, Bob 99
Moore, Ellis 131
Morphy, Paul 39
Morris, McKay 4, 128, 136
Mosher, John Chapin 165
Murchison, Mrs. John Reed 186
Murphy, Esther 104, 132, 153
Murphy, Genevieve 103
Murphy, Gerald 49, 104, 124, 125, 127, 132, 135–136, 148, 149, 193
Murphy, Sara 49, 124, 125, 127, 132, 148, 193

Natalie Scott: A Magnificent Life 134
National Security League 55–56
Neaf, Emile 164

New Orleans Junior League 5, 81, 111, 112, 129, 149
Newcomb College 31, 81, 95
Newton, Esther 153
Nott, Phillip 164

Oak Alley Plantation 7, 27, 120–121, 122, 134, 167, 168, 172, 173, 174, 187
Oak Hill Plantation 41
O'Donnell, Peter 57
O'Kelly, Mrs. John G. 32
O'Kelly, Lucille 32
O'Kelly family 141
Old New Orleans 182
Oliver, John 172
On Approval 157–158
On the Job 183
One Hour of Romance 173
One Lucky Fellow 12
Onoroti, Joe 98
Orleans Club 164
Orme, Richard 27, 78, 98, 100, 111, 130, 133, 134, 135, 171, 172, 181, 186, 192
Ott, K. Brad 188
Our Hearts Were Young and Gay 103

Paoli's 177
Paramount 3, 8, 138, 148
Pardue, Shermon (Shine) 67, 100
Parker, Dorothy 125
Parker, John, Jr. 67
Parker, Virginia 50
Parkhurst, Claire 31
Parlo, Dita 152
Passion Flower 139
Patio Royal 6, 39, 79, 90, 91, 147
Paul Morphy Book Shop 38
Paulet, Madame 105
Pearson, Gabrielle Thomas 43
Pearson, James Thomas 43–44, 45
Pearson, Richmond 43, 45
Peirce, Waldo 105–106, 157, 166, 193
Pelican Bookshop Press 128
Perez, Frank 129
The Perfect Alibi 136
Perkins, Anthony 101
Perkins, Osgood 101
Perkins, Rebecca 31, 99, 100
Perry, Ida 139
Le Petit Salon 163, 164, 179–180, 188
Le Petit Théâtre du Vieux Carré 34, 35, 37, 50, 64, 95, 100, 119, 126, 146, 147, 151, 157, 158, 161, 163, 180–181
The Philadelphia Story 132
Picasso, Pablo 125
Pitot, Genevieve 7, 31, 128
Porter, Cole 125
Powell, William 139
Pratt, Mrs. Theodore 70
Preminger, Otto 6

Index

Prescott, Allen 172–173
Preston, Kiki 6
Pride House 122
Princeton University 2, 41, 43, 44, 45, 46, 47, 48, 55, 89, 95, 96, 115, 136, 186
Prohibition 4, 7, 88, 126
Provisty family 141
Provosty, Michel 67
Pugh, Florence 50
Puoch, Marie Ernestine Baudoin (Mrs. Ernest Puoch) 19–20
Purcell, Gertrude 111
The Pursuit of Priscilla 44, 45

Quartier Club 34, 37, 38, 70, 71, 72, 76, 163
Quartz Arts Ball 170

Raffles 4, 9, 148
Rathbone, Basil 139, 148
Rathbone, Mrs. J. Cornelius 98–99
Rathbone, Ouida 139, 148
The Real Thing 100
Red Cockatoo 113
Reds 105
Reed, John 105
Reed, John Shelton 8, 70, 81, 153, 160
Reilly, Charlotte 80, 84
Reinike Academy of Art 176
Reynolds, Lewis E. 12
Rogers, Herman L. 173
Roosevelt, Teddy 141
Ross, Charles 26
Roussel, Elise 80, 100
Russell, George H. 20
Russell, Laura 108
Russell, Lollie Eustis 20
Ryan, Allan, Jr. 136
Ryan, Thomas Fortune 136

Saenger Theaters 4, 5
St. Nicholas 42
St. Paul's School 38
Sainte-Beuve, Charles Augustin 34
Samuel, Mrs. Monte (Helene) 154, 158, 167, 176
Sand, George 117
Santacroche, Mary Nell (see Mary Nell Ivey)
Saunders, Cay 96
Saxon, Lyle 64–65, 70, 128, 173, 174
Scales, Jane 99
The Scar 44
Schaff, Louis Valentine 151
Schertz, Helen Pitkin 34, 35, 36, 95, 119–120, 128, 163
Schulberg, B.P. 3
Schwartz, Albert 61
Schwartz, Myrthe Stauffer 54, 61
Schwartz family 141
Schwing, Samuel 119
Scott, C.C. 24
Scott, Mary Frances 24

Scott, Natalie 15–16, 22, 34, 36–37, 38, 50, 64, 69, 72, 73, 77, 80–84, 86, 87, 94, 96, 99, 101, 102, 103, 104–105, 106, 109, 112–113, 114, 115–116, 117, 119, 120, 123, 125–126, 127, 128, 132–133, 134, 146, 149, 167, 177, 205
Scott, Sidonie Provosty 167
Seaman, Harold 21
Seaman, Maude Eustis 13, 14, 21, 108
Segovia, Andres 136
Sessums, Cleveland 180–181
Shadows-on-the-Teche 8
Shaw, George Bernard 146, 147
Shawn, Ted 168
Sherwood Anderson and Other Famous Creoles: A Gallery of Contemporary New Orleans 128
Show Boat 160
Silenzi, Mrs. William 109
The Silver Cord 147–148
Simmons, Mrs. Joseph B. 93
Simonin, Mrs. Maurice 109
Skelly, Hal 139
Skinner, Cornelia 103
Slidell, Eileen 94, 131, 134
Slobotsky, Israel 175
Smith, Elise 78, 100
Smith, Gordon 80
Smith, Marguerite (Peggy) Mason 39, 77, 78, 100, 111
Smith, Mary Janet 80
Soniat, Leon 67
Souchon, Marion 23, 34, 39
Soulle Business School 84
South Wind 163
Southern Yacht Club 28, 32
S.P.C.A. 77–78
Spencer, Dorothy 118, 154, 158
Spratling, William 7–8, 69, 70, 81, 128
Stanton, Frederick 12
Stanton Hall 12
State of the Union 191
Stauffer, Dorothy Russell Dickason 57–60, 61–62, 98
Stauffer, Elizabeth Myrthe Taylor (Betty) 52, 54, 57, 58, 64
Stauffer, Ike 54
Stauffer, Isaac Hull 52
Stauffer, Louise 54
Stauffer, Myrthe 54
Stauffer, Richard (Dick) 54, 64
Stauffer, Walter Robinson 52, 54, 58, 59, 64, 78, 158, 188
Stauffer, William (Willie) 54, 64
Stearns, William 48–49
Steele, Catherine 59
Stein, Gertrude 105, 106
Stevens, Aline Richter 183
Stewart, Andrew (Buddy) 6, 14, 19, 20, 21, 86, 132, 134, 135, 150, 151, 166, 183, 184, 185, 187, 188, 189, 191, 192

Index

Stewart, Andrew (Katty's grandfather) 14, 17
Stewart, Andrew (Katty's uncle) 7, 27, 91, 120, 122, 134, 158, 172, 188
Stewart, Beatrice 124
Stewart, Donald Ogden 124
Stewart, John 26, 152, 168
Stewart, Josephine 7, 27, 91, 120, 121, 122, 134, 158, 167, 172, 187, 188
Stewart, Katharine Eustis (Kittie) 7, 11, 12, 14, 17–18, 19, 20, 21, 22, 23, 27, 28, 29, 32, 38, 84, 86, 87, 90, 91, 93, 94, 96, 98, 102, 104, 105, 106, 107, 108, 109–110, 111, 126, 130, 132, 133, 134, 135, 136, 137, 146, 147, 150, 151, 152, 153, 156, 164, 168, 171, 172, 173, 177, 178, 179, 184, 187, 188, 189, 191
Stewart, Mattie Kemp 183–184, 189, 192
Stewart, Therese Josephine Pharr 26
Stewart, William P. (Will) 6, 11, 14, 15, 17–18, 19, 20, 21, 22, 23, 26, 27, 28, 32, 80, 86, 91, 94, 96, 98, 103, 134, 136, 150, 151, 152, 159, 164, 166, 172, 184, 185, 187
Stone, Mrs. John W. 78
Stouse, Margaret Ferrier 39
Stouse, Walter Pierre 39
Strange Interlude 152
Stravinsky, Igor 125
Street of Women 101
Stuart, Donald Clive 43, 44
Stuart, Ruth McInerny 140
Such Men Are Dangerous 148
Suffrage House 29
Sullivan, John L. 161
The Sun Also Rises 106
Sutro, Alfred 95
Sutter, Nan C. 62
Swann, Kay 6
Sze, Maimie 166

Tangletoes 110
Tarkington, Booth 45
Tau Sigma 28, 34
Taylor, Richard (Dick) 52, 54, 112, 189
Taylor, Sarah (Knoxie) 141
Taylor, Zachary 23, 52, 54, 56, 112, 141, 189
Taylor, Zachary (Walter's cousin) 141
Teissier, Lois 134
Teissier, Mr. and Mrs. Louis 134
Tender Is the Night 124, 125, 136
Testing 183
Tharp, Jessie 36
This Side of Paradise 46
Thomas, Katherine 28, 31
Thornton, Sarah 54
Tobin, Eliska 26
Tobin, John William 24
Tobin family 141
Triangle Club 43, 44, 45, 46, 47, 95, 96, 136, 186
Trouble in Paradise 97, 98
Troutman, Ivy 105, 106, 166, 172

Tulane, Paul 158
Tulane University 42, 51, 69, 81
Tullis, Garner H. 165, 166, 169, 186
Tusson, Maria Ann 161
Twain, Mark 11

United Artists 148
Valery Nicholas House (Casa Flinard) 64–65, 66, 69–70, 71, 72, 73, 74, 75, 79, 200
Van Brunt, Laura Russell 20
Van Dyke, Henry 44–45
Ventadour, Fanny Craig 82, 128, 133, 166
Vigo, Jean 152
Villa America 125, 149
Villa America 49
Villare, Pierre 77
Viosca, Rene A. 176

Walker, Stuart 88
Walls, Elizabeth Gilbert Barber Dickason 58, 59, 60, 62, 63, 99–100
Walls, Frank 63, 99–100
Walmsley, T. Semmes 67, 159
Warner, Reuben 136
Washburn, Mel 173
Washington Artillery 56, 57, 61, 63, 67, 176
Waters, Mr. and Mrs. Arthur C. 186
Waugh, Alex (Alec) 158
Waugh, Arthur 158
Waugh, Evelyn 158
We Cover the Battlefront 183
Webb, Millard 138
Weicker, Lowell, Jr. 54
Werlein, Elizabeth (Betty) 5, 37, 86, 149, 157, 163, 191
Werlein, Parham 79–80
West, J.S. 175
Westfeldt, Burdette *see* Huggins, Burdette
Westfeldt, George 118
Westfeldt, Gustaf 179
Westfeldt, Martha 118
Westfeldt, Wallace 187
White, Albert Sidney 20, 23, 25, 26, 28, 31, 33, 89, 91, 93, 95, 103, 106, 167–168, 171
White, Albert Sidney, Jr. (Sid) 25, 26, 191
White, Celestine de la Ronde 23
White, Ellen Tobin (Mummy) 20, 23, 24, 25, 26, 27, 28, 31, 33, 34, 89, 91, 93, 95, 106, 120, 145, 157, 163, 171, 174, 188
White, Ellene (Tita) 20, 25, 26, 32, 38, 39, 76, 77, 106, 141, 142, 167, 171, 176, 188, 191, 192
White, John 25, 187, 191
White, Maunsel (Moosie's nephew) 2, 25–26, 28, 74, 95, 104, 105, 106, 112, 145, 157, 161–163, 165, 167, 171, 188, 189, 190, 191, 192, 193
White, Maunsel (Moosie's uncle) 25
White, Maunsel, Sr. (Moosie's great-grandfather) 23–24, 167, 171
White, Maunsel White, Jr. (Moosie's grandfather) 167

White, Miles 122
White, Sue Bryan 95, 161, 190, 191
White League 188
The White Rose 8
Whitesell, Joseph Woodson (Pops) 128–129, 205
Whitney, Elise 158, 172
Wiegand, William 9, 165
The Wife Saver 172
Wild Oats Lane 88
Wilde, Oscar 7, 45
Wilkinson, Elizabeth 69, 72, 75
Williams, Laurence M. 181
Williams, Margaret 181
Williams, Phil 98
Williams, Tennessee 27
Wilson, Edmund 46
Wilson, Woodrow 45
Windsor, Duke and Duchess of 173
Winship, Althea 19–20, 26

Winter, Val 164, 182, 183
Wolfe, Thomas 115
Wood, Elizabeth 100
Wood, John 168
Wood, Ruth 29
Woodward, Hazel Ellis 8, 42, 74, 183
Woodward, Jo, Jr. 173
Woodward, Joseph 8
Woolley, Monty 125
Woollcott, Alexander 180
Wurtele, Lois 157
WWL 182, 183

Yale University 55, 57, 141, 185
Young, Roland 101
Young, Stark 111
The Youngest 107, 186

Zemurray, Samuel 158
Zemurray, Sarah 158